Your Macroeconomic Edge

Your Macroeconomic Edge

Investing Strategies for Executives in the Post-Recession World

Philip J. Romero

First published in 2011 by Philip J. Romero
Business Expert Press, LLC
222 East 46th Street, New York, NY 10017
www.businessexpertpress.com

ISBN-13: 978-1-60649-320-5 (paperback)
ISBN-13: 978-1-60649-321-2 (e-book)

DOI 10.4128/9781606493212

A publication in the Business Expert Press Economics collection

Collection ISSN (print): 2163-761X
Collection ISSN (electronic): 2163-7628

Cover design by Jonathan Pennell
Interior design by Scribe Inc.

First edition: November 2011

10 9 8 7 6 5 4 3 2 1

Printed in the United States of America.

Abstract

Businesspersons and investors have been conditioned to anticipate that after a period of turbulence following the "Great Recession," conditions will return to "normal." For the preceding generation (from 1982 to 2007), "normal" was the economic "Great Moderation": a period of low inflation and low unemployment that brought on high growth in asset values.

Those days are gone. This book reviews the major, and largely inescapable, trends that will make the next generation a more challenging investment environment in all developed economies: an aging population and an overextended government. California today captures the challenges that will be faced by the American economy over the next decades.

After summarizing these trends, the book outlines investing strategies for individuals and companies can use this new environment. It provides an extended case study in how greater economic literacy can offer readers an advantage for understanding the opportunities, and threats, presented by long-term trends.

Keywords

Aging, bonds, BDC, Brazil, budget, California, China, currency, debt, deficit, demographics, devaluation, dollar, economics, emerging economies, entitlements, ETF, fertility, fiat money, finance, fiscal, Greece, India, inflation, investing, long term, macroeconomics, MLP, monetary, money, PIIGS, REIT, Roth, stagflation, stocks, tax, utility

Contents

Preface

To the Reader: Why This Book?

The final few years of the decade of the 2000s demonstrated, with a vengeance, how economic forces can wreak havoc with our daily lives. A brave few used their economic literacy to recognize and take advantage of this once-in-a-decade opportunity to get rich. Whether you wish to get ahead, or only to keep your head above water, understanding the economy is no longer optional.

Unfortunately, most economics courses are long on theory and short on practical applications. It is usually left up to the student to identify real-world examples of the abstract concepts they encounter in textbooks. Busy executives, balancing work responsibilities with the demands of executive education, have little patience with the purely theoretical. Real examples can reinforce learning through illustration, making it relevant. Although many textbooks try to do this, the volume of material they must cover leaves little room for extended illustrations, and those few that are included typically have a strong "toy example" flavor. This book fills that gap.

This volume is a companion to a traditional economics text. It focuses on two applications of economics: (a) for individual investors and (b) for corporate developers (e.g., strategy and M&A specialists). The emphasis in most of the chapters is on individual investing, because all of us will be investors, so we can accumulate the assets we need to retire someday. But significant corporate implications are also addressed in the final chapter.

The core premise of this book is that an executive's knowledge of economics can allow her to identify, and act on, threats and opportunities before competitors do. These competitors may be other firms in your industry, or other investors (individuals or institutions) who may bid up (or down) the price of an asset you wish to acquire or to sell. The need to track broad outside forces that can affect the environment within which you compete will come as no great surprise to you, but the utility of economics to do so may.

The majority of this book is a discussion of two great long-standing and interrelated forces affecting the developed world's economies—the fiscal tsunami of government financial profligacy and the demographics of declining birth rates—because they will shape our economic and business environment for decades to come. It presents these forces, and their implications, in a series of short chapters. Each concludes with a brief summary. Those pressed for time may wish to scan the summaries first and dive deeper into those chapters most pertinent to their interests.

This book was written in the midst of the Great Recession in 2009 and early 2010, based on research and thinking of a few years earlier, in 2005 to 2008. Because events in the world economy unfold quickly, some small details are now dated. (For example, the 2007–2009 recession has now officially been declared over, although the economy has been gaining altitude quite slowly, as this book predicted.) But since the book concentrates on long-term trends that will unfold over decades, any obsolete items are quite minor. I am often asked how well my predictions made in the mid- and late 2000s had stood up to the events of 2010 and 2011. The greatest surprise was the speed at which my forecast became reality.

While most of the book is an extended case study of the environment investors will face over the next 10 to 20 years (and is particularly relevant to anyone with a long investing time horizon), the penultimate chapter outlines how economics can be used in corporate strategy decisions, with emphasis on corporate development such as M&A and divestitures. I've attempted to use as little jargon as possible, and no graphs. I assume no prior economics education, although you may well find that your worldly experience has informed you about the economy more than you had realized.

Several appendices provide background. One is a primer on long-term investing (emphasizing investing for retirement) for beginners. Another is an introduction to international economic forces that can shape the market for assets. Suggestions for further reading are available in a resources appendix. Finally, a guide to relevant business school case studies related to each chapter is included for instructors who use case teaching methods.

The economic world evolves continuously, so new information will be added at my website: http://lcb.uoregon.edu/forms/profile/profile.html ?id=362&format=full. Check it out for news and commentary on themes explored in the book and on the evolving world economy.

May your continuing economic education be rewarding, in every sense of the word.

Philip J. Romero
Beaverton, Oregon
August 2010

Acknowledgments

Like any knowledge product, this book is the result of a lifetime of learning. Along the way I have been blessed by generous and talented teachers. I can only name a small fraction of those to whom I am indebted.

The need to make ideas actionable to improve the world has been a constant refrain among my mentors. First and foremost, Pete Wilson, who has a keen understanding of the potential and limits of use of government power to achieve positive change. Next, George Shultz, who began professional life as an accomplished labor economist but made history as Ronald Reagan's partner in defeating communism and confirming the superiority of capitalism.

I have been fortunate to work in several organizations that define "world class," and each has left its mark on me. Most recently, the Wilson administration, arguably the last successful governorship of what was once our most successful state. In my early career, George David and Karl Krapek of United Technologies patiently endured my transition from Cold Warrior to aspiring corporate strategist. Earlier still, Jim Thomson, Paul Davis, Richard Darilek, and the late Bruce Goeller taught me how to think rigorously about a wide range of public policy issues.

A number of people have generously reviewed and commented on this book. What you are reading is much kinder to the reader due entirely to their advice. I am grateful to the faculty, staff, and students of California State University's College of Business and Economics, where I had the honor of serving as its dean from 2008 to 2010, during which time I drafted this manuscript. Special thanks go to Susan Bergstrom, Hsing Fang, John Isaacson, Dong-Woo Lee, and Andrew Winnick. My arguments have been sharpened by reviews of a number of finance and economics students at CSULA and the University of Oregon, with particular thanks to Miriam Bolton for proofreading the manuscript.

Finally, the greatest investment of time came from two people who helped me strip out the economics jargon and make this book of value to a wide range of readers. This book would not exist without the contributions of Paul Romero and Lita Flores. I hope this book helps you protect your assets from the storms ahead.

Prologue

No one has ever made money over the long term betting against the American economy. The United States consistently ranks near the top of world competitiveness rankings, because of its flexible markets and the relatively light hand of government thereupon. It has the deepest and most liquid capital markets on the planet, which can reallocate capital from failing businesses to promising ones in a blink of an eye. As a result, America has one of the world's highest rates of formation of new businesses. Since the first sector to emerge from every recession over the last generation has been small business, the nation which led all others downward into the recent global recession can reasonably be expected to lead the world back out.

Despite my confidence in our economy's ability to withstand anything natural economic forces can throw (and have thrown) at it, I don't have the same confidence about what our political leaders can do—and have done already. This is not a partisan point. While many are criticizing the Obama administration for record deficits, it is almost certain that there was no alternative to forestall a continued downward deflationary spiral that would have replayed the Great Depression.

America has been committed on the road of higher taxes and accelerating inflation for decades, because of decisions made by our "leaders" in both parties. This profligacy is not confined to Washington, DC: state legislatures and city councils have also made trillions in promises that can't be redeemed, unless someone pays much more. That "someone" will be all of us, but most particularly those who our current leaders consider "rich"—that is, those households that earn more than about $100,000 per year.

If you have been fortunate enough to work and save a decent nest egg—say, several hundred thousand dollars—against your future retirement, **this book is about how to avoid the coming raids on that nest egg over the next few decades**: specifically, the second and third decades of the 21st century. It describes actions you can take in the next few years to guard against the depredations from Washington and your state capital.

The seeds that will grow into these twin forces—much higher taxes and much higher inflation—were planted bit by bit over the past several decades. Politicians of both parties are equally guilty. Although the recession of the latter years of the first decade of the century displaced these challenges temporarily, they will return with a vengeance when economic growth resumes.

It isn't hard to find bears in the woods these days. A historic drop in both stock and bond indexes since their peak in late 2007 has made a mockery of much traditional investment advice. Many congenital optimists suddenly reversed field, and euphoria turned to gloom.

Besides the newly bearish converts, there have always been the "permabears"—those authors who have been predicting doom, without much evidence, sometimes for generations. This book will be different in four important ways:

- First, I'll draw on my experience making economic policy for the nation's largest state, California, for an understanding of the effects of government actions on the economy and the irresistible temptation politicians face to act irresponsibly.
- Second, I'll show you substantial and compelling evidence of nearly irreversible trends that will drive continued irresponsibility by our "leaders."
- Third, I won't insult your intelligence with alarmism or bombast. I know that you can't *really* diversify your retirement. You have only one future, and I want yours to be protected from the depredations of your government. I am positioning my own personal finances based on the scenarios outlined in this book. I have no better way to demonstrate the seriousness of my convictions.
- Finally, this book is less about "investments" than it is about *protecting* your investments, whatever they are. Beginning in 2010 you have an opportunity to take some straightforward steps that could save you tens to hundreds of thousands of dollars in lower taxes later, if you follow the suggestions made here.

Your financial planning has already taken body blows: escalating health care costs mean that your nest egg must be stretched farther each year; increasing longevity means you can't help but worry about outliving your money; and the recent massive decline in asset markets decimated your savings. I take these threats to your retirement seriously, because I face them, too. I want to arm you with the knowledge you need to *act* and to protect yourself from the threats to come.

If you are so fortunate as to have insulated yourself from the coming tidal waves, pay particular attention to the chapter on corporate strategy applications. I hope that you will lead companies I invest in.

PART I

Why the Great Moderation— and Its Bull Market— Won't Return

CHAPTER 1

Introduction

Avoiding Californication

Once a proud and vibrant state that exercised such strong influence to be called a "hegemon," it now slides downhill in genteel, sclerotic decline. Its generous welfare system is supported by an ever-shrinking number of taxpayers, because high taxes and regulations have driven most young, ambitious entrepreneurs to greener pastures, leaving behind the old and the dependent. The government is experiencing declining tax revenues, despite raising tax rates several times and imposing taxes on products and activities that previously were exempt. Government makes up for inadequate revenue by borrowing more and more, spooking investors who have downgraded its bonds and who demand ever-higher interest to loan the state their funds. Escalating debt payments magnify the vicious cycle of borrow, tax, spend, and decline.

The American empire that has been a dominant fact of life in world politics and finance for three generations is slowly waning. This book outlines the main trends that are driving this decline. The so-called Great Moderation of the past generation (1982 to 2007)[1]—when inflation and unemployment were both low, and the stock and bond markets responded with double digit increases for many years in a row—will not be repeated in the coming decades.

This means that every Baby Boomer who counts on a benign investment environment like the past 25 years to compensate for insufficient savings needs a new retirement plan. This book also describes steps you can take to protect your nest egg from rough seas ahead: higher taxes, higher inflation, and slower growth.

California's Cautionary Tale

Any book that purports to outline what will happen in the economy and asset markets over several decades deserves to be taken with several trillion grains of salt. But the future is already here, in several European countries (e.g., Greece) and in at least one U.S. state: California. As you probably know, California has faced a mammoth "structural" deficit—that is, a deficit that persists even in boom times—because it chronically spends more than it collects in taxes. State leaders have made multiple attempts to plug the gap with gimmicks and sometimes with higher tax rates. I say "tax rates," not "taxes," because somehow, mysteriously, the added revenues predicted by tax increase supporters never materialize.

The reason? Entrepreneurs and others who are unwilling to pay high taxes find ways to avoid them. A phalanx of accountants exists to help them. But once available tax shelters have been exhausted, there is always another option: leaving.

In the past few years, California has gone from a state that received the largest number of immigrants to a "sending" state: More California residents moved out than moved in. In an increasingly globalized world, voting with your feet to leave behind dysfunctional, poorly governed homelands will become an increasingly common lifestyle choice. Emigration is a rational response of anyone whose ambitions are stifled by cultural or political circumstances at home. Such economic refugees will not only be Third World peasants but First World professionals, working or retired.

So while the trends and events outlined herein still lie in America's future, you can see them unfold in the present in the travails of the Golden State. (California received that name in an era when the appellation wasn't ironic.)

I have a unique perspective on California's self-inflicted wounds and their power to predict America's eroding position in the world. In the 1990s, I served as chief economist to California's last successful governor, Pete Wilson. My role was, essentially, to help turn back the tide of excessive taxes, regulation, and spending so that California's once-vibrant private sector could again create jobs and prosperity. The state's economy transformed from last in the nation to first—from losing 1,000 jobs per day to creating 1,000 new jobs each day. I spent the 1980s at the Rand

Corporation, conducting studies for the Pentagon and the intelligence community about methods to reduce threats to American security. So I have experience with how domestic politics affects international relations and vice versa.

I am also a Boomer, one who was too heavily invested in equities (common stocks) when the market crashed in late 2008. In effect, my portfolio was allocated as if I was still in my 30s (when I first began investing); I had not become gradually more conservative as my investing horizon shortened.

The Great Recession was a very powerful wake-up call, for families and for nations. Historians will probably look back on it as the end (or at least the beginning of the end) of the American Century, and a transition to whatever will replace it. I will not label the new century; that would be presumptuous at so early a date, and in any case, this is a book about personal finance more than the international system. But any Boomer who fails to recognize the new realities will ensure that their financial future is a disappointment or worse.

You should view anyone's confident predictions about the future, including mine, with skepticism. But you can see America's future unfolding today in California's present. Pay close attention, because my goal is to help you avoid having your savings Californicated.

How Empires—and Nest Eggs—End

Whether you know it or not, you are living through the peak and decline of the American empire. It was an empire of economic and financial power, not political conquest. Many called it a "hegemony." Its demise was long predicted but slow to arrive. The Great Recession that began in 2007 not only started in the United States but also signaled the crest of its imperial wave—a good run of arguably about four generations. The next generation will be a historic transition into an unknowable era in which other nations may assume global economic leadership—or no one may lead at all.

Historians of the 22nd century will chronicle this passage, which will repeat similar transitions that have occurred over the centuries. Citizens of the declining power may not be able to take such a long view. In particular, Baby Boomers have much more immediate concerns. Boomers came of age in an era of unprecedented affluence and counted on the good times to last forever, or at least through their retirements. Boomers, chastened by the financial meltdown of the past few years, have thrown their spendthrift habits of the last decade into sharp reverse, turning a savings rate that was negative (i.e., households borrowed to spend more than they earned) into one provoking worry it will dampen the recovery. Anyone whose retirement plan is premised on a return to the Great Moderation of 1982 to 2007—when inflation and unemployment were quiescent, and asset markets earned double digit returns year after year— needs another course correction.

This book arms you for the rougher seas ahead. It outlines two major trends, both domestic and international, that will make the next few decades far less benign for savers than the last few.

- *Taxes.* Will rise by a factor of 2 or 3, especially on the incomes or wealth of the so-called rich—which may be defined by politicians as low as $100,000 in income per year.
- *Economic growth.* Will be substantially lower than the long-term trend 3% of the post–World War II era; perhaps 1% or 1.5% per year (i.e., Western European–level growth and unemployment rates).
- *Asset prices.* Lower growth in overall economic activity will mean suppressed corporate earnings and, therefore, lower stock prices.
- *Inflation.* The unsustainable promises U.S. governments (federal, state, and local) have made for decades will lead to "monetization" of the national debt—the continued printing of money that will make the dollar worth less and lead to higher prices.

In a word, *stagflation.* Those with long memories will recall the late 1970s, when unemployment averaged 8%, inflation reached 13%, and the prime rate topped 21%. Dust off your leisure suit: the '70s will be back.

Many investment books sensationalize possible economic threats. This book will not warn you of "the next great depression," "the end of the dollar," or any other such apocalypse. The future will be more challenging than the past, but the challenges can be coped with, especially if you use the next few years to prepare. In particular, opportunities are opening in the near future that can preserve hundred of thousands of dollars of your nest egg's purchasing power.

The End of the American Empire

Rome ended, according to Gibbon,[2] when its decadence caused it to rot from within, so that bands of primitive nomads could push their way in through an open front door. The Ottoman Empire met a similar fate, after centuries as the "sick man of Europe." In both cases, there was no single turning point, no instant in time that clearly delineated the beginning of the empire's collapse. The peak and decline required centuries. Often an empire's end was briefly forestalled by some miracle that offered a temporary new lease on life, such as the discovery of rich gold deposits in Latin America that kept the Spanish empire on life support for centuries. Amy Chua[3] argues that in these and other cases the fatal disease was insularity and intolerance. Nations that had thrived by opening to the outside world—inviting in foreigners and their ideas, learning from other cultures, and improving by competition with them—rotted from within once they closed their doors, and their minds. Avoiding hubris and xenophobia is very difficult for a dominant company—ask General Motors' shareholders—or a dominant empire, and none have managed it for long by historical standards.

The most successful empire in recent history, that of the United Kingdom (its very name connoting imperial reach), fell more swiftly, but not in an instant. Britain had invented and prospered from the Industrial Revolution, but other countries—particularly its erstwhile colony the United States and Germany—perfected it. Although labor productivity (value produced per hour of worker's labor) in the United Kingdom had grown faster than the European average from the beginning of industrialization and throughout the 19th century, that lead began evaporating by early in the 20th century, as more productive competitors overtook Great Britain (most of all, the United States, and more malevolently, Germany). Productivity is the fundamental determinant of prosperity: individuals, or societies, can't earn more over the long term than the value of what they produce. Englishmen were no longer the richest citizens of the planet, and the empire on which "the sun never set" was, by the 1920s, becoming rapidly less affordable.

Two wars killed the British Empire: the Great War (World War I) to preserve the European balance of power, at a vastly higher cost than dozens of Britain's past wars had required, and World War II, to ensure the survival of democracy itself. Britain financed these wars through generous loans from allies, most of all the United States. Arguably, the final chapter of the empire began soon after World War II in 1946, when Britain was refused one more loan from the United States. But the empire did not fully collapse until decades later, when Britain withdrew from most of its possessions east of Suez in the early 1960s.

Two key themes emerge from the history of empires. First, they do not rise or fall in an instant, but gradually. Second, the seeds of decline are economic—the overextended imperial economy cannot support its commitments—as well as cultural and political, and they take generations to germinate.

This book applies these lessons to examine the state of the U.S. economy today and for the next generation, in order to guide those who are planning for their own financial futures. No group craves such information more than Boomers, a population of roughly 75 million whose leading edge is reaching the traditional retirement age of 65 years, and whose trailing edge may be sending their last child to college. All Boomers need to accumulate assets (i.e., save), because they have witnessed the demise of defined benefit pensions, but few have saved adequately.

The recent recession has caused Boomers to put their spendthrift habits of the early years of the decade into sharp reverse: Savings rates that were near zero—even negative in mid-decade—have now climbed back toward (but still below) historic averages. Having belatedly regained the saving habit, Boomers need every possible advantage to preserve the purchasing power of whatever they have managed to accumulate and to grow it to meet the needs of lengthening life spans. They are understandably very interested in what will happen to their late-acquired wealth.

This book will outline the main forces that will affect developed economies' (especially American) economic performance over the investment horizon of most Baby Boomers, roughly the next 25 or 30 years:

- *Your government is bankrupt*: Promises by all levels of government—to seniors, to public employees, and more recently to foreign investors—cannot be sustained without sharp increases in taxes that will arrest economic growth. Worse alternatives are also available that will lead to accelerating inflation. Chances are that all will be tried, and we will live with their side effects.
- *The world is aging*: Prosperity in many formerly poor countries and the emancipation of women has brought enormous social and economic benefits but also some side effects. Working women have fewer children, so society has fewer workers. At the same time, the elderly are living longer, thankfully. Most benefits schemes in developed countries were premised on a ratio of workers (who pay the costs) to beneficiaries (who receive the benefits) far above current levels, much less future ones. As the rest of the world prospers and aspires to a middle-income lifestyle, this demographic challenge is becoming ubiquitous. This will mean less innovation, less saving, less investment—and therefore slower economic and asset price growth.

Together, these two forces, as well as their second order and side effects, will mean a very different savings and investment climate in the next decades compared to that of the past generation.

This book will not delve in detail into any of these trends. My job is to review that specialized literature and synthesize its implications for your financial planning. For those readers who wish to go deeper, the bibliography and resources sections suggest places you can start.

Plan for the Book

After this introduction, this book is divided into two main parts. Part I, the "macro" section, summarizes these forces and their broad economic implications. Part II, the "micro" section, outlines responses to the macro trends: steps you can take to begin to prepare so that you can preserve your wealth in the more challenging times ahead.

In Part I, some chapters include a scenario that illustrates its main themes.

"Scenarios" are essentially short stories: miniature works of fiction, usually written as future news stories or historians' articles, about the trajectory of hypothetical future events, which will make abstract economic themes more tangible. The first scenario, which illustrates how the United States may be taught a dramatic lesson about its fiscal vulnerability, follows immediately after this introduction.

Will the future play out exactly as these scenarios suggest? Almost certainly not. But these trends are powerful and virtually inevitable. Although the world of 2025 won't look exactly like that described in these scenarios, a reader from that time should recognize his present in my accounts of our future.

Although I have deliberately tried to keep the unavoidable economic and financial jargon on a short leash, readers unfamiliar with any phrases or concepts may find it helpful to consult one of the appendices: a primer on retirement planning and investing; a primer on international economics and finance; and a glossary. In each, I've tried not to merely define terms, but interpret them and explain why you should care.

Nagging Worries: Boomer FAQs

The recession has forced Boomers to relearn the virtues of thrift, in a hurry. This book can help them keep what they've saved. It can help answer questions such as

- *Can I count on Social Security*, or other pensions (for those vanishing few who still have them)? Chapters 3 and 4 outline the inescapable demographic truth that the United States and virtually every other nation of middle income or better is getting older, making it ever more difficult to maintain the generous pensions and benefit systems designed for a different era.
- *How can I shelter my income from rising taxes?* Returning 20th-century-era benefits systems to solvency in the 21st century will almost certainly require much higher taxes. These will come on top of those needed to pay for the binge of government stimulus spending that softened the recent deep

recession. While no one likes taxes, those on fixed incomes are harmed most because they cannot compensate by earning more. Fortunately, there is a way to make much of your savings grow entirely tax free; chapter 9 explains how.

- *What will happen to the dollar, and the prices I pay?* The government's alternative (or worse still, supplement) to higher taxes is to begin reneging on its debt commitments: either all at once (default) or gradually (by debasing the currency, that is, causing inflation). Neither is good for the dollar, your investments, or the prices you pay, as outlined in chapters 4 and 5.

- *What will happen when foreigners stop lending to us?* Americans' high level of consumption (and consequent low rates of savings) were only possible because foreign countries have been willing to lend us hundreds of billions of dollars per year. This is possible because American consumers send roughly the same sum overseas every year to buy these countries'— especially China's—exports. Economists call this situation an "imbalance" and have argued for years that it needs to be balanced through less consumption by Americans and more consumption (and lower exports) by Chinese. This rebalancing has already started. Chapter 4 describes its effects on the U.S. economy, and Boomers' savings.

- *Are the Chinese buying up the world's resources?* Fast-growing economies need vast infusions of resources, particularly agricultural products, energy, concrete, and metals (e.g., for making steel). China alone engineered nearly $30 billion in acquisitions in 2008, the last year for which data are available, from next to nothing in 2003: 36 major deals in mining and metals, 32 in energy, and 54 in other sectors.[4] As much of the former "Third World" grows richer, it will have rich world appetites and will compete for the same resources. In the first half of 2008, prices of each of these commodities rose at double-digit rates, elevating Western consumer prices at rates that caused great concern. While inflation ebbed during the recession, it will return. Anyone on a fixed income now, or who expects to be sometime in the future, should prepare for rising prices. Chapters 3 and 5 elaborate on this point.

What Inflation?

As I write this in early 2010, the greater immediate challenge is deflation, not inflation. There is still considerable slack in the American economy—we are only using about 70% of our manufacturing capacity. Unemployed workers, and businesses, aren't in the habit of raising prices, because they know their competitors will undercut them and keep them unemployed.

But within a few years, even what is expected to be a very anemic recovery will gain momentum, and that slack will be reabsorbed. When banks finally begin lending again to private businesses, the increase in the money supply will fuel inflation. This may be a 2015, not a 2010, problem, but it will persist for many years, including the duration of many Boomers' retirement.

You should approach any book containing predictions, including this one, with more than a dollop of salt. But most of the developments described herein are highly likely to occur at some point in the next 20 or 30 years. Long life spans mean that the period once called "retirement"— when we no longer rely on a full-time job as our primary means of economic support—can easily last at least as long.

My aspiration is that *Your Macroeconomic Edge* will differ from most current affairs and economics books in being accessible to readers with no grounding in technical fields, and by giving you specific recommendations for steps you can take to protect your savings and your future. Boomers have a second chance to build the assets they will need to support a fulfilling lifestyle in the decades to come. I want to help you keep whatever you've accumulated.

Scenario 1: Military Victory, Economic Defeat: The Three Day War With China

By Dustin Yu
Dateline
April 30, 2030
Oil City # 3, Spratly Islands, South China Sea

This is the fifth anniversary of the Three Day War.

This brief struggle between the planet's most powerful nations—China and the United States—resulted in an ignominious defeat for the United States, the world's former "hyperpower." It brought memories of America's much bloodier defeat in Vietnam in April 1975.

While it is too early to render an authoritative verdict, it appears that the Three Day War was a far more significant turning point in world history than was Vietnam. When the dust settled few could deny that global power relationships had profoundly changed.

Single events rarely determine the fate of great powers. Their rise or fall is usually the result of decades, even centuries, of actions. The Three Day War dramatically punctuated the end of a long period of ebbing preeminence for the United States.

The Buildup

The so-called unipolar world of the 1990s—in which the United States survived as the only superpower after the implosion of the Soviet Union—planted the seeds of its own demise long before. First, China had enjoyed blistering economic growth since opening its economy to foreign trade and investment in the late 1970s. "Rising China" gained in self-confidence as its middle-class grew, a process that accelerated into the first decade of the 21st century, and only began slowing in the following decade, under the weight of its incompletely reformed economic system and fast-aging demographics.

At the same time, U.S. economic growth relied increasingly on foreign capital—most of all from those most prodigious of savers, Chinese households. Much of that surplus capital went toward purchasing U.S. treasury securities, both because of their safety, and to depress the value of the yuan by propping up the dollar. Most commentators remained sanguine about this symbiotic relationship—American consumers buying Chinese manufactures, and Chinese savers (through their government) recycling their proceeds to sustain the American consumption habit. They argued that this codependency assured that both countries had strong reason to maintain it.

This first began to change in the recession that commenced in late 2007. It began in the U.S. housing sector, but quickly spread through the financial sector, and through a worldwide credit crunch, to the rest of the "real" economy in all the industrialized countries. As the rich countries' economies contracted, their imports fell even faster—much faster—which undermined export-led economies such as China's. The Communist Party's hold on power depended on maintaining rapid economic growth, so despite an unprecedented economic stimulus, seeds of festering discontent germinated during this recession.

When industrialized countries recovered in the first half of the second decade of the 21st century, the same codependence and "global imbalance" (excess savings in one country; excess consumption in another) revived, albeit at a more moderate scale. Although steps were taken to try to reduce the imbalances—for example, greatly increased taxes in America—they had relatively modest effect. By 2015, the U.S. trade deficit was 12% of GDP, with almost half of it with China alone.

In the meantime, the Chinese regime was becoming more and more insecure. Riots in Guangzhou and other cities by unemployed migrants from the countryside underscored China's vulnerability due to its extreme dependence on exports. The aging population demanded more and better health care. And China's growing role on the world stage had its price as the military consumed more resources.

Military Assertiveness

China's thirst for oil led it to an aggressive diplomatic, and later military, stance. As early as the mid-2000s China was engaged in securing long-term supplies of key industrial commodities. As major fields of newly discovered oil were found in the South China Sea, China asserted its mineral rights, backed up by a growing "blue water" navy. There were showdowns with Japanese, and in one case, American, naval vessels, but all were resolved without serous incident—and with China firmly occupying its claims.

The Taiwan Crisis

Whipping up nationalism is a time-honored strategy for tottering regimes, one that the Chinese leadership had used before. As the effects of the "one child" policy aged the country—by 2020, China's median age was already higher than America's—growth slowed. Millions of underemployed single males, raised in an era of growing prosperity, faced decades of stagnation while waiting for the older generation to die. And the newly muscular military was eager to claim its place.

If China's slowing economy and demographics were the powder keg, the Taiwanese elections of 2030 were, in retrospect, the match. The opposition Democratic People's Party won national elections in a dramatic upset. They ran on an independence platform that many political observers viewed as a desperate come-from-behind strategy. The Chinese leadership kept silent during the campaign, knowing that any attempt to influence the election would backfire. But within hours after the results were broadcast, Premier Li announced that "the DPP [had] violated the democratic rights of our brethren across the Straits" by stealing the election. "The People's Liberation Army is prepared to liberate our fraternal brothers and sisters to reestablish order and democratic rule." The oddly named People's Liberation Army Navy (PLAN) established a blockade of Taiwan.

It has since been revealed that behind the scenes the Chinese had been engaged in a frantic effort to stave off this calamity, of the "renegade province" finally, officially breaking away. Using the United States as an intermediary, they had privately offered the incumbent Taiwanese government a virtual blank check as long as they stepped back from the political brink. But the DPP was the clear underdog and believed they had nothing to lose, so they refused to honor agreements their predecessors had made.

Soon the "fighting" was not only metaphorical. At dawn on April 27, a Chinese frigate fired on an American destroyer that was asserting free passage through the blockade. Shortly after noon on the 27th, a Song-class diesel-electric submarine sank a Japanese civilian tanker bound for Taipei. Within hours, the three American aircraft carriers that had rushed to the area had sunk all four Chinese submarines being tracked in Taiwanese waters, after one carrier took a missile hit that killed dozens on its flight deck and suspended flight operations for days. The remainder of the PLAN pulled back under Chinese air cover from the mainland.

The state-run Chinese media had mobilized public opinion against the "Taiwanese oligarchs" and "their American enablers." Because the sharp defeat at sea had stung, the Chinese leadership could not turn back. So they played their strongest and most destructive card.

At the opening of the bond markets in New York on April 28, the People's Bank of China began selling U.S. Treasury securities. Bond prices fell sharply and interest rates rose by 9 full percentage points. As sales volume far outdistanced historical records, panicked investors joined in. By 11:00 a.m. on April 28, a full-blown run on the dollar was on.

This was the first known effort to crater a currency as a tool of statecraft in almost a century. The last time, in 1956, the United States had forced Britain and France to withdraw their invasion of the Suez Canal Zone by dumping the pound sterling. Now it was on the receiving end of currency warfare.

Within 36 hours, the Chinese has sold $3 trillion in American securities, roughly three-fifths of their foreign reserves. Of course, they lost heavily along with any other holders of U.S. debt, which is why their strategy had been long considered self-defeating. Estimates of Chinese losses range from $600 billion to $2.4 trillion. But as retired Foreign Minister Lin told CNN, "Some national interests are more important than profit."

The dollar was dealt two nearly simultaneous blows. After the Chinese sold treasuries, they moved the proceeds out of dollars and into gold. The price of gold soared from about $2,000 per ounce before the crisis to $9,600 at the close on April 29. The sudden surge in this traditional and very visible indicator of dollar weakness drove panic selling of dollar-denominated assets beyond only treasuries. By the time trading was suspended at 11:43 a.m. on April 29, the dollar had fallen 84% from its level 2 days earlier.

President Chelsea Watkins bowed to a superior force and withdrew the Seventh Fleet from the South China Sea. The State Department announced that "the U.S. has no desire to intrude on what is a fundamentally domestic dispute within China. We have no more right to interfere with Chinese law enforcement than the Chinese would if there was a domestic disturbance in San Francisco."

On April 30, PLA troops began disembarking at Taipei's Sung Shan Airport, and Chinese marines began landing at Tanshui and Hsinchu. Senior DPP officials were placed in protective custody. There were a few incidents of protest, but the PLA dealt with them efficiently and with little bloodshed.

There were in all just under 1,000 casualties in total: 77 on the flight deck of the carrier USS *Nimitz*; 14 U.S. air crew shot down; an estimated 900 Chinese sailors on four submarines and two surface ships that were sunk by the U.S. Seventh Fleet; and approximately 10 Taiwanese civilians killed in the early hours of the occupation. Tragic as these deaths were, they were minor compared with the scale of the Chinese victory—in the marketplace, if not on the high seas.

Thus ended the Three Day War. Ironically, the very high-tech might that had won the military conflict for America had also absorbed so many resources for so long that it helped secure the U.S. economic defeat long before the shooting started.

Aftershocks

The Three Day War clearly established China as a coequal, at least, of the United States on the world stage. Chinese leaders were careful to control their triumphalism—after all, they had lost the shooting war. Also, they knew that several other countries such as Brazil were rising just behind China, and could soon make a plausible case for global economic leadership. But Chinese economic dominance, although fragile, was now impossible to deny.

As in most wars, for both sides the aftermath of the conflict dealt a severe blow to their economies. The drastic decline of the dollar meant that all imports jumped in price, which accelerated inflation from the 5% to 6% levels of the preceding few years well into the double digits. High import prices drove down trade, which brought on a mild recession in China, precisely the situation from which the Chinese leadership had tried to distract its populace.

Over the next few years, several long-standing American allies—Australia, Pakistan, and Japan among them—eased farther away from their traditional close relationships in favor of greater deference to China. Japan, which for 80 years had relied on American military guarantees (originally against the Soviet Union), now formally requested the removal of all military personnel from its soil. Five years on, the United States has thus far delayed its evacuation (to the consternation of successive Japanese cabinets), but most observers see it as imminent. For one thing, the wholesale exit from the dollar signaled the official end of its 80-year run as the world's reserve currency. (Warning signs had been evident for most of the prior few decades.) The United States simply could no longer afford a far-flung network of bases. Withdrawal from Europe began in 2017 and continues today. Ninety-seven percent of a much-shrunken U.S. military is now stationed within its borders, versus less than 60% a generation earlier.

The military vacuum has been filled only partly, mostly by China, India, and Brazil. (Russia's armed forces remain large but underfunded and inferior to first-line militaries in its manpower and technology.)

Chapter 1 Summary

- This chapter sets the economic forces that dominate this book in larger historical context: the rise and decline of empires.
- Empires decline slowly, then suddenly. Typically, their mortal wounds have been self-inflicted over several generations. The British Empire took three generations to unwind, from its peak in the late 19th century to its official close in the mid-20th

century. Historians of the future will likely date the official close of the American Empire to the early 21st century, with the peak coming a generation or more earlier, perhaps in the 1980s.

- There likely will be no single successor to American hegemony. The Three Day War scenario describes a hypothetical dramatic transfer of global leadership to China due to American economic vulnerability, with several other powers (India and Brazil in particular) nipping at China's heels.

CHAPTER 2

The Fall, Rise, and Slow Crash of California, 1981–2010

Baby Boomers who remember the 1950s and 1960s think of California as an Arcadia. The twin mobilizations of World War II and the Cold War brought hundreds of billions of dollars in defense spending to the aerospace cluster of Los Angeles County and the web of military bases that included the Bay Area and San Diego. All that money attracted migrants by the millions, making California the nation's largest state by the early 1960s (surpassing New York). It also paid for a wave of investment in public infrastructure: highways, universities, and a water system that made the desert bloom.

A generation later, California's population was more than double what it had been in the early 1960s, but its infrastructure was no more developed. In fact, that investment had not even been maintained: the state had some of the worst roads in the nation, congested and pothole-strewn. One estimate put the average cost per driver of poor road conditions at more than $700 per year. The generation of the Baby Boom had squandered its inheritance from the GI Generation.

Crummy public services did not stem from any laissez-faire philosophy of low taxes and light regulation. In fact, California had plenty of both. Its total tax rate placed it in the top third of states. By some measures of competitiveness, it was near the bottom.

The cycle of crisis, leadership, investment, rebirth, complacency, and decline has been repeated several times in the past few generations. California is again at a point in its history when it appears its best days are behind it. No one can be certain how rebirth will begin again. *Whether* it begins has significance far beyond the state's borders: it may determine our national future as well.

California's recent economic and fiscal history is worth telling because it carries lessons for the nation and, therefore, for the entire world economy.

In full disclosure, I was a participant in some of the events described here (in the early and middle 1990s) and a commentator on others (in the 2000s). No pretense of objectivity is made; this chapter reflects a distinct point of view: that California is taxing, regulating, and spending at levels well beyond those needed to ensure prosperity. This incontinence reflects a crisis of governance that, while unique in detail, has close parallels in Washington, DC, and a distressingly wide range of democracies.

The End of Glory: The 1980s

The Cold War fueled California's rise to preeminence in the 1940s through 1970s. The impact was both direct, through historic spending on defense, and indirect, through government programs boosted by competition with the Soviets, most especially the space program. The burst of federally funded technological innovation gave birth to the microprocessor in 1971 and the personal computer around 1980. These industries were headquartered in Northern California, while defense and aerospace clustered in Los Angeles and San Diego counties. Between half and one third of all U.S. employment in related high-tech industries resided in the state.

The last great sprint of the defense economy came in the 1980s. Ronald Reagan was elected president with a commitment to strengthen America's defenses to stand firm against the Soviet Union. Defense spending roughly doubled as a share of national gross national product, or GDP. At the same time, one of the distant progeny of the Cold War, the personal computer, was in its infancy, with enormous commercial growth potential. PCs penetrated American households faster than any appliance had before.

All these possibilities brought capital and brainpower to California. The rapid increase in economic activity brought even faster increases in tax revenue, because of the state's heavy reliance on personal income taxes, which rise quickly in booms—then crash in busts. Elected leaders surfed this wave of growing revenues, even under one of the state's most conservative governors, George Deukmejian. Revenues grew by 12% annually for the two decades between 1960 and 1980, much faster than population (2% per year) or the state economy (8.4% per year). California became a tax-intensive state.

In the immediate postwar years, those taxes paid for historic investments, earning taxpayers a superior return by generating economic growth that more than paid for their initial cost. In many years, the state's economy grew twice as fast as the nation's, even when the country was growing quickly as it shrugged off the lingering effects of the Depression and enjoyed the demographic dividend of the Baby Boom.

But by the 1970s those high taxes were being devoted not to investment but to consumption. Highway construction ground to a halt as an act of state policy. College campus expansion slowed to a trickle. But in the pattern of President Lyndon B. Johnson's Great Society, an increasing share of state spending went to transfer payments, distributing wealth from the shrinking portion of the tax base who paid taxes to the growing portion "in need" and therefore exempt from taxation.

The beginnings of fiscal reckoning came in June 1978, when voters overwhelmingly passed Proposition 13, which limited property taxes cities could levy on homeowners. Prop. 13, as it is well known, was the torch that lit the national bonfire of tax revolt that swept Ronald Reagan into the White House two years later.

Paradoxically, among Prop. 13's many side effects was an expansion of state government. Property taxes (which Prop. 13 cut) were the primary funding source for schools, a local responsibility. To soften Prop. 13's blow, the following year the legislature approved a "backfill" in which state revenues were directed to school districts. This was possible because the state that year enjoyed a temporary surplus and necessary because recent federal court cases had mandated a subsidy from rich districts to poor ones to more closely equalize educational opportunity, which the court deemed subject to the equal protection provisions in the U.S. Constitution. So an ironic side effect of a tax revolt was a huge expansion of Sacramento's spending as the state became the main funder of K–12 schools. Today, the subsidy represents nearly half of state spending, and education interests (especially the teacher's union) dominate state budgetary politics.

Despite the clear cri de coeur by voters in Prop. 13 and the Gann expenditure limit that followed in 1979, spending continued to climb.

The tax revolt slowed its rate of ascent, but only modestly—from a 12% annual pace in the 1960s and '70s to a 9% pace in the 1980s. Any of these rates well exceeded the rates of growth in GDP, population, prices, and all combined.

This continued profligacy was possible because the Cold War entered a new, and ultimately terminal, phase with Ronald Reagan's election in 1980. To respond to a rising Soviet Union, Reagan increased defense spending at double-digit annual rates, rising by about 150%, from $134 billion in 1980 to $304 billion by 1989. About one fourth of those funds, and a larger share of the increase, came to California, allowing the state to forestall the inevitable fiscal reckoning day.

The 1990s: Crisis and Renewal

Defense spending peaked in 1989 and then fell slowly throughout the 1990s, creating a "peace dividend." But even peace has its casualties. When the relatively mild and brief national recession of 1990–1991 arrived, California was hit much harder. The state's recession was roughly four times as deep and four times as long as the nation's,[1] because of the drag on the state economy from declining defense purchases.

Coinciding with this defense downsizing-magnified recession, California also suffered from the hangover after the party of the 1980s: a public policy environment distinctly hostile to business. Boom times had permitted the creation of numerous state mandates on business that discouraged firm creation or expansion. The state Council on Competitiveness appointed by new governor Pete Wilson in 1991 and chaired by Peter Ueberroth termed the state a "job killing machine." Government excesses that were tolerable when the economy was growing—like a land use process that required years to permit a new factory—were unaffordable now that companies were battling for their very survival.

California's economy declined during the recession at a multiple of the nation's and so did state finances. California is more dependent on income taxes than most states—more than 50% of total general fund revenue comes from this tax. Furthermore, California has one of the most progressive income tax structures of any state. Those with incomes of more than $200,000 pay more than half total income tax revenues but account for less than 5% of taxpayers. So, in practice, far less than 5% of

California citizens provide more than one fourth of state revenues. (Proportions are similar, though not quite as dramatic, at the federal level.) Some years, the difference between a state surplus and deficit hinges on the choices of a handful of billionaires.

Much of the income earned by those prosperous taxpayers comes not from wages but from investments. Their incomes surge in bull markets and crash in bear markets. As a result, state income taxes explode when asset markets are rising—as the stock market did in the 1980s and 1990s and as the housing market did in the 2000s. But when markets crest, as they generally do just before an expansion turns to recession, so do tax revenues. Aggravating the fiscal problem, government spending generally rises in recession, as more people are unemployed and qualify for various anti-poverty programs (and California's are among the nation's most generous). Plummeting revenues and rising caseloads lead to sharp increases in state deficits.

Pete Wilson was elected California's governor in November 1990. A recession had already begun 4 months earlier, although few yet realized it. As he relates the story, a meeting soon after the election with outgoing governor George Deukmejian was regularly interrupted by the state finance director (equivalent to director of the Office of Management and Budget) reporting on the decline in the state's fiscal situation, almost by the minute.

By the time Wilson was inaugurated in January 1991, the state faced a general fund deficit of tens of billions. As Wilson described it, "It was like a family that suddenly had lost a third of its income." His early attempts to apply a fiscal tourniquet included a mix of spending cuts and tax increases—a surcharge on upper bracket taxpayers (making the income tax even more progressive) and temporary taxes on a variety of goods previously exempt from sales tax (immediately known as the "snack tax"). Wilson, a moderate Republican from San Diego not closely affiliated with the highly conservative state GOP that was dominated by rural interests, found himself making strange bedfellows with Democrats, led by Speaker Willie Brown, the self-proclaimed "Ayatollah of the Assembly," to pass his emergency 1991–1992 budget.

But while the national recession had bottomed out by the spring of 1991, the continued erosion of the defense budget, combined with an exodus of small businesses fleeing an unfriendly tax and regulatory climate, perpetuated California's downward plunge. Arguably, some of the emergency measures put in place, such as the income tax surcharge, probably made the situation worse, since many high-income filers are business owners. By spring 1992, California faced an even larger deficit than the year before. A lengthy impasse in the legislature led to payments to vendors and employees being made in IOUs after the new fiscal year began in July 1992, because the legislature lacked the legal authority to spend money without an enacted budget.

While Wilson acted to control the expanding fiscal emergency, he simultaneously attempted to rally the public to recognize the self-inflicted wounds from anticompetitive public policies adopted in better times. At the policy level, the aforementioned Competitiveness Council outlined a checklist of measures to allow the state to compete effectively with other states for new business. Ueberroth's council set the policy agenda for many economic reforms over the next few years.

One centerpiece was taxes. Wilson appreciated that "you can't tax your way to prosperity," and he regretted the tax increases he had been obliged to propose when he entered office. By 1993, he was ready to try another approach: *cutting* taxes to stimulate economic activity. The emphasis was on reversing the upper bracket increases of 1991 to eliminate a disadvantage in the state's competition for small businesses and targeted tax breaks to lure new large businesses, particularly manufacturing facilities. The narrowness of these cuts made them palatable to enough Democratic legislators to achieve passage in the legislature, with invaluable support from Speaker Willie Brown.[2]

After Wilson's reelection in 1994 and his abortive bid for the Republican nomination for president in 1995, the policy agenda became less about reversing the excesses of the 1980s and more about breaking new procompetitive ground. Initiatives included the restructuring of the electric industry from three vertically integrated monopolies (Southern California Edison, Pacific Gas & Electric, and San Diego Gas and Electric) into a market in which in principle any customer could buy power from any willing provider. This was good GOP politics, and probably smart policy, since California needed to be beyond business reproach to emphasize the change from the "ABC (anywhere but California)" days. Many of these initiatives depended on spirited implementation, which often did not survive the change of governors in 1999.

By the middle of the 1990s, California's deep recession—then the worst since the 1930s—had blossomed into a sharp recovery, then a record-breaking expansion. In a few short years, the economy transformed from one that lost 1,000 jobs per day to one that created 1,000 new jobs per day. The state's fiscal picture improved commensurately, so that Wilson could propose further tax cuts in 1996 and enact the elimination of the vehicle license fee "car tax" in 1997 on the grounds that it was regressive.[3]

These short paragraphs emphasize the results, not the struggle to achieve them. Every anticompetitive policy was originally created to achieve some other objective and had passionate constituencies defending it. Public employee unions, including the large and politically powerful teachers union, were opposed to tax cuts because they feared the loss of union jobs paid for by those taxes. Unions exercised virtual veto power because of their generous campaign contributions to Democratic candidates, who repaid with their votes in the legislature. Assemblyman Roger Niello of Sacramento summarized this when he said, "The unions don't just have policy influence. They really have policy control."[4] But many incumbents felt vulnerable in bad economic times and were persuaded by Brown to break with the unions to support tax cuts. It also helped that the most prominent supporters were moderate Republicans from Silicon Valley like state Senator Rebecca Morgan and Assemblyman Jim Cuneen, as well as moderate Democrat Ted Lempert, whose districts had much to gain if electronics plants could be attracted or retained.

In addition, these reforms came at a price. A concurrent push to convert redundant defense and aerospace skilled workers into teachers resulted in a large portion of California's teachers being poorly qualified, especially in districts with high rates of poverty. Of course, "qualified" meant "certified," and educational reformers argued that certification requirement put primary emphasis on fluency in pedagogical fads at the expense of subject-matter knowledge. More teachers were needed because of a Wilson-initiated push to lower class sizes in early grades, although the evidence in support of such a move was spotty and anecdotal. Nevertheless, California teachers were among the highest paid in the nation—testament to their clout with legislatures and school boards.

Reform's Retrenchment in the Early 2000s

By the late 1990s, the Internet was beginning to achieve its full commercial promise, and stocks of many companies associated with this new technology were bid up to stratospheric levels. This "dot-com" bubble was not unlike previous technology-based bubbles, including that of the 1920s, which originated with the new technology of radio and the disruptive technology of widespread electrification.

Because California state revenues are built on the one-legged stool of capital gains, the late 1990s was feasting time in Sacramento. There were further tax cuts, and public employee unions assured they claimed their share of the windfall. In particular, the powerful prison guards union extracted double-digit pay increases from the legislature and new governor Gray Davis. Previous governors, including Wilson, had also treated the CCPOA (California Correctional Peace Officers Association) very well. Wilson was particularly supportive of a sharp increase in prison construction, which added new CCPOA members. But the magnitude of the wage concessions Davis agreed to was without precedent. Sacramento insiders interpreted this as a desperate move to pay back an ally for campaign contributions that helped to elect Davis in 1998 and reelect him in 2002. Davis had a well-deserved reputation as obsessed with fundraising, which would be his undoing in the 2003 recall election.

Similarly, on the strength of reassurances from the California Public Employees Retirement System (CalPERS), in 1999 the legislature made the retirement formula significantly more generous, adding hundreds of billions to future liabilities.

All this spending was possible because of the flood of revenues that accompanied the dot-com bubble. The Internet industry was largely centered in Silicon Valley, so its explosive growth swelled state coffers. But asset markets often overshoot—Amazon's price-to-earnings ratio reached into the hundreds, and many firms went public with no earnings at all. In April 2000, the bubble finally burst, presaging what became another mild and brief national recession. But while the 2001 recession was not again accompanied by defense downsizing—in fact, just the opposite after the September 11 terrorist attacks on the Pentagon and World Trade Center—the consequences for state revenues were similar. Sacramento was abruptly pushed, again, from feast to famine.

Although the California constitution calls for the governor to submit a balanced budget to the legislature each year, there is no way to mandate realism in budgetary assumptions. To respond to the reopening fiscal gap in the early 2000s, budgets became more and more breathtaking in the range of "smoke and mirrors" tricks employed to pretend a balance. Some of these tricks had long histories, including under Wilson, but their breadth in the 2000s was unprecedented. Each budget simply "kicked the can down the road" (in Governor Schwarzenegger's phrase) into the next year, when a different group of decision makers would have to deal with it (thanks to term limits, passed by the voters in 1990). The phrase "structural deficit" (i.e., a deficit that persists even in normal or boom times) became common argot among Sacramento budget wonks.

The legislature and Davis also reinstated several taxes that had been eliminated earlier during the early 1990s reforms, including reimposition of higher tax rates for upper-income filers. Along with a range of tightening environmental rules that made it increasingly difficult to site a business facility in the state, "anywhere but California" reappeared in business's vocabulary.

In essence, the legislature and Davis had exploited a temporary windfall from the dot-com bubble to make permanent commitments of state expenditures—many of them to public employee unions, not coincidentally. Each of their successors was now saddled with a permanently higher level of expenditures.

In addition, in 2000, the hidden flaws in the electricity industry restructuring passed in 1996 surfaced. When the plan was adopted, electricity demand growth appeared to have plateaued, so substantial surpluses were forecast with attendant falling prices. But by the winter of 2000–2001, the opposite had occurred. Several years of dry weather slowed stream flows to a trickle, diminishing available hydropower, which normally supplied about 10% of the state's electricity. At the same time, supplies of natural gas, which fired nearly 50% of the state's generators, were curtailed amid charges of market manipulation by pipeline and energy trading companies, including Enron. The wholesale price of electricity in the West skyrocketed. But under the restructuring law and the California Public Utilities Commission's (CPUC) interpretation, utilities were subject to price caps on what they could charge retail customers.

(Policy makers had not expected these caps to be ever binding, because they had anticipated an electricity surplus.)

The result was shortages of electricity at the least likely time of year—winter. Brownouts and rolling blackouts that had been occasional and local on hot summer evenings were now common and pervasive. The Davis administration focused its energy for weeks on finding someone else to blame, and then in desperation it committed further billions to long-term power purchases from out-of-state suppliers. Within weeks, the crisis had passed, but the state had taken on another multi-billion-dollar permanent commitment.

Perhaps the greatest long-term damage done in the early 2000s was political, not fiscal. Every decade, legislative district lines are redrawn based on new census data. Incumbent legislators oversee the redistricting. Commonly, legislators draw district lines to ensure a large majority of voter registration in the party of the incumbent in that district. When this first occurred in 1812 Massachusetts under the leadership of Governor Elbridge Gerry, some of the resulting districts were shaped like lizards, termed by wags as "gerrymanders." The term has since become a verb because gerrymandering is so common: Voters don't choose their legislators; incumbents choose their voters. The leader of the 1980 California gerrymander, Congressman Phil Burton, referred to the resulting map as "my contribution to modern art."

Gerrymandering is the enemy of true accountability (which is the essence of democracy) because "safe" districts inhibit challenges to incumbents, and indeed, more than 95% of the members of Congress who stand for reelection are returned by the voters. Those in the minority party—Republicans in California, whose registered voters were outnumbered by Democrats by margins of roughly 3 to 2—believed that the absence of competitive districts meant that their party held a proportion of seats well below their actual popularity. In California, GOP legislators largely came from inland, rural districts: the cities and the coast were safely Democratic.

The most corrosive effect of gerrymandering was the rise of partisanship. Because districts were drawn to be safely in the hands of one party or the other, the general election was irrelevant; only the primary mattered. Primary election turnout is dominated by the party's base—the true believers who tend to the ideological extreme.

Consequently, winning candidates usually had strong ideological leanings. Few moderates survived this process. When combined with the high expense of campaigns that mandated constant fund-raising (often from ideologically skewed special interests), the stage was set for ideological polarization.

A rare exception occurred after the 1990 census, when Pete Wilson rejected the legislature's concoction and threw the job to the state Supreme Court. In fact, putting a GOP governor in place to counter the legislature's gerrymander was a key reason many GOP leaders had rallied behind Wilson's candidacy, despite their tepid support for many of his moderate positions. Truly competitive districts allowed a handful of moderate legislators to lead many of the landmark bills passed in the early and mid-1990s. On the GOP side, these included the aforementioned Morgan and Cuneen on tax cuts and Steve Kuykendall on electricity restructuring. Among Democrats, Dede Alpert and Ted Lempert on education and Steve Peace on electric restructuring implementation led historic legislative initiatives that helped shape the post-1990s recession economy.

After the 2000 census, the legislature produced another incumbent protection plan, but this time Gray Davis signed it without protest, thereby guaranteeing the continued tenure of the very legislators who had put the state on an unsustainable fiscal path. Speculation in Sacramento was that he was paying back Democratic legislators as his generous giveaways to unions had done before.

The Mid-2000s: Recall and "Postpartisanship"

The cumulative unsavoriness of Davis's actions—relentless fund-raising, accusations of "pay to play" policy deals, intervention in the 2002 GOP primary to ensure that the weaker candidate was nominated, exacerbation of the structural deficit from giveaways to union contributors—peaked in the 2003 campaign. The recall (essentially an impeachment decided by voters) manifested enough voter anger against Davis to handily eject him from the governor's office and sweep Arnold Schwarzenegger in with a majority in a very crowded field of possible replacements. Schwarzenegger's core issue was stopping "the crazy deficit spending."

By 2004, the growing structural deficit—most of it financed through short-term borrowing—could not be deferred any longer. Politically, the recall had made clear that failure to rein in spending credibly would put even ultrasafe incumbents at risk. Schwarzenegger and the legislators quickly concocted a debt restructuring plan that converted tens of billions in short-term borrowing into long-term "economic recovery bonds," which were approved by the voters.

This was probably the greatest, and the last, element of Schwarzenegger's postelection honeymoon. Within months, the legislature had blocked his efforts at spending control, including a plan to limit future pension payments by mandating defined contribution retirement plans for all future workers.[5] Schwarzenegger concluded that nothing less than fundamental political reform was necessary. But since Democratic incumbent legislators would never agree, he resolved to use his star power to take the case directly to the voters, in the form of a handful of reform initiatives that he qualified for the November 2005 ballot. These included initiatives to create an independent redistricting commission, to increase standards for teacher tenure, to place new state employees in a defined contribution retirement plan, to create a state expenditure limit, and to require that union leaderships disclose their political spending to their members.

Schwarzenegger's mistake was to take on the entire range of political adversaries all at once. All elements of the spending lobby—public employee unions, teachers unions, nonprofits that received government dollars, and the legislators they elected—bitterly opposed the suite of measures and outspent the forces of reform by 5 to 1. This spending included a barrage of campaign commercials, many of which brazenly lied about the measures' deficiencies. For example, one oft-aired commercial claimed that Schwarzenegger planned to suspend survivor payments to the widows and orphans of slain police officers. Schwarzenegger found himself surrounded and virtually without allies, because his natural ally— business—stayed neutral in fear of being punished in the legislature.

When the entire slate went down to defeat and Schwarzenegger's approval ratings under the union onslaught sank to barely double-digit levels, he turned abruptly from a moderate Republican to a "postpartisan." He cooperated more extensively with legislative Democrats—so much that many Republicans argued he had been completely co-opted. The most visible change was an increased emphasis on environmental initiatives at the expense of short-term economic growth. (Schwarzenegger argued that many of his initiatives would stimulate the growth in "green jobs" that would more than compensate for any loss of traditional jobs.) For example, AB 32 put in place a state "cap and trade" system to control greenhouse gas emissions. This was much more popular in the boom of the mid-2000s than in the post-housing-bubble recession that followed. At this writing, an initiative has qualified for the ballot to suspend the AB 32 mandates until the unemployment rate drops below 5.5%, which is not likely for several years.

Schwarzenegger's postpartisan line in the sand—if he drew any at all—related to taxes. He claimed complete opposition to any tax increases, in light of their poor record in the Davis years. However, he did not hesitate to propose "user fees" that were virtually indistinguishable from taxes. This began in his abortive health care reform plan that mimicked a 2006 Massachusetts reform law passed under then-governor Mitt Romney and presaged the Obama plan of four years later. But inventive expansion of "fees" and taxes really kicked into high gear in the late 2000s recession, when state revenues plunged again. For example, the 2009–2010 budget proposed several temporary increases in sales taxes. A follow-up initiative in May 2009 to extend their duration went down to defeat at the polls by almost 2 to 1.

Today, the structural deficit is still as troublesome as ever. Each year policy makers concoct a "solution" that papers over a deficit in the range of several tens of billions, only to find that a continuing recession (California's unemployment rate is nearly 3% above the nation's already high rate) makes a mockery of these clever fictions. In fact, on the occasions when deficits are partly closed by substantive changes, those changes (such as the temporary 2009 sales tax surcharges) often exacerbate the problem. That is why Schwarzenegger has been reasonably firm against tax increases.

The deficit problem would be far worse but for stimulus funds provided by the federal government. In fact, 2010's proposed "solutions" in Sacramento and in several cities depended heavily on fanciful assumptions about supposedly imminently arriving federal subsidies.

Gridlock

The structural deficit has been obdurate because the spending lobby is so powerful. Over the years, they have engineered spending programs that their members treat as entitlements. The situation isn't quite as bad as in Greece, where 1 in 3 workers is on the public payroll, and some have resorted to violence to protest the austerity demanded by the European

Union and the International Monetary Fund as the price of their spring 2010 emergency bridge loan. But California public employee unions are not beyond intimidation and fraud to protect their hard-won gains. That the taxpayers who pay their salaries enjoy nothing like the same level of protections does not temper union leaders' passion; it merely demonstrates that more workers should be government workers.

Many of the problems could be readily solved if politicians did not secretly find them convenient. For example, the vast majority—some say as much as 95%—of general fund dollars are earmarked for specific purposes by long-term contracts, voter initiatives, and court rulings. This makes a mockery of the supposed flexibility of the "general fund." But these programs serve the same political purpose as entitlement programs at the federal level: They allow continued, and growing, spending to reward specific constituencies without the messy and embarrassing prerequisite of an actual legislative vote. Politicians can decry "ballot box budgeting" without actually proposing any changes needed to regain fiscal discretion—because with discretion comes responsibility and accountability. Better to get the political benefit of dispensing state largesse without the political cost of actively choosing.

In a similar way, the requirement of a two-thirds legislative majority to pass a budget or tax increases is singled out as a barrier to fiscal progress, because as long as the majority party (Democrats) holds less than two thirds of the seats, a handful of Republicans can hold up fiscal bills. This happens nearly every summer, often delaying budgets by many months, sometimes leading to the IOU situation mentioned earlier, which was briefly repeated in 2009. Here again the two-thirds requirement helps the agenda of Democratic leaders: They have an enemy—"obstructionist" Republicans—they can blame and rail against in the fund-raising battle.

A number of other political reform issues have garnered attention—an open primary, elimination or relaxation of term limits, tightening eligibility requirements for initiatives—but most suffer from the same problem. Those few who thrive under the status quo have far more motivation to resist reform proposals (including spending millions to defeat them at the ballot box) than do the forces of reform. As with free trade, political reform benefits the many only modestly, but it costs the few greatly. The few fight harder for the status quo and usually prevail.

By early 2010 Schwarzenegger was officially a lame duck, with declining clout. (Arguably this had begun several years earlier.) Soon the dam holding back tax increases will burst,[6] and California will join states like New Jersey and New York in setting rates so high that more than half of a middle-class paycheck, at the margin, goes to federal, state, and local taxes. Not coincidentally, such states have the highest unemployment rates of any state with a diverse economy.

As California Goes . . .

Informed readers will recognize that, although the details differ, there are strong parallels throughout the developed world:

- Unrestrained spending that leads to persistent structural deficits.
- Escalating tax rates that never seem to generate the additional revenue predicted.
- Torpid businesses, and especially low rates of new business formation.
- A growing number of "tax consumers" and a shrinking number of "tax producers."
- Above-average unemployment that persists long after the rest of the nation is in recovery.
- Per capita income that is underpacing the nation, both because of limited economic growth, aggravated by escalating in-migration by the poor, and out-migration by the productive.
- Partisan gridlock ordained by a political structure designed to preserve the status quo, which prevents economic reform.

The previous paragraph not only describes California but could apply to virtually any Western European country today, and increasingly applies to the United States as a whole. Western Europe, with its generous safety net and extreme employment protections, is the envy of many liberals, who consider its generosity worth its price of high chronic unemployment.

The United States and California share some attributes with Europe, although the demographic dimension is more muted in California. But

America also has some advantages that could allow it to avoid the worst elements of Europe's and California's future. The balance of this book will go into some detail about both the structural problems and opportunities. The final chapters offer some ideas for how the reader can respond to the future outlined herein.

Chapter 2 Summary

- California is a case study for how an ossified political structure causes creeping insolvency. Examining California's recent political history provides a leading indicator of the fate of many developed economies, including much of Europe, Japan, and the United States.
- California has been in long-term decline for 50 years but not without periodic corrections (temporary booms).
- Periods of resurgence (defense boom in the 1980s, the Internet bubble of the late 1990s, the housing boom of the early 2000s) have bred complacency, leading to self-inflicted wounds by successive governments.
- The persistent causes of decline include
  - Tax rates and regulations beyond those of competing jurisdictions such as Texas
  - Structural political rules that sustain gridlock
  - Special interests that impose costs on general taxpayers
  - Result: per capita income has grown slower than the national average
- The long-term implication has been a slow death spiral.
- This pattern is being duplicated in many developed economies, including in the U.S. federal government.

CHAPTER 3

Your Country Is Getting Older, and Your Government Is Bankrupt

General Motors spent decades in crypto-bankruptcy, borrowing money to stay afloat and selling assets to keep its creditors at bay. Its basic problem (besides the unpopularity of its core product) was that it had made promises to its employees and retirees that were premised on constantly rising sales. For most of the past decade, it was apparent to observers that GM's key demographic assumption was no longer true: that its employee base would shrink and be saddled with the support of a still-growing retiree population. Finally, the recent recession murdered GM's autonomy: the company solicited a $50 billion capital infusion from the federal government and in exchange ceded their independence to the White House and Congress.

Something like what happened to GM (and Chrysler) in 2008 will almost certainly happen to the federal government, and many state and local governments, in a future recession. It will have exactly the same cause: commitments of benefits to current and former workers that are unsustainable given predictable demographic trends.

You have probably heard something about the trends this chapter will describe, but its significance may have been lost amid the more urgent challenges of the recent recession. Also, the issue has received little serious attention from our elected leaders. But while government finances are arcane, they will have very real consequences for your lifestyle and your assets. This chapter describes the domestic fiscal challenge. Chapter 4 adds an international dimension. Chapter 5 integrates these themes to show the likely effects on your savings and your purchasing power. Chapters 8 and 9 outline steps you can take to protect your assets.

Demography Is Destiny

Economists' records as forecasters make astrologers look good. But demographers are on much firmer ground. After all, an excellent predictor of the number of 20-year-olds 20 years from now is the number of births this year. While demographic surprises are possible—for instance, the surge in immigration to the United States in the 1980s and 1990s—the broad outlines of our population can be predicted decades in advance.

Two demographic phenomena are already shaping our economy today and will do so even more profoundly in the future.

Fewer Babies

As developed nations' economies relied less and less on agriculture in the 19th and 20th centuries, families moved to urban areas. For a newly urban family, having large numbers of children was no longer an economic asset. Better sanitation and health care also meant a much lower rate of infant mortality, alleviating the need to compensate by having many children. In addition, as women became emancipated from their historic role as homemakers, they often earned enough to make it expensive to have many kids (and leave the workforce for awhile around each birth). Consequently, birthrates have fallen sharply. This decline in fertility was first observed in Japan, later spreading to Western Europe, but it has also been a fixture of American demographics for at least three decades.

Demographers measure this change of behavior by the "total fertility rate" (TFR). It captures the average number of children born per woman in her lifetime. A TFR that produces just enough births to replace deaths would be just above 2.0, say, 2.05. (The extra .05 compensates for infants who die in childbirth.) A society with a TFR of 2.05 or so would have a stable population—it would not shrink or grow without immigration.

America's total fertility rate was nearly 4.0 around the tail end of the Baby Boom, defined by demographers as the mid-1940s to the mid-1960s. At that time, many were concerned about a population explosion. The TFR fell below 2.0—that is, below the replacement level—in the early 1970s and has stayed there up to the present. (It has, however, risen from a low point of 1.8 throughout the 1980s, closer to 2.0, presumably due to increased immigration of couples from countries with higher birthrates.)

Fewer births today means fewer 25-year-olds a generation hence. The decline in TFR has pervasive effects on nearly every industry: fewer toys sold after 5 to 10 years; fewer tickets to rock concerts after 15 years; fewer college students after 20. And, most significant, to the broader economy: fewer workers after 25 years. The implications of this are discussed next.

Longer Lives

Medical advances have added almost 1 year to the average life span each decade. Male average life spans in 1950 were 78 years, while today they exceed 81 years. The trend is even more dramatic for females: from 81 years in 1950 to 85 in 2000.

We can be grateful for the extra life we can enjoy. But our retirement and entitlements systems were premised on much shorter life spans. When Social Security was enacted in 1935 and granted eligibility to citizens when they reach age 65, average life spans were not much longer: to about age 67. Today, a worker who retires in his or her 60s has a high probability of collecting retirement benefits for at least 20 years and quite possibly 30 or more.

Effects on Retirement Benefits

These demographic facts collide with the underlying premise of our entitlement programs. Contrary to popular belief, any contributions we made as workers are not saved in some personal account to be used later when we retire. They were spent immediately to pay benefits of those already retired (just as those recipients' contributions had been used to pay earlier retirees).

Such a "pay as you go" system—as Social Security, Medicare, and most private pensions are, at least partially—works only so long as the incomes of current workers (who are paying into the system) are as large as the current benefits the system is committed to pay. When total worker income declines (e.g., because the number of workers shrinks), the system is revealed as the Ponzi scheme it is.[1]

In a nutshell, this was GM's problem, too. Huge improvements in manufacturing productivity in the 1980s and '90s meant that GM could produce a given number of vehicles with far fewer workers. By the mid-2000s, the company's rolls had fallen to 200,000 workers, but it had one million retirees, whose benefits were paid from the production of the reduced ranks of those still working. Health care benefits were particularly expensive, because health costs have risen several times faster then even manufacturing productivity (which has grown quite rapidly). Health benefits for GM's growing number of retirees were a key factor in its spiral into insolvency.[2]

This demographic implosion will be particularly stark in the next few decades, as the Baby Boomers retire. The oldest Boomers are now in their mid-60s. Over the next 20 to 25 years, most of these 80 million people will leave the workforce. The generation that will succeed them is barely half the size. Even if many Boomers delay retirement or work part time after their official retirement date—as many have improvised in the recent recession in response to huge bear market declines in their assets—the United States still will see a dramatic rise in its "dependency ratio"—the ratio of those not in the workforce to those still working.

The federal government has, through the Medicare and Social Security programs, instituted and sustained a Ponzi scheme of historic proportions. These two entitlement programs[3] have made commitments of $50 to 100 trillion in excess of foreseeable revenues, with the lion's share due to Medicare. Equivalent commitments by state and local governments to their own retirees—often far more generous than pensions of equivalent workers in the private sector—are of similar scale.

"Trust funds" into which these entitlement programs have invested temporary surpluses (i.e., have bought government bonds) will allow these programs to keep operating for a period after their income falls short of their expenses. For Social Security, its trustees predicted in 2008 that the system would fall into operating deficit in 2017 but be able to cover its losses from the trust fund until 2041. Then the recession hit: payroll taxes plunged, and many individuals "retired" early because they were forced to by circumstances. The dates just mentioned will almost certainly be revised downward by a few years.

A Confiscatory System

Both these entitlement programs are financed entirely through payroll taxes. In theory, they are paid equally by both the employee and their employer. But in practice, all of the tax comes from employees' wages, since employers can reduce their wages to pay for the tax.

Payroll taxes are inherently regressive. That is, unlike income taxes, in which higher-income earners pay a higher proportion of their income to the IRS—termed a *progressive* system—the reverse is true. Payroll taxes are flat (i.e., the rate stays constant) regardless of income up to just more than $100,000 in wages; then they are zero at higher levels. So an employee earning $200,000 pays payroll tax on only the first $100,000 of his income and nothing thereafter. His effective payroll tax rate is, therefore, half that of an employee who makes $100,000 or less.

These programs' benefit structures are likewise regressive—regardless of how much you earned while working, your Social Security benefits are capped at less than $30,000 per year. Nevertheless, it remains surprising that Americans have (grudgingly) accepted this regressive payroll tax, which has risen much faster than incomes. Likewise, Medicare taxes will rise again under the Affordable Care Act (a.k.a. "ObamaCare").

Implicit and Explicit Debt

The *explicit* national debt held by the public—that is, omitting any government securities held by government itself, such as the Social Security trust fund—is in the neighborhood of $15 trillion. Generally, debt specialists focus not on the absolute dollar amount but on its size relative to that of the national economy with which it is associated, in other words, the ratio of "debt to GDP." This facilitates comparisons across borrowers (nations) and gives a very general idea of the ability of the nation to cover its debt obligation.

The average debt-to-GDP (gross domestic product) ratio for the United States in the late 20th century was about 40%. It exceeded 100% during and after World War II as the nation borrowed to pay for a massive mobilization. Thereafter, it fell gradually as a growing economy ballooned the denominator of the ratio, reaching its low around 1980.

The debt-to-GDP ratio has climbed sharply several times in our nation's history: in the Civil War, during World War I, and to combat the Great Depression. In each of these times, the nation faced an existential crisis that justified borrowing from future revenues to confront a current emergency. But in each instance, after the crisis the nation ran surpluses, so the ratio came down. (Andrew Jackson paid the debt off entirely— a debt-to-GDP ratio of zero—in the 1830s.) Arguably, preventing Great Depression 2.0 mandated similar "crisis" borrowing today. But there was no emergency that justified the borrowing of the 1980s, 1990s, and early 2000s.

This line of reasoning makes a larger point: the issue is not the debt per se, but what the increased borrowing bought for the money. Financial professionals approve of households taking on debt if it goes to purchase an asset with a return greater than the cost to service that debt. A classic example is a college education: it may cost $100,000, but it will add $1 million or more to the student's lifetime earnings.

Most of the federal borrowing in recent decades went for consumption, not investment. In this, our government mirrored the millions of households who secured home equity loans earlier in the decade to spend not on economic assets but on upgrading their lifestyle. Borrowing to consume only makes sense if your income (from which you will service the loan) rises faster than the loan costs do. Families earlier this decade can be excused for not anticipating a recession that would devastate their incomes, but governments cannot claim to be surprised by demographics.

Furthermore, our nation is in a much less favorable position to service a large federal debt than we were 50 years ago. First, our average age was considerably younger (remember the Baby Boom). Second, our relative youth meant bright prospects for strong economic growth, yielding growing tax revenues to service the debt. Finally, our creditors were "captive"—almost exclusively our own residents. Today, by contrast, nearly half the debt is held by foreigners. The implications of this are taken up in the next chapter.

But the $10 trillion or so in national debt is only the *explicit* debt. There is a parallel *implicit* debt, which is much larger: the $50 to 100 trillion in retiree entitlements, depending on demographic and economic assumptions, as mentioned above. In other words, the problem is 10 times bigger than you thought.

To put these programs in perspective: In the late 20th century, the federal government spent about 20% of GDP in total (its revenues were slightly less, hence the chronic small deficits). By the middle years of this century, these two entitlement programs plus debt service will *alone* consume about 25% of GDP, more than all the revenues the government earns. California has similarly had a "structural" deficit—one that never closes, even in boom times—for about a decade and has borrowed perpetually, suffering repeated debt downgrades to the lowest level among the states.

None of the above figures include the implicit and explicit debts of cities, counties, and states, which are of roughly similar magnitude to the federal government's burden. So the coping strategies Washington will try in the coming decades will be mirrored by similar attempts in state capitals and city halls.

Debt Versus Deficit

When any entity—a business, a household, or a government—spends more in a given year than it earns, it has run a *deficit*: the annual difference between income and outgo. If the entity does not have assets it can sell to cover this difference (e.g., savings in a bank), it may be able to borrow from creditors. That borrowing is added to the stock of past borrowing, that is, the entity's *debt*. So a given year's deficit is added to the accumulated debt; that is, the accumulation from past deficits.

If the federal government's level of debt was at an acceptable level— say, 40% or 50% of GDP—it could maintain that debt level if it ran deficits of 2% or 3% of GDP more or less perpetually, as long as the economy (i.e., the source of debt service payments through tax revenues) was growing at a similar rate.

Even very large deficits can be justified if they are a necessary price to achieve some critical national objective: such as winning a war in which the nation's survival is at stake, as in World War II. This is the argument made by those in government for running a deficit in excess of 10% of GDP in the recent recession: The deficit inevitably rose because the recession simultaneously suppressed tax revenues (because the unemployed have no income to tax) and ballooned entitlements (e.g., for food stamps), and because aggressive fiscal stimulus was necessary to avoid a far worse downturn.[4] But the result is that projected deficits into the next decade will cause the debt-to-GDP ratio to rise from about 60% to close to 90% by the end of the decade and more than 100% soon thereafter.[5]

Why Reform Has Been So Long Deferred

The arrival of the Baby Boom bulge to entitlement eligibility has been predictable for two generations, and lengthening life spans have been a long-established fact as well. So our leaders cannot claim to be surprised. In fact, there have been a number of efforts to more closely align entitlements' expected costs with expected revenues. But far more often, Congress has increased benefits without regard to costs—or made unrealistic assumptions about economic growth to rationalize overly optimistic revenue forecasts to make their increased benefits appear to pencil out.

The politics behind this dynamic illustrate the proverbial "law of unintended consequences." Social Security illustrates nicely. As conceived in the early 1930s, it was intended as a program to support the indigent elderly—in other words, an income redistribution program. President Franklin D. Roosevelt realized that it could not pass Congress in that form, so he redesigned it to make it universal: Every worker contributed, and every contributor collected benefits after age 65. But the indigent earn a higher return on their contributions than the wealthy do. Effectively, an income redistribution scheme over time morphed into a middle–class entitlement. Universality created a very large and powerful constituency for the program, but that very constituency has blocked most efforts at reform. The only enacted reform in recent memory was the Greenspan Commission of the early 1980s, which raised payroll taxes and the retirement age. Its charter obliged Congress to vote "yea or nay" without amendment.

The Consequences of Inaction

Scholars like Boston University's Lawrence Kotlikoff, the Congressional Budget Office (CBO), the Peter G. Peterson Foundation, and the Concord Coalition have examined the growth in entitlement liabilities and their effect on the federal budget. As noted earlier, since World War II federal spending has averaged about 20% of GDP. By the middle of the next decade, entitlement spending *alone* will exceed 10% of GDP, rising to more than 20% by the middle of the century. Even if all other spending is held in check, total federal spending will rise to close to 35% of GDP by then. In other words, *within most Baby Boomers' lifetimes it will be impossible to meet the government's commitments without historic reductions on other programs, increases in taxes, or (most likely) both.* Since Congress has shown no stomach for serious reform of entitlements, it will be obliged to make major changes elsewhere.

All options are painful. In broad strokes, they include the following:

- Raise the ceiling on the payroll tax from just over $100,000 to a much higher income, or abolish it entirely.
- Set a much higher payroll tax rate, at least for higher incomes.
- Reduce benefits prospectively for those retiring after some future date or those born after some past date.
- Raise Medicare premiums to catch up with medical inflation.
- Index entitlement payments to a slower-escalating base.
- Devote a growing share of general revenues to pay for these programs (already nearly half the federal budget), which would require increases in other taxes such as income or corporate taxes.

You can make your own prediction as to the likely mix of benefit reductions, spending reductions, and tax increases. From past experience, it seems certain that tax increases will bear most of the load. Analysts such as Kotlikoff have estimated that tax increases in excess of 100% will be required if Congress acts immediately and much more if they continue to delay.

This problem has existed for decades. But added to it is a more recent fiscal challenge: the enormous ($1 trillion to 2 trillion) deficits the federal government is now running to counteract the recent recession. These have only aggravated, and accelerated, America's day of fiscal reckoning.

Awareness of the need for long-postponed frugality is mobilizing anti-government insurgents throughout the industrialized world, with the Tea Party getting most of the attention in the United States. Perhaps unsurprisingly, Western European governments, who have sinned the most and longest, show the most rhetorical support for a newly discovered austerity. This issue divided the G-20 summit in Toronto in June 2010. It seems likely to pose a heavy price on incumbent politicians in future elections, as it did in spring 2010 primaries in the United States.

The Stakes: Lackluster Economic Performance

Scolds like me have for decades warned of dire consequences from continued high-deficit spending. But proponents have correctly argued that our day of reckoning never seems to come. This is what Vice President Cheney meant in 2002 when he said (incorrectly) that "deficits don't matter."

You now know the reason America's financial comeuppance has been so slow in arriving: Foreign investors have provided the capital to replace that not available from domestic savers. These investors have done so in part because they believe they can earn a superior return in the world's heretofore most dynamic large economy, and because some investors—particularly the Chinese and Japanese central banks—have depressed the value of their own currencies by selling them and buying dollar-denominated assets. The next chapter will argue that this flood of investment will wane, for financial and demographic reasons.

It is quite reasonable to ask: At what point does a nation become *too* indebted? When will its debts undermine investor confidence, driving up either interest rates or tax rates that bring on stagnation? Two former International Monetary Fund economists, Carmen Reinhardt of the University of Maryland and Kenneth Rogoff of Harvard University, have answered this question: The "wall" gets hit at a ratio of government debt to GDP above 90%.[6] After that, economic growth decelerates, and higher unemployment becomes chronic. The United States will reach that threshold within a very few years. By some measures, it already has.

Above this threshold—or even before—bond vigilantes and speculators will sell off assets in the nation's currency—especially government bonds. This will either increase interest rates to a level where the debt can no longer be serviced, force tax increases to pay down the debt faster (but drive economic growth into the cellar), or lead authorities to monetize the debt and cause accelerating inflation. Often a combination of all of the above occurs. Reinhart and Rogoff examined more than 1,000 historical examples of national debts across dozens of countries, stretching back to the 12th century. They found that for each increase in the nation's debt-to-GDP ratio of 30%, GDP growth fell by about 1%. Debt ratios above 90% led to subpar economic growth with elevated inflation. At this writing, Greece's situation is the latest object lesson.

Because the dollar remains the world's reserve currency, foreigners are forced to accept a certain amount of American profligacy as long as they accept dollars. (If they fled the dollar, they might not be able to transact business as easily in another currency.) So the United States might be able to relax the 90% debt-to-GDP threshold somewhat. But as foreigners are witnessing our upward-spiraling debt, they are diversifying away from the dollar. America may soon lose its special status and be obliged to live within the same constraints as every other nation.

A Certainty: Higher Taxes

Americans have enjoyed historically low income tax rates in recent years. The nominally temporary tax cuts of the early years of the previous decade are scheduled to expire in 2012, although President Obama and the Senate leadership intend to extend them for those taxpayers earning below $200,000. Regardless, for many of us *the days of low taxes will soon be behind us. In the future, we can anticipate paying double or triple our current level of income tax.*

The prognosis is equally bleak for city and state income taxes, because most jurisdictions have made excessive commitments also—in this case to public employee retirees. Local jurisdictions will almost certainly raise taxes, as many did in the recent recession. Some without income taxes will probably institute them or create a substitute such as a value added tax, or VAT (as has been under discussion in California and in Congress).

Income tax may not be the specific tax that bears the burden of raising the trillions in added revenue needed. Government bodies have shown infinite imagination in expanding other taxes such as sales or property taxes or creating whole new ones (as a VAT would be in the United States, although it is widely used elsewhere).

As severe as these effects of an aging population will be, America will feel them much less than every other developed nation, as long as we continue to receive numbers of (mostly young) immigrants. (But this dynamic may also change, as illustrated by the *El Norte* scenario in chapter 4.) Rising developing economies like India or China will face even more abrupt shocks, because their rapid economic growth is compressing into a few decades medical, social, and demographic changes that took a century in the developed nations. Many investors hope that growth in emerging markets will compensate for problems at home. The next chapter will demonstrate that while salvation (and subsidy) has come from overseas for the past few decades, that door will be closing.

Scenario 2: The Deficit Trials of 2027

"Deficit Trials Bring Guilty Verdicts Against Three Former Presidents, Dozens of Senators and Congressmen," *USA Today*

Salt Lake City, Nov. 11, 2027—The trial of three former presidents and several hundred congressmen and senators concluded today in guilty verdicts for some of the nation's most eminent former officials, on charges of "financial crimes against American taxpayers."

The trial began over two years ago after the federal deficit reached 22% of GDP and interest rates exceeded 15%, signifying the government's great difficulties in borrowing. The federal budget for fiscal 2028 allocated 35% of revenues to debt service, despite eight tax increases between 2011 and 2026 that have raised tax rates to 2.5 times the rates of the beginning of the century.

Special prosecutor Patrick Kennedy had to employ two novel arguments to even hold the trial at all: First, that former elected officials could be held liable for the effects of official decisions they made in office. And second, he got the court to ignore the statute of limitations to include officials in office as far back as the 1970s. (Many of the defendants were bypassed because they are deceased.)

Kennedy argued, and the jury upheld, that the defendants had as public officials "knowingly committed the nation's finances to an unsustainable path" that had "wrecked our currency, plunged our country into a permanent recession, and cost untold families their livelihoods and their savings."

Defendants will be stripped of their government pensions and benefits and have a 50% tax surcharge imposed on all their future earnings. The court acknowledged that "the scale of the crime means that the punishment cannot possibly provide full restitution. But it is hoped these punitive damages will send a strong message to our current leaders: ignore future generations at your personal peril."

Supporters of the defendants criticized the ruling, and the trial itself. "We have criminalized a lack of perfect foresight," said former White House chief of staff Joe Clemmons outside the courthouse. "Public life is about making decisions that balance risks and benefits. Officials shouldn't be penalized for good faith decisions that, unexpectedly, contribute to the deficit."

But the jury was having none of it. Jury foreman Consuelo Ortega noted that "we've known since the 1960s that the number of workers would shrink. The Social Security and Medicare trust funds have been underwater for decades, and most public employee retirement systems are in worse shape still. Yet these officials, and countless others, raised benefits over and over again for both public employees and entitlement recipients, knowing full well they could never be paid for. They can't argue that the consequences have been any kind of surprise."

Prosecutor Kennedy considered but chose not to file corruption charges, although he has made clear that he believes personally that these officials benefited from their decisions via campaign contributions from lobbyists who supported benefit increases they approved.

The convicted defendants will spend time in federal prison, ranging from 6 months to 5 years, in addition to the required monetary restitution.

The trial cast a shadow over American politics long before the verdicts were rendered. Eighty-three congressmen—over 3 times the normal number—have already announced that they will not seek reelection. In three fifths of those seats, no candidate has announced his or her intention to replace them. Political analysts expect similar or greater proportions of U.S. Senate seats to be affected. There are also 120 uncontested state races identified to date.

The financial markets reacted positively to the news, having already priced in the expected convictions. The Dow Jones Industrial Average rose 3.2% to 462.

Chapter 3 Summary

- Over the past century, rich world economies have urbanized and emancipated women. Urbanization and greater female workforce participation have eliminated the economic benefits of large families, reducing birthrates to levels below replacement rates.
- Declining birthrates and longer life spans have led to rising dependency ratios (the ratio of older nonworking adults to younger working adults).
- Despite this long-predicted demographic reality, governments have continued to promise ever more generous benefits to retirees—mainly because older constituents vote and contribute to political campaigns far more than do younger members of society.
- These benefits cannot be sustained at current tax rates. This is especially the case in nations with high median ages and low tax compliance, such as Greece.

CHAPTER 4

Cutting Up America's Credit Card

International Demographic Trends

America is far from the fastest-aging rich nation. Almost every European country has for decades had a fertility rate well below the 2.05 children per woman replacement rate threshold and has a median age well above ours. As other countries become more prosperous, they are graying, too. Japan's fertility rate, for example, is even lower than Europe's, and Japan essentially prohibits immigration, so it cannot rebuild its age-depleted workforce.

For the past several decades, much of the dynamism in the world economy came from East and South Asia. As China and India opened their economies to trade—that is, to the disciplining forces of capitalist competition—their growth exploded: for China, more than 10% per year from 1980; for India, nearly 7% per year since 1991. Both followed the model pioneered by Japan, South Korea, and later other Asian tigers: high rates of domestic savings that were invested in export industries that serve the tastes of the industrialized (Western) world. China became the world's factory, and India became its call center and IT department. More people—hundreds of millions—entered the world's middle class in a shorter period than any time before in world history.

This triumph for globalization has shaped the 21st century world. The entry into the world economy of "three billion new capitalists" (in Clyde Prestowitz's phrase)[1] was a massive disinflationary supply shock that suppressed prices and, therefore, wages for many workers who produced traded goods and services (and so sparked a backlash in much of the rich world against international trade). America became the "importer of last resort" as consumers took on more debt to buy more stuff, especially imports. The symbiosis of Chinese savers and American consumers led Harvard historian Niall Ferguson to describe them as economically a single country—"Chimerica."[2]

Asia's entry into the industrialized ranks was not without its challenges, for instance, to United Auto Workers members who faced mortal competition from Toyota and Honda. It also transformed for the better the lives of billions of Asians and helped hundreds of millions of Westerners. Look in the cart of any Walmart shopper, and you will see a collection of wants satisfied at significantly lower prices, because of the rise of Asia.

Asia's influence goes far beyond cheap goods. Much of the income Asia's exporters earn is saved; China has the highest savings rate in the world. Those savings are invested, with much of the investment coming to the United States. Chinese foreign direct investment (FDI) in American companies in 2008 alone provided the capital to create at least 3,000 jobs.[3] (Most Chinese investment in the United States is not FDI but rather purchases of financial assets to suppress the value of the yuan.) Japanese FDI in the United States, exemplified by Honda's Accord factory in Spring Hill, Tennessee, or Toyota's Camry factory in Georgetown, Kentucky, has been revitalizing dying communities since the 1980s; in 2008, it was nearly 100 times that of China.

The largest Asian investment in the United States is by sovereign wealth funds and central banks in securities issued by the U.S. Treasury Department—that is, U.S. government debt. What Ben Bernanke in 2005 called the "savings glut" became a glut of money chasing American investments. By March 2009, China held more than $1.1 trillion in U.S. treasuries or agency debt (e.g., FNMA [Fannie Mae] bonds), equivalent to about 8% of American GDP.[4] This ocean of cash bid up the price of treasuries, bidding down interest rates. This in turn drove demand for all sorts of assets, raising prices sharply, most notoriously real estate before its crash in 2006–2007 after the Fed finally began to raise rates again.

Less well known until recently is how much this Asian savings glut allowed the U.S. government to borrow without restraint, running record deficits. Asian demand for treasuries kept interest rates very low (facilitated by the Federal Reserve, which kept short-term rates very low—negative in real, inflation-adjusted terms—for three full years after the 2001 recession). This made it cheap to borrow (i.e., to run a deficit).

It also appeared to be foolish to save, since interest rates were very low so savers saw little return. These conditions led to the housing bubble of the early and mid-2000s and to its crash after the Fed began raising rates in 2006.

In sum, America's prosperity has been shaped by Asian savers since this century began.

Cutting Up the Credit Card

The gravy train of Asian money will come to an end, for two reasons. One has received extensive media attention, and one has not.

First, any casual observer knows that the rate of borrowing by the U.S. government in the past few years is unsustainable. Certainly, a reader of the previous chapter will have no doubt. Publicly held debt relative to GDP, that is, relative to the U.S. economy's ability to pay back that debt, rose from about 40% in 2000 to almost 60% in 2007, *before* the recent deep recession. Efforts at stimulus implemented in 2008 and 2009, combined with the explosion in entitlements outlined in chapter 3, are expected by the Congressional Budget Office to drive federal debt above 100% of GDP very soon.[5] Only a few other rich countries—Greece, Italy, and Japan—are more indebted, and all are in danger of bankruptcy.[6] Investors are worrying aloud about this with increasing frequency. The magnitude of U.S. indebtedness is so well known that the Chinese vice premier has lectured Treasury Secretary Timothy Geithner in public.[7]

Second, even if we can somehow convince Asian savers to keep buying U.S. assets, *the savings glut will dry to a trickle*. This isn't because Asians will become less *willing* to invest but less *able* to invest. In a word: Asia—and the rest of the world outside the G-7 rich country club—is aging, fast. These countries will see a similar demographic transition to the one described in chapter 3.

One- and No-Child Policies

As the formerly poor countries of the world reach middle-income status, two demographic changes are occurring, just as they did for the rich countries in the 20th century. First, life spans are lengthening as sanitation and medical care improve. Second, young couples are delaying childbearing and having fewer children than their parents and grandparents had.

Nicholas Eberstadt of the American Enterprise Institute is a close student of demographic trends and one of the first analysts to demonstrate that the birth dearth was not only a rich-country phenomenon. His work draws heavily from the UN Development Program (UNDP). The decline in births, and consequent rise in the median age of each country, is a side effect of growing prosperity: For the millions who moved from poor rural farm villages to urban megalopoli (300 million in China alone), large families became a liability, not an asset. As more women became educated so they could become financially independent, the cost of children rose because of the mother's lost wages. These trends should be celebrated, but they have consequences.

Take two countries that have for generations been the poster children of overpopulation: India and China. Between them they hold almost half the world's population—nearly 3 billion people.

China has long maintained a one-child policy: Couples are limited to a single child (often a boy, in Chinese culture), with stiff fines for violators. By definition, the ratio of children to woman is far below the replacement rate of approximately 2.1; by law, it is not much above 1.0. According to Eberstadt, the far smaller new generation to succeed their parents will raise China's median age above America's by 2020. China's median age was little more than half of America's less than two generations ago.[8] As Eberstadt has said, China will be "the first country to grow old before it grows rich."

India's average per capita income has risen from $280 in 1987 to $950 today.[9] But averages are misleading. As in China, the new prosperity in India has been geographically concentrated. In China, economic growth has been strongest in coastal provinces, especially in the southeast (e.g., in Shanghai or Guangzhou) and less so in the northeast (e.g., Manchuria, home of heavy manufacturing and walking-dead state-owned enterprises, or SOEs). In India, the boom in technology services and finance has been concentrated in the south, such as Bangalore and Mumbai. Other regions—inland China and northern India—without ready access to world markets have experienced much less growth. The difference in per capita incomes between southern Indian states, such as Karnataka, and northern states, such as Punjab, can be a factor of 3 or more.[10]

Regional economic differences have demographic consequences. In India, the fertility rate (number of children per woman) in prosperous southern states is below the replacement rate, while in the north, it is as much as 4 times as high. In China enforcement of the national one-child policy is laxer in the inland rural provinces, and of course, more children are an asset to farm families.

Nevertheless, it seems to be an almost ironclad rule that as societies get richer, their women bear fewer children. The impoverished exceptions are all the more noteworthy as they become rarer. According to the RAND Corporation, the fertility rate has fallen sharply in the past 50 years on every continent except Africa. Even Asia and Latin America, long bedeviled by a population growing faster than resources, now have fertility rates at or just above replacement levels.[11]

This will lead to profound implications for the West, including for the U.S. federal budget and for your portfolio. Young, growing populations, like young households, save part of their income to make it available later when they can no longer work. Aged populations spend down that accumulated wealth. So, in the next few decades, *Asian savings rates will fall markedly*. America's line of credit will dry to a trickle.

Effects on the Federal Budget

Early last decade, as federal deficits rose from a surplus of $236 billion in 2000 to a deficit of $375 billion in 2004, then–Vice President Cheney famously said that "Ronald Reagan proved that deficits don't matter."[12]

On the surface, Cheney had a point: Deficits run in the 1980s—from 5.1% of GDP in 1985 to 3.9% in 1990—were not followed by the rise in interest rates that most economists had predicted. Federal borrowing required by the deficits was expected to compete with private borrowing. With a fixed supply on investment capital, this competition was expected to bid up the price of funds. The economists' cliché was that federal borrowing would "crowd out" private sector borrowing.

In fact, 30-year treasury bond rates fell from 13.45% in 1982 to 7.78% in 1986.[13] Why? Because the supply of capital to the United States was *not* fixed: foreign investment surged starting in 1983.[14] The United States was viewed by many overseas investors—especially central banks and sovereign wealth funds—as the place to earn superior risk-adjusted returns. Foreign capital, along with some (quite modest) savings by the Baby Boomers as they came into adulthood, helped create the bull markets of the 1980s and 1990s. So foreign investors largely underwrote the federal deficits of that era, misleading Cheney to believe that "deficits don't matter."

The trend of foreign subsidy of federal borrowing, particularly by the Chinese and Japanese central banks, accelerated in the early 2000s. These export-led economies heavily bought treasuries to prop up the dollar and depreciate their own currencies to support their exports. (By depressing the price of their currencies, these countries promoted exports, since those exports were cheaper in dollars.) Brad Setser of the Council on Foreign Relations estimates that three fourths of China's foreign reserves were invested in treasuries or "agencies" (government-backed independent organizations, such as Fannie Mae) as recently as 2007, before the People's Bank of China began diversifying into other currencies.[15] With the sharp decline in the U.S. housing market in 2006–2007, the value of mortgage-backed agencies plunged, and China began heavily buying treasuries to compensate. This continuous demand for U.S. government debt enabled the borrowing binge of the first half of the 2000s decade under President George W. Bush and Republican Congresses. For example, the passage of Medicare Part D prescription drug coverage in 2003, the largest new entitlement program in generations, was entirely financed by borrowing.

In the decade of the 2000s, China's overseas investments grew more than 10-fold, from about $200 billion at the beginning of the decade to nearly $2.5 trillion by 2009, with nearly 90% in reserves held by the People's Bank of China (central bank), mostly in government securities such as U.S. treasuries. This explosive accumulation of assets was driven by an exceptional savings rate, reaching nearly 50% of disposable income in recent years.

But the rising tide of Asian capital will soon be flowing out, as older Asians consume more and save less. The 2007–2009 recession prompted waves of fiscal stimulus, leading to a U.S. federal deficit in the neighborhood of $2 trillion—more than 14% of GDP—in fiscal 2010. This spooked Wall Street and especially foreign investors. But as chapter 2 outlined, runaway federal, state, and local liabilities existed well before the recent recession or the Obama administration, although they may have made it worse.

Scary Scenarios

The combination of growing federal borrowing needs with shrinking Asian lending will almost certainly lead to one of the following scary scenarios:

- *Bond vigilantes.* Investors—domestic and foreign—will shun treasuries, so the government will need to offer higher and higher rates of interest to attract funds. This afflicted Greece in spring 2010, requiring a trillion-dollar bridge loan from the European Union and International Monetary Fund. As the "risk-free rate" treasuries set the floor on most other interest rates, all rates may rise. As businesses find borrowing money more expensive, they suspend research or expansion plans. Economic growth stalls. There may also be another reason for this scenario: higher taxes to try to rein in private borrowing. Taxes would have the same effect on economic growth, perhaps worse.
- *Printing presses.* The Federal Reserve could replace ebbing Asian funds by creating their own out of thin air. The cost, of course, is inflation: If the supply of money rises much faster than the supply of goods and services it can buy, their prices will go up. Implicitly, the purchasing power of money will go down, that is, inflation will accelerate. This is always a risk with fiat money—that is, money whose supply isn't constrained by the limited supply of whatever commodity on which it is based, such as gold. The United States has been using fiat money since 1971. Running the printing presses "monetizes the debt"—debt service payments are made in decreasingly valuable dollars, so the real cost of the debt declines. This scenario is discussed extensively in later chapters.

Which scenario will come to pass is a political choice, not an economic one. Financial markets seemed to be anticipating these in mid-2009, as treasury sales were weak, rates rose, and the financial talking head programs were full of inflation warnings based on the Obama deficits.

What was missed in those discussions is that (a) these problems long predate President Obama and were brought on by largesse in both parties; and (b) they cannot be resolved merely by persuading the Chinese (or other investors) of our determination to cut the deficit and defend the dollar. What will change is not Asian *interest* in investing in U.S. securities but *ability*. As Asian societies age, their savings rates will plummet, making less capital available worldwide for any investment purpose, including for American securities. Retired Asians will need to *sell* their American investments to provide income.

Before the effects of aging Asian demography really begin to bite, China is already using its dollar holdings to buy hard assets, mainly natural resources.[16] This creates a larger income stream, hedges against dollar devaluation, and diversifies away from the dollar, which are all prudent acts.

While the sharp drop in Asian demand for treasuries will be the most dramatic—because its earlier rise was so steep—the drought in capital will apply to most other investment as well. Not only the government's credit card will be cut up but most American businesses' as well. This will seep into everyday transactions: Home mortgages, car loans, and consumer credit card rates will all rise, and lending standards will tighten. If the printing presses aren't run with abandon, it will be a good time to be a lender, because your capital will be in short supply and will command a good price. But it will be a bad time to be a borrower. Of course, if the debt is monetized, these positions will be reversed: Inflation lowers the value of income to lenders from debt service as it lowers the price to borrowers.

The result is that the stay of execution our economy—and your portfolio—has enjoyed because of the influx of Asian capital will come to an end over the next few decades. The combined increase in federal demand for capital and decreased Asian supply of capital will mean some combination of slower growth, higher interest rates, or accelerating inflation. Forecasting the mix is a job for political pundits, not economists, but my bet is we will see some of all three.

This future is almost inevitable and will do great harm to any savings you've accumulated for retirement. But there are steps you can take to protect yourself, which are described in Part II.

Scenario 3: The Tide Goes Out

"Where Have All the Foreigners Gone?" *Financial Times,* October 7, 2016

Orange County, California—Lynette O'Keefe, a real estate agent in San Clemente, California, had built an excellent relationship with Chinese investors looking for bargains among bank-owned houses and apartment buildings left behind when the 2006–2007 housing boom crashed. Her Berlitz course had provided her a basic Mandarin real estate vocabulary, which her clients appreciated. These investors needed education in American real estate norms, of course, as she would in Chinese norms. But they paid cash and weren't afraid of Orange County prices.

Reflecting on the events of this summer and fall, she realized that she had not had a single new foreign buyer approach her since April. Since that time, calls had dwindled, and stopped around Labor Day. Many foreign investors who had taken advantage of a surplus of available houses were now adding to that surplus by listing the homes they owned as investment properties for sale. O'Keefe's purchase business had dried up, while its sales business had great promise—but only if more buyers came forward.

"I was known in certain circles in Shanghai as the 'agent of choice' to help them find a suitable investment here," she said. "As volume has dried up, so have my commissions. The Chinese are no longer coming. Now they're leaving."

All over the country the same story is being repeated: Chinese investors, who once seemed to have an insatiable appetite for dollar-denominated assets (including houses), now are fleeing the dollar in droves. The polite term for it is "diversifying out of the dollar." The People's Bank of China has been doing it quietly for five years, reducing its disproportionate exposure to U.S. treasuries by helping Chinese companies buy up hard assets such as commodity supplies around the world. This trend accelerated after the August 2014 earthquake in

Sichuan Province mandated a multi-trillion-yuan rebuilding program, keeping Chinese investment at home for the foreseeable future.

What has been a boon for the sellers of these hard assets has been something else for American former recipients of Chinese capital, like O'Keefe. As China has slowly reduced its purchases of dollars that suppressed the renminbi exchange rate, U.S. interest rates have climbed, with the 10-year treasury note at 8.66% yesterday. This has reduced access to capital to American companies and boosted mortgage rates (and deterred O'Keefe's buyers).

Only with the absence of new flows of investment from China do Americans realize just how dependent on them America's economy had become. Economists from the Council on Foreign Relations estimate that the reversal of the flow of capital between China and the United States—from inflow to America to outflows—cost the economy about 0.8% GDP growth: 0.6% due to the end of inflows, and 0.2% due to the current level of outflows.

These are direct effects alone. O'Keefe's reduced income means she will spend less, reducing the incomes of all the retailers and service providers she patronizes. High interest rates mean that small businesses don't invest in expansion, including hiring new workers or rehiring laid-off workers. Economists believe that these "indirect" effects could be up to twice the size of the direct one. Several million jobs could be lost: about a million due to direct effects, and two million more from indirect effects.

"Until the economy is weaned off the foreign investment drug, it will have withdrawal symptoms," says Robert Ferguson, a Chapman University economic forecaster, who provided the above estimates.

The sharp change in Chinese investment behavior has its roots not in the United States, but in Chinese policies. China's one-child policy has reversed its formerly uncontrollable population growth. But fewer children mean more old people, relatively speaking. The elderly Chinese population that saved—and invested—so much when it was working is now hunkering down in retirement.

Furthermore, Chinese leaders realized almost a decade ago that they relied too heavily on dollar-denominated assets, partly because China wished to prop up the dollar relative to its own currency, in order to stimulate the export jobs that maintain the regime's hold on power. As they have diversified, they have also changed what they own, now emphasizing the raw materials that China's continued growth needs. Some private Chinese investors have been slower to redeploy their investments, but, at least in Orange County, it has happened with a vengeance.

O'Keefe is philosophical. "I can parlay the knowledge and relationships that helped me sell to Chinese, to now help them sell to others. The problem is, there are few native buyers now. I fear that my owners haven't woken up to the price reductions they are going to need to take."

Chapter 4 Summary

- An aging population is not only a rich-world phenomenon—median ages are rising rapidly in emerging markets, at several times the rate it occurred in developed economies.
- Many of these newly old nations have been the main sources of capital for developed economies. But older societies, like older households, need to spend, not accumulate, capital.
- Some emerging economies will soon need their capital at home and will begin repatriating it. Reduced foreign capital will lead to higher interest rates and slower economies in developed economies that borrowed heavily, most of all in the United States.

CHAPTER 5

The Devil's Bargain

Inflation for Stimulus

What does all this mean for Baby Boomers trying to grow—or at least protect—their savings so that they have assets to spend in later life when they can no longer work? The picture isn't pretty:

- Over the next few decades, expect to pay 2 to 3 times as much in taxes per dollar of income you earn.
- Your investments will grow far more slowly, because the economy will be stagnant due to higher taxes and interest rates.
- Prices in general will rise faster than in the past few decades, with prices for goods and services consumed by the elderly rising the fastest.

These trends mean you will get to keep less of your income. In addition, your income's purchasing power will steadily ebb.

Do not despair: Part II describes several key steps you can take, starting immediately, to protect yourself. First, this chapter will integrate the information from prior chapters to describe the economic future Boomers can expect as they retire.

The Impact of Higher Taxes: Stagnation

An axiom of economic thought is that when you raise the price of something, less of it is purchased. That is the logic underlying the standard "demand" curve. A tax on an activity is the price of engaging in that activity; for example, income taxes penalize the earning of income (i.e., working). A great deal of economic evidence from across nations and states demonstrates that higher tax rates discourage additional work.

Edward Prescott, a 2004 winner of the Nobel Prize in Economics, has demonstrated that one main reason unemployment rates are higher in Western European countries than in the United States is because higher income tax rates lead people to work about 10 hours less per week. Likewise, if consumers have less disposable income, then they purchase less, which causes employers to cease hiring workers to produce goods and services that are no longer demanded.

The United States has conducted several "natural experiments" about the economic effects of tax rates. High-tax states, such as New York and California, have lower economic growth and lower in-migration compared with low-tax states, such as Texas and Florida. People "vote with their feet." At the national level, tax rate reductions, such as in the mid-1920s, the early 1960s, the early 1980s, or the early 2000s, coincided with an acceleration of growth in gross domestic product (GDP) and a decline in unemployment. Although these facts are disputed in the political world, there is little disagreement among economists. In general, as the economy expands, the share of taxes paid by the highest earners rises as well (due to progressive taxation), so prosperity is not earned on the backs of the poor or middle class. (The recent boom in the early and mid-2000s was a partial exception.)

Greater economic activity means greater wealth, because an asset is valued based on its cumulative future earnings. During the Great Moderation of low taxes, America's real net worth (i.e., correcting for the effects of inflation) climbed from $25 trillion in 1980 to $57 trillion in 2007.[1] Adjusted for inflation again, the value of the S&P 500 index of stocks—a common proxy for the broad U.S. stock market—climbed by a factor of about 8.[2]

It's not hard to understand why: If unemployment is low, most of those who want to work can do so; they use their paychecks to buy goods and services or to invest. This supports stock prices, directly through investment demand or indirectly by helping companies grow sales. In addition, low taxes on investments encourage more investment, and that increased demand for assets drives up their prices. Bull markets are common side effects of reduced taxes.

Unfortunately, the opposite is true when taxes rise: consumers have less disposable income, so they cut back on spending. Companies sell less volume, so they lay off workers, aggravating the slump. Poor corporate performance makes those stocks less attractive. Stocks' average price to earnings (P/E) ratio slides downward, and earnings also decline because of poor economic performance. This creates a double-whammy downward pressure on stock prices. In the 1970s, P/Es fell from well above 20 to much less than 10 because of similar conditions. Stocks remained flat for almost a decade.

Stagnation's Effect on Your Nest Egg

To illustrate the possibilities, the S&P 500 stood at 1,126 at the end of 2009, with a P/E of 22.7 (already above historic averages). Earnings grew during the 2000s boom by 6.73% per year, a rate not likely to be repeated. Let's be generous and assume a 5% rate of earnings growth each year. If the hostile tax and demographic climate reduce the index's P/E to its historic average of 17—also an optimistic assumption—by 2020, the S&P 500 can be expected to grow just 2% per year. This is about one tenth as much as investors came to expect in the great bull market of 1982 to 2007. Less optimistic assumptions could easily lead to *negative* growth in stock prices.

Those with memories only of recent stock market history may believe that stock prices' long-term trend is ever upward, notwithstanding occasional corrections or vicious bear markets, such as after the dot-com bubble burst in 2000 or the housing bubble burst in 2007. However, this is also an artifact of the 25-year bull market that attended the economic Great Moderation. Over a long period, stock prices will be driven mainly by two things: (a) earnings, which will be anemic under rising taxes, and (b) investor confidence, which will erode in a malignant macroeconomic environment. (If you need evidence, see the panic of late 2008 and early 2009 for an extreme example.)

This is not an indictment of all stocks. However, success in the market will not be possible by simply buying and holding an index fund, as was true for the past generation. Chapter 8 will outline some principles for stock selection under these much more challenging conditions.

The More Subtle but Serious Danger: Inflation

The American experience with the effects of high levels of debt mimics the experience of other countries over the centuries, according to Reinhart and Rogoff.[3] Countries with high levels of debt (above 90% of

GDP) have no good choices. Raising taxes or cutting spending will slow economic growth, but growth would slow anyway under the higher interest rates that speculative attacks on the currency would make inevitable. The least painful approach may be to monetize the debt, printing money to flood the world with dollars, driving down their value and the real cost of servicing that debt. Unfortunately, this also leads to accelerating inflation, while not fully avoiding stagnation. For a recent example, see the 1970s.

The growing and unavoidable entitlements crisis almost certainly will not be solved entirely through tax increases. These programs have such entrenched constituencies that serious benefit cuts are even less likely. The federal government has another weapon at its disposal to alleviate its fiscal crisis: running the printing presses and letting the value of the dollar decline, so that the debt will be worth less.

Scenario 4: El Norte

Senlac Indian Reserve No. 411, Saskatchewan, September 8, 2022

"Freeze!" said the rough voice of a Canadian Mountie in the pitch-black night in the Canadian Rockies. The 14 men and women, most from the Phoenix area, scrambled into the woods by the side of this deserted country lane.

The Royal Canadian Mounted Police (RCMP) officers who had been alerted to this group of illegal immigrants sprang their trap. Twelve were captured and two escaped the net. "They will undoubtedly wander north through the forest," said Sgt. Steven Loh of the Moose Jaw RCMP station. "But these American suburbanites aren't prepared for an Arctic autumn. Eventually they will be cold, hungry, and desperate, and will turn themselves in."

Illegal immigration was long a chronic problem for America. The United States has a 2,000-mile border with Mexico, which provided ample opportunities for Central Americans to slip undetected into "El Norte" and join the 20 million illegal residents. Today, Canada faces its own illegal immigration problem, and Canadians are as conflicted about it as Americans were a generation ago.

From Immigration to Emigration

How did the United States, the world's greatest recipient of migrants for centuries, become a sending country?

The "Land of Opportunity" ceased being opportune. There were two primary causes.

First, American mothers did not have enough babies to replace prior generations as they died off. In addition, medical advances and lifestyle improvements lengthened lives. As a result, the average age of the population climbed, from the low 30s late in the 20th century to the low 50s today. Nearly one in three Americans is older than 65 years.

Second, those older than 65 years voted in far larger numbers than younger generations. What they voted for was more generous benefits for themselves, paid for by higher taxes on those still working. Economic risk taking at which American entrepreneurs excelled came to be replaced by much greater caution, because older populations are less innovative and because highly taxed populations do not invest in risky ventures. Therefore, the rate of formation of new firms—long an American economic strength—dropped by 75%. Because small firms have been the primary source of new job growth for decades, unemployment rose. "Full employment," which was once defined as 4% or 5% unemployment of the workforce, now means 15% unemployment, levels that a generation ago were only experienced under depression conditions.

The first signs of the demographic reversal from immigrant receiving to emigrant sending occurred in the recession of the late 2000s. Immigrants who had flocked to America to join the construction industry found themselves unemployed and unwelcome when the housing bubble burst. Many "self-deported" south to their home countries.

That recession also greatly expanded U.S. federal deficit spending, leading to a scramble for tax revenues to limit the deficit's growth. Higher taxes slowed the recovery from the recession and the strength of the subsequent expansion. Throughout most of the last decade, U.S.

economic growth has rarely exceeded 1% per year, and unemployment has stayed at or near double-digit levels.

Young people, both immigrants and natives, faced unemployment rates as much as twice the already high national average. Ambitious twentysomethings sought opportunities overseas: first in Australia, New Zealand, and Singapore and later in many "emerging market" countries, whose fiscal condition was far better than at home.

By 2015, the effects of climate change were affecting water supplies in the arid American Southwest (although there it was disputed whether the change was man-made or part of a natural climate cycle). Serious droughts had occurred four out of five years. Property values that had finally begun to recover late in the 2010 decade from the aftereffects of the housing crash now reversed and began falling more gradually, as families found the Sunbelt no longer tenable because of water shortages.

The same economic and climatic forces that made the American Sunbelt inhospitable by 2020 had opened up swaths of the Canadian North to development. The first illegal migrants were recent American college graduates, who slipped into Canadian cities, especially Vancouver and Edmonton. This wave began around 2012. The second wave of unemployed and forcibly "retired" professionals, beginning in 2016, favored the new towns springing up south of the Arctic Circle, especially in the west.

Today, Canada's income tax rates are several percentage points lower than the United States'. Unemployment rates are less than half of U.S. unemployment rates, especially in the booming oil sands regions of Alberta. If remittances by American migrants to families back home were an "industry," it would be the United States' eighth largest. For some high-tax U.S. states, such as California and New Jersey (whose unemployment is well above the national average), remittances are their single largest source of income.

Canadian Ambivalence

Canada is still a sparsely populated country, with a population smaller than California's (before the great emigration). Labor shortages are common. In addition, Canadians are a friendly, open people.

Therefore, their first instinct is to welcome the "whitebacks" from south of the border. ("Whiteback" was a nickname first bestowed by a Toronto comedian; it quickly stuck.) However, those whitebacks are posing burdens on social services and competing for jobs in an economy that labors under a large state sector.

Professor Ian McDermott of the University of British Columbia is a scholar of comparative national attitudes about immigrants. Contrasting American attitudes toward illegal Mexican immigrants in the 1990s versus Canadian attitudes today, he observes, "Americans then feared that immigrants were stealing their jobs. Canadians today fear that they steal their welfare." But he notes the irony that, while for generations Canadians have accepted a larger role for government than Americans, today millions of Americans have fled their home country because of the oppressive effects of an expanding government.

The new arrivals in Canada come from opposite ends of the age spectrum: the ambitious young and the dependent old. The average age of the migrants is older than Canada's natives, but younger than America's. Developing countries in the 1960s and 1970s worried about a "brain drain" to the West. America is experiencing a "youth drain" that is exacerbating its economic challenges.

Canadian hospitality is being sorely tested. News accounts report occasional violence against whitebacks. However, provincial prosecutors have resisted trying these cases under hate-crime statutes. Perpetrators are generally charged with misdemeanors, an indicator of the growing mood that such acts are borderline justified.

Prime Minister Sylvia LaRocque sums up the crosscurrents of Canadian attitudes:

> While some of my countrymen have scorned the U.S. for its brutal embrace of the free market and failure to protect the disadvantaged, they should have been careful what they wished for. Today, America has the Western European disease of a rich social safety net, high taxes, and a sclerotic economy. Unfortunately, hard-working Canadians are coping with the side effects of American misgovernance.

Chapter 5 Summary

- The collision between rising extravagant promises and fixed resources leaves American governments—and those of most developed countries—only three options:
  - Cut spending severely, far more than most politicians (and the special interests that elect them) can countenance—the Tea Party notwithstanding;
  - Raise taxes by 200% or more, which would be self-defeating because it will slow economic growth, drive up entitlement spending, and exacerbate the fiscal problem; or
  - Inflate the debt away by expanding the money supply ("monetizing" the debt as the Federal Reserve's "quantitative easing" policy pursued).
- Monetization of government debt is the most likely outcome, but not until after vain attempts at spending cuts and tax increases have been tried first.
- The end result will be slower growth and higher inflation: *stagflation.*
- Declining economic opportunity will have demographic consequences. The United States may cease being a receiving country for striving immigrants and become a sending country instead. Some Indian and Chinese nationals are already repatriating home where there are better prospects.

CHAPTER 6

Surprise Bailouts

What if I'm Wrong?

In 1989 Yale historian Paul Kennedy published *The Rise and Fall of the Great Powers.*[1] For a work that was primarily historical, it elicited great controversy, because it predicted that the American leadership position among nations would erode, at least on a relative basis. From a historian's perspective, this forecast seemed indisputable: hegemonies are impermanent, as this book has confirmed. At the time, Japan was the rising power: its lower cost of capital and apparently invincible industrial policy fostered companies that produced goods—cars, electronics, appliances—better and cheaper than Western competitors. And the Soviet Union had been a rising military threat less than 10 years earlier.

What terrible timing. Japan's economy fell into a deep postbubble torpor soon after in 1990, and the Soviet empire imploded between 1989 and 1991. The 1990s were, in fact, a time of unparalleled American economic, military, and cultural global dominance, leading by the early 2000s to a growing backlash against American "hyperpower" (the word "superpower" no longer captured it). This was expressed in French resistance to American designs in the Middle East and, most tragically, in al-Qaeda's deadly attacks in 2001.

Even a casual review of long-term forecasts will reveal that many "inevitable" events never happened or unfolded very differently from earlier projections. Anyone with the hubris to describe the future needs to leaven their presumption with the recognition that surprises may occur that will overcome the supposed inevitable they predict. This chapter outlines some possible surprises that could intrude.

Economic Surprises

Productivity Revolution

American anxiety about "Japan as Number One" (another popular book from the early 1980s) occurred against a backdrop of sharp differences in comparative labor productivity. Recall that, on average, improvements in living standards are limited by improvements in productivity: employers can't pay workers more than the value of what they produce. American productivity, which had grown at about 3% per year for the generation following World War II—fast enough to allow incomes to double in less than 25 years—had fallen into a deep stupor in 1973, along with the rest of the West. Japan, by contrast, accelerated, easily outstripping American productivity growth. This was the economic backdrop of a pervasive angst that preoccupied observers of the U.S. economy in the 1980s.

There was precedent: the U.S. had overtaken Britain 75 years earlier, for the same reason: American industrial productivity leaped ahead of Britain's in the late 19th and early 20th centuries. The two World Wars supplied the coup de grace that ended British global dominance.

Around the same time (1980) that American economic anxiety reached its peak, a new invention came to market: the personal computer. Knowledge workers became much more effective, as software programs replaced legions of pink-collar staff (receptionists, bookkeepers, file clerks, etc.). While those surviving professionals produced far more value per hour than they could before, for a decade and a half those gains were not visible to economists. A wag noted that "you can see the effects of computers everywhere . . . except in the productivity statistics."

All this finally began to change in the mid-1990s. The productivity revolution began in 1995 and, for the most part, has not let up since. It is likely that it took a decade and a half for firms to reengineer their business processes to take full advantage of the new technology. Another possibility is that the full potential of PCs could not be harnessed until they were netted together by the millions, that is, until the Internet was widely used.

Productivity improved in America first and then quickly spread to other countries as their companies strived to remain competitive. In the meantime, Japan botched its attempts to reinflate its postbubble economy, which has remained in a crypto-recession for most of the past two decades.

This book has argued that an aging population will be less productive, and the high tax rates necessary to cover the government's promises will suppress investment and hence productivity. These trends should occur in every aging country that has huge unfunded liabilities—that is, almost every country, developed and developing. But some new technology or technique may be invented that has as pervasive an impact as did the personal computer and the Internet.

What might that breakthrough be? Venture capitalists the world over are investing to make it a reality. Here are a few possibilities:

- *Materials.* Nanotechnology is already moving out of science fiction to practical application. New materials that are stronger, lighter, or cheaper (or all three) because of engineering at the molecular level will enhance existing products and lead to new products and whole new industries. In the early years of the nanotech revolution, the technology isn't likely to improve productivity significantly, because it will still be new and production volumes will be small. But as manufacturers gain experience, they will manage significant productivity improvements every year, as they have in each segment of the industry. As nanotech affects a growing range of products, it will also have an expanding effect on productivity.
- *Artificial Intelligence (AI).* In the 1980s, automation replaced many routine manual tasks, such as those on many factory floors. Many manufacturers today "employ" more robots than people. Automation has had less effect on professional occupations because rising education levels in developing nations have allowed many poorly paid (by developed standards) accountants, programmers, software engineers, and lawyers to perform "outsourced" work for Western clients, connected via the Internet. But as AI advances, it will reach a level for which it is possible to replace even inexpensive, outsourced professionals with software. An accounting firm, for example, might process 100 tax returns entirely electronically, relying on humans only to spot check. This would clearly allow the

surviving professionals to leverage technology and "produce" much more value per labor hour.

- *Biotechnology*. The manipulation of genes has already enhanced seeds to make them more drought or disease resistant, giving produce longer shelf lives, greater nutritional value, or therapeutic properties. It has also led to new pharmaceuticals. Soon customized products (drugs, produce) will exist tailored to consumers' genetic characteristics. Over time, biotech firms will move further up the value chain, developing more expensive products (such as drugs) that command higher prices, and whose producers therefore generate more value per worker.

Here are a few other "breakthroughs" that are much talked about but not so likely to have broad economic impact:

- *Green jobs.* Production, installation, and servicing of renewable energy, energy conserving, and non-fossil-fuel-consuming transportation will be good for the planet, but not obviously good for the economy. Fossil fuels have had pride of place in our energy portfolio for so long for a reason—they're cheap. Replacements from newly developed technologies will at best likely cost the same and will probably cost more. In fact, it may be necessary to force a rise in the price of energy to make renewable sources cost-competitive. In general, while many of these jobs will be politically correct and "cool," they will replace analogous noncool jobs in the energy and transportation industries. Being new, these occupations will at first not produce at the scale to allow for improved productivity compared with existing industries with great experience in achieving economies of scale. It is more likely that these industries will depress productivity growth than enhance it.
- *Computing.* Skeptics argue that although the computing industry has been relentless in producing new products (most recently smartphones like the iPhone), the microprocessor industry is reaching the limits of the possible. Computer chips have already been miniaturized down to atomic level. But

industry insiders scoff at this, claiming that they will soon operate at the *sub*atomic level via quantum computing. Either way, it seems that while greater miniaturization will make new "smart" products possible, it isn't evident that those products will further change the way we work. It is not clear when the historic point of diminishing returns will be reached in this industry or whether it already has.

Another productivity revolution is entirely possible and, like its predecessors, thoroughly unpredictable. If one occurs, it will probably start in the economy with the most entrepreneurs who see the commercial potentials in new scientific breakthroughs. In the last century, the United States clearly had an unbeatable advantage in creating new businesses and, therefore, in economic dynamism. America will still have a better position than many other developed nations, but its position is far less assured as "the rest" rises.

Revitalization Through Immigration

America's relative openness to immigrants has undoubtedly been one of its great sources of economic strength for more than a century. In his book *The Next Hundred Million: America in 2050,* Joel Kotkin shows that he believes this will continue.[2] Certainly the United States is less grudging in its hospitality to immigrants than Western Europe, where open anti-immigrant discrimination is a fact of life, or Japan, which is effectively closed to immigrants.

This difference may be an example of the innate common sense and pragmatism of Americans. But attitudes can change with economic and demographic conditions. Anti-immigrant sentiment tends to be countercyclical (i.e., moves opposite the business cycle): It tends to peak with unemployment and fall as jobs become more available. However, demographic changes are longer lasting.

Judging by Europe and Japan's examples, as a population ages, it becomes less receptive to immigration. Such a trend is manifestly irrational, since younger immigrants can revitalize an aging population. As individuals become more cautious and less open to outside ideas as they age, not surprisingly, so do whole populations.

In 2003, *The Economist* magazine reported on an international poll conducted by the Pew Foundation. It asked the question, "Which is more important for government: To guarantee that no one is in need; or to provide individuals freedom to pursue their goals?" The proportion that chose redistribution over opportunity correlated exactly with the country's median age. In Italy, the oldest of the countries surveyed, "need" was chosen over "opportunity" by more than 3 to 1. In the United States, the youngest of the countries, the proportions were nearly reversed ("opportunity" was chosen over "need" by well more than 2 to 1). Britain, France, and Germany—with older populations—each had attitudes much more like Italy's than like America's.

So while optimists like Kotkin count on continued high levels of immigration to renew America as they have done for over a century, that cheery prediction depends on avoiding a backlash against those immigrants. However, it is fair to say that if any large developed nation has a chance of keeping its doors open, it is the United States.

The limits of immigration as a demographic solution are taken up in more detail in chapter 7.

Great Depression 2.0

The world recently avoided a repeat of the 1930s Great Depression because policy makers—most of all Fed chairman Ben Bernanke—had studied its lessons and knew what to avoid: not doing enough. Avoiding a deflationary spiral like the 1930s, or like Japan's in the 1990s, required desperate and aggressive measures. As of this writing in early 2010, the developed world seems to have avoided a catastrophe but still endured a near-record downturn. While GDP seems to have stabilized, employment may not have yet bottomed out and will take years to recover. A great backlash has emerged as critics such as the Tea Party argue that many antirecessionary policies were actually counterproductive.

Leaders and financial functionaries fight the last war, so the next time the world faces into the chasm of a deep recession, central banks may not do too much but too little. The resulting deflation will aggravate the tendencies toward stagnation described elsewhere in this book, but they may overcome the tendencies toward inflation.

The Flight to Safety

In troubled times, investors flee risk toward safety. In late 2008 as markets crashed, money rushed from stocks and bonds into the world's purportedly "safest" asset, treasuries. Spreads, or differences in interest rates, between other types of bonds and treasuries reached record levels.

A geopolitical crisis or severe economic downturn could certainly see a repeat of this pattern. Generally, such a flight lasts no longer than—often even less than—the crisis that precipitated it. Credit spreads that widened to historic proportions in late 2008 were already returning to normal levels by mid-2009.

Arguably, this flight to safety occurred in spring 2010 when hundreds of billions in capital left Europe for the dollar. Greece's misfortunes were America's temporary good fortune and forestalled the day when many of this book's predictions will come to pass.

Skeptics will respond to my thesis by arguing, correctly, that many other developed nations have accumulated even more debts than the United States, on top of a faster-aging population (see Greece). But as long as some countries in the world are reasonably well-managed—with a rule of law to protect investors, transparent and liquid markets, and a modest government sector that siphons away resources from the private economy—dollar assets will be less attractive by comparison.

There undoubtedly will be crosscurrents to the basic trend of dollar devaluation this book describes. But long-term trends described herein seem to have a much higher chance of occurring than not.

Capital Controls

The U.S. government may try to mandate away the trends described here by imposing controls on the flow of capital out of the country. This is highly unlikely at present because it would kill Wall Street. Investors will not invest in a place unless they are confident they can repatriate their money when they need it. But as capital increasingly moves overseas as foreigners diversify their investments, it will become less unthinkable as a desperate measure to protect the dollar. It will probably be presented as a tool to thwart and prevent "speculators," as it was in several Asian countries in the late 1990s and again more recently.

Capital controls have a checkered history, most recently as used by some Southeast Asian nations during their currency crises in 1997–1998. The problem with capital controls is that the cure is often much worse than the disease: Investors who can't get their money out of a country will never put more money into it. Capital controls may help a nation's currency in the short run but harm it—by drying up supplies of foreign investment—for many years to come.

Such controls are nearly unthinkable in American practice. But be warned: if you hear the treasury secretary protest too much, as he did in early February 2010 about America's AAA bond rating, it is often the sign of a failing rearguard action.

Geopolitical Surprises

Even if the American economy performs better than expected, the empire will still fade, unless the geopolitical world evolves in very different ways. Here are some possibilities that would change our forecast.

Collapse of China Into Civil War

The primary alternative to the United States for global leadership is China, for good reason: China has more than 4 times America's population, a rapidly rising GDP that will overtake the United States' early in the next decade at current rates, and significant financial reserves (i.e., it is a massive creditor, not a debtor). If you believe Chinese economic statistics, its own stimulus—the world's largest in proportion to the country's GDP—seems to have kept GDP growth robust even in the face of a crash in exports because of deep recessions in its main markets. By early 2010, China was *cooling off* its economy to deflate a growing Japanese-style property bubble.

As noted in the Three Day War scenario, China has some significant structural problems. It also has a history of fragmenting away from central government. Any number of sinologists have speculated about the remaining life span of the current communist regime. Within the next few decades, the frustrations of a population no longer satisfied with material progress without democracy could lead to violence and separatism, with ambitious politicians and military leaders all too willing to get in front of the parade. A hundred years ago, such men were known as "warlords."

An implosion in China by no means guarantees the preservation of American dominance, because several other members of the so-called BRIC nations—in particular, Brazil and India, both vibrant and rowdy democracies—may be able to surpass China's position in the future.

Aging Competitors

The United States is hardly the only country aging. In fact, it is the youngest developed country now, and its margin may soon widen if it maintains relatively high levels of immigration. Most major developing countries are likewise aging rapidly as they grow more prosperous, although from a much younger starting point. China, for example, will have a median age higher than the United States by late in this decade.

If America's competitors age faster than the United States (because of lower birthrates and immigration rates), their chance for greater dynamism will evaporate. Essentially, they will experience a slow motion version of Japan's relative decline and fall since the 1990s.

However, even if America's relative position is favorable, its absolute position will not be. Japan's or China's eclipse will not make American commitments any more affordable (in fact, it may exacerbate their costs). Even if a "multipolar" world does not come into being in 2025 because of lost economic vitality in a wide range of countries, that will not mean the "unipolar" world will be sustained.

Crisis or War

A geopolitical crisis would likely drive investors into the arms of whichever seems to be the strongest and safest currency. In late 2008, that was the dollar and the euro. In late 2009, it was gold. In early 2010, it was the dollar and gold. Future crises and wars will trigger further flights to safety.

Climate Change

Although there is a fierce dispute about whether gradually warming temperatures are anthropogenic (caused by human actions) or a natural trend, there is little disagreement that the climate is changing. Like any major change, it will produce winners and losers. Losers will include nations grouped near the equator, which generally are poor and have few resources to help adapt. Winners are less clear, but will probably include nations at high latitudes, and nations with large concentrations of industries that can exploit the changing climate, such as renewable energy systems manufacturers, foresters, nuclear power manufacturers and operators, and utilities that can cost-effectively sequester carbon. New industries will cluster in countries with a hospitable business climate. Increasingly, such a benign policy environment is increasingly found in well-managed developing economies.

Climate change will remake the world's geopolitical map in ways that are difficult to predict. America has some advantages (a relatively innovative economy) and some disadvantages (a large share of its population and industry located in arid environments). It is difficult to say whether climate change will help or hurt Americans' hegemony.

Delaying the Inevitable?

No one today can say what date historians will ascribe to the end of the American empire. This book has argued the historical chapter began closing in the great recession of the late 2000s. But there are at least two reasons the close of the American century may be postponed a little longer.

Slow Recovery From the Recession

Paradoxically, the very event—the recent recession—that signaled the empire's eclipse may sustain American dominance a little longer. If the recovery is as slow and anemic as most economists in early 2010 expect, the considerable slack capacity will be deflationary and continue to counteract the inflationary effects of loose money and government overspending. In the argot of the investment markets, the Fed may not be able to execute its "exit strategy" very quickly. As of spring 2010, the Fed appears to have postponed that exit by at least 1 year compared with its original schedule.

This scenario is a repeat of 2009. Massive fiscal and monetary stimulus did not have their "normal" effect of bringing fast growth and inflation, because they were countervailing equally strong forces of stagnation and deflation due to the deleveraging many firms and households were forced to implement.[3] That stimulus arrested the economy's slide downward, but as of early 2010, it has not been enough to turn recession into a strong recovery.

Continued strong headwinds from deleveraging—as many economists expect—will postpone the inflationary effects of rising government expenditures. The suppressing effects of tax increases to pay for those expenditures make such an anemic recovery likely. But this will only delay, not prevent, the inflation predicted in this book. It will occur whenever the economy returns to full employment, more likely in 2015 than in 2011.

The (Over)Privileges of a Reserve Currency

Reinhart and Rogoff's extensive historical research has indicated that economies begin experiencing severe stagflationary effects when the ratio of government debt to GDP exceeds 90%. According to the Congressional Budget Office, federal debt will exceed that threshold by late this decade. If state and local debt is added, we have crossed it already.

Controlling the world's primary reserve currency has its privileges. Because so many international transactions are denominated in dollars, there is an "artificially" strong demand for our currency. (This is in addition to the artificial demand associated with Asian efforts to suppress their own currencies by bidding up ours.) For example, American importers have been able to buy foreigners' exports by paying in their own currency. Most importers overseas cannot do this. As long as the dollar maintains that favored status, lenders will offer the United States some extra latitude. So the threshold for the dollar before stagflation sets in may not be a debt of 90% of GDP but 100% or 105%. At predictable rates of spending, this more permissive limit only delays the day of economic reckoning by 1 or 2 years.

It is for exactly this reason that increasingly foreign investors—government and private—have begun diversifying their holdings away from the dollar, as discussed elsewhere. The 90% threshold should not be shrugged off. America might hit its "wall" even sooner.

All but Certain

I am a congenital optimist about the American economy, and our history has borne me out thus far. The "end of the American dream" obituary has been prematurely written many times before, including in the late 1930s during a decade-long depression and in the late 1970s when we had our first brush with stagflation.

America always seems to pull itself out of its slumps. The United States attracts the ambitious risk takers of the world and offers them an environment in which they can pursue their opportunities—if we don't tax or regulate them away.

I don't see the future described here, in which the late 1970s repeats itself 50 years later, as a permanent condition. Eventually, the great good sense of the American electorate will propel into leadership the 2020s versions of Ronald Reagan and Paul Volcker. In the meantime, it will be rough seas ahead, especially for Boomers who are already behind in the race to accumulate enough assets to retire comfortably. Historians may write that the period of high debt, high inflation, and slow growth was temporary, but Boomers preparing for their futures cannot take such a long view.

Any sweeping prediction for several decades in the future cannot be considered certain. Any of the above events could nullify, or at least delay, this book's predictions. Even some of these apparent game changers are less than they seem. I would never suggest betting all of your investments based on the trends outlined in this book, but I will be redeploying the majority of mine.

Chapter 6 Summary

- While a number of "wild cards" could surprise us, most will only be temporary corrections to the general trend outlined in these chapters.
- Since this book was completed in early 2010, the main surprises (rising commodity prices, revolutions in the Middle East, and an electoral backlash against big government in several rich countries, including the United States) have accelerated, but have not reversed, the trends described here.

CHAPTER 7

Will Immigration
Rescue Us?

America has made and remade itself several times in its history through new demographic infusions from overseas. Optimists argue it will do so again.[1] This chapter examines the viability of immigration as a demographic tool of national policy.

We begin with a caveat. Immigration is a highly charged, emotional issue. Some of the material in this chapter may appear "anti-immigrant." Individuals who were not born in the United States—or their children—may take some of this quite personally. This chapter addresses all immigrants as a group (with the exception of a brief digression regarding illegal immigrants as distinct from those who settle in the United States legally). By definition, any group that comprises millions of individuals will include many who resemble the general group, and many others who are quite different. No simple generalization will apply to all. But that does not invalidate the generalization.

The Decline of Declinism

Although the United States' fertility rate barely exceeds the level necessary for births to replace deaths, it is still half again higher than Europe's or Japan's, so America will age less rapidly than any other developed economy. This is largely due to immigration: many immigrants come from nations with higher birthrates, and they bring their fertility behaviors with them (at least they do at first). In addition, most immigrants are young adults in their peak childbearing years, so they lower the median age through their own presence and that of their children.

As a result, many immigration advocates suggest increasing rates at which the United States accepts immigrants as a strategy to enliven an otherwise aging population and renew America's dynamism, as immigrants have done so often before. Opposed are those against immigration: nativists who see the country's complexion and culture changing into unfamiliar hues; some union leaders in low-skilled industries who see eager new arrivals as a competitive threat; and no-growthers who wish to forestall population pressures and the ecological stresses they bring.

Proimmigration advocates generally have the facts on their side (with some very important provisos mentioned later). Opponents have narrow economic self-interest allied with deep emotion and hostility to foreigners. These polar attitudes have made immigration reform an exemplar for Washington gridlock.

To see the future, if our present ambivalence toward immigration is sustained, look no further than Western Europe. Most European countries have fairly liberal immigration policies enshrined in their laws. Actual attitudes, however, are something else. The combination of a generous welfare state and limited economic opportunities has encouraged immigration by those needing government support and discouraged that of entrepreneurs and the highly skilled, who can find better opportunities elsewhere, such as in North America or in Australia.

Millions of low-skilled immigrants have been segregated into European ghettos, with the active assistance from natives' prejudices. The 2004 riots in the *banlieues* of the Paris suburbs were a dramatic expression of immigrant frustration at their exclusion from French society. In most Western European countries, many immigrants cannot be productive in a postindustrial economy—there simply are not many jobs for those with only a few years of education. Added to this is native resentment of foreigners, especially when so many drain the public coffers.

Even the few exceptions, such as Britain and Switzerland, which in the past showed comparative tolerance, are acting much more "European" these days toward immigrants. And even the handful of countries such as Denmark and the Netherlands, which have policies intended to require a measure of immigrant assimilation, have not escaped serious problems and native backlash.

Self-Selected Risk Takers

The canonical immigrants of the late 19th and early 20th centuries were poor but ambitious peasants seeking economic opportunity in the United States that they could not find at home. Despite the great handicaps associated with adjusting to a new culture, according to the conventional wisdom, these immigrants assimilated quite successfully. Whatever the limitations of their schooling or English skills, they or their offspring blended fully into the "melting pot" and within a few generations converged with natives economically.

Up until the late 20th century, that folklore was largely correct. Any list of eminent American scientists, performers, industry leaders, or writers was disproportionately populated by immigrants. But as George Borjas of Harvard's Kennedy School (himself a Cuban immigrant) has dramatically demonstrated, that began changing in the late 20th century as the composition of arriving immigrants changed. There are two elements to this change: education level and sending country.

New immigrants have customarily had less education than native-born U.S. residents. But not all: a minority come with more education than the average American. While only about 1 in 4 natives has earned an undergraduate degree or higher, the rate is about 30% among immigrants. One in three Silicon Valley founders and CEOs is an immigrant, and most have advanced degrees.

Incomplete Assimilation

At the same time, those immigrants with less than a high school education are twice as prevalent as natives—34% versus 16%. In general, educational attainment among natives is fairly evenly distributed, with 83% of natives having at least graduated from high school, thanks to compulsory secondary education. New immigrants cluster heavily at the top and bottom of the educational spectrum, with about one third holding at least an undergraduate degree, one third without a high school diploma, and one third in between.

One hundred years ago, a strong back and a solid work ethic were sufficient to secure the American dream for most immigrants. They still are enough for most of the new arrivals who start small businesses, which they do at several times the rate of natives. But in a postindustrial economy, by far the largest proportion of jobs go to "knowledge workers," and those without education are severely handicapped. Furthermore, English proficiency tends to rise with education, so those relatively uneducated immigrants face enormous obstacles of language to integrate into the mainstream economy.

In addition, the mix of sending countries has changed significantly since the 1965 immigration law essentially abolished national quotas. Previously, the bulk of immigrants came from Europe (especially southern and Eastern Europe). Today, their sending countries are much more diverse, although the majority come from Latin America (mainly Mexico and Central America). Many of these countries provide very limited public education, with private education out of reach of many poor families. So while the prototypical Indian doctors or Chinese engineering students still settle in the United States, the more common immigrant is a poor peasant from southern Mexico with less than 6 years of schooling.

Such educational and English deficiencies pose huge obstacles to assimilation. Borjas's research confirms this. He examined the wages of immigrants compared with natives for several arriving cohorts, each about 10 years apart, entering between the 1950s and the 1980s. The average incomes of those who arrived in the 1950s began about 10% behind the average of natives, but rapidly—within 15 years—exceeded that of natives. But each succeeding cohort started farther behind, and they never caught up. The 1960s cohort started 13% behind natives and was still about 5% behind 30 years later. The 1980s entering cohort began 25% behind and then fell farther behind over the next decade. The pattern is one of degrading waves of immigration, each economically less successful than those before.

Why assimilation is a receding dream is the subject of Jacob Vigdor of Duke University's Immigrant Assimilation Index. Vigdor measured immigrant assimilation by comparing their rates of various metrics to those of natives. He tabulated economic, civic, and cultural metrics into a single composite index. Vigdor's economic assimilation compares average immigrant wages to natives, similar to Borjas's work. Civic assimilation uses measures of civic participation such as rates of voter registration and of voluntary military service.

Not surprisingly, across all immigrant groups, assimilation rises over time, with economic assimilation the highest and civic assimilation the lowest at first (soon after arrival). Therefore, civic assimilation rises the most over the next few decades. No component of assimilation falls in the years after arrival. Vigdor also found that successive waves of immigrants from a particular country arrive less assimilated and assimilate (i.e., as a group adopt the economic, civic, and cultural characteristics of natives) more slowly than the wave before. This is completely consistent with Borjas's economic findings. One could speculate about a "production function" of immigrant waves: Those with the best chance of success emigrate first, those with poorer prospects following later.

The most interesting of Vigdor's findings is the stark difference in assimilation trajectories for immigrants from different countries. Immigrants from Canada, Cuba, the Philippines, and Vietnam have the highest rates of assimilation. In two of these countries, English is very prevalent. Immigrants from Mexico and El Salvador have the lowest assimilation rates. Differences in education and English proficiency probably explain most of these disparities.

No Economic Rescue

Whatever degree of assimilation was historically achieved by immigrants, their children and grandchildren typically achieved economic outcomes that equaled and in some cases exceeded that of natives. For the children of relatively recent immigrants, that pattern cannot be confirmed, since not enough years have passed since the parents' arrival. But there is reason to be skeptical, in light of the disadvantaged position at entry and subsequent economic retrogression of recent arriving immigrant cohorts. Their children have a great deal of ground to make up, and they begin with great handicaps—that is, they know no English and have very low incomes.

One manifestation of this trend is in the rate of dependence on government benefits, tabulated by Borjas.[2] Among natives, just under 8% received some form of government-supplied cash payments (such as Aid to Families with Dependent Children or food stamps) at the peak year of 1980. By 2000, this rate had fallen to 7%. But for immigrants throughout this period the rate of dependency has been higher, modestly so in

1980, but much more so by 2000. As Borjas has put it, immigrants seem to assimilate quite well on at least one dimension: reliance on the welfare state.

While working in California state government, I examined the net fiscal effects of *illegal* immigration on state finances.[3] I found that for every dollar illegal immigrants paid in taxes, they consumed five to seven dollars in government subsidies. Such a disproportionate result is not surprising for a group of generally low-income individuals: Our tax structure is highly progressive (i.e., the wealthy pay a disproportionately larger share of their incomes in taxes, and the poor pay the opposite). At the same time, the structure of government benefits is skewed in the opposite direction, with the poor receiving the vast majority (by design). The democratic polity has chosen this for ourselves—*but only for those who reside here legally.*

The National Research Council and other prestigious social science researchers generally confirmed these conclusions: Illegal immigration may be a moneymaker for the federal government, which collects Social Security and Medicare payroll taxes from illegal workers who can never collect benefits. But it is a money-loser for states and cities, which must provide the federally mandated services.

By 2007, I had updated this 1994 study and found that illegal immigration had continued apace, nearly tripling over 1994 levels, and dispersing far beyond the handful of states that had earlier absorbed 83% of illegals. The new arrivals were even poorer than their predecessors, so they now consumed eight to twelve dollars for every dollar they paid in taxes. To an order of magnitude, the difference between expenditures and revenues was comparable in size to California's entire structural deficit.[4]

Thus, Americans' ambivalence about immigration is well grounded. Educated and skilled immigrants invent new technologies and launch start-up companies that have been a source of tremendous dynamism. But such talented people are a diminishing proportion of more recent immigrant cohorts.

The bulk of new arrivals crowd the lower rungs of the labor market, with limited skills that restrict their upward mobility. While many do "jobs Americans won't do," this is partly because their mere presence suppresses wages in those jobs.

Discouraging Modernization

Research on the economic effects of immigration is generally equivocal or neutral. Studies that compare cities and regions with high rates of immigration to those with low rates generally find the high-immigration areas grow faster. But the causal direction is difficult to determine: Do more immigrants spend more and so create jobs, leading to economic growth, or does high growth attract more immigrants? The summary finding has been that the net effect is about neutral: Immigrants both "positively displace" some natives from employment—that is, create more jobs than they absorb—and "negatively displace" others. Both well may be true, with the positive effects occurring because highly skilled occupations have a larger market for their services, while occupants of low-skilled occupations face greater labor market competition.

The greater long-term problem stems from the effects of this low-skilled labor surplus on productivity growth. Many industries achieved in the 1990s and 2000s a productivity miracle, as they found ways to use computer technology to automate functions previously performed by low-skilled humans. Higher productivity growth cost the poorly educated employment—one of the main reasons real wages among those with less than a college education have been slowly declining for 30 years. But those able to master the challenge of working with the new technologies were able to produce more and could earn more. Technology-based productivity growth has been the key to prosperity since the Industrial Revolution.

But new machines cost money. Why automate when there is a ready supply of eager, poorly educated workers who can do the routine tasks that would otherwise be undertaken by productive but expensive machines? Immigration at the low end of the labor spectrum has almost certainly retarded the productivity growth of many industries with high immigrant participation, including construction, retailing, and health care. It seems plausible that the stagnation in wages, including of the educated middle class, is at least partly due to this productivity drag caused by a surplus of poorly educated workers. This trend is likely to continue, since most lists of the fastest-growing occupations have heavy representation from low-skilled jobs.

In sum, the particular composition of recent immigrants is not likely to provide much dynamism to the American economy in the next few decades. While it may be a mistake to assume that their children or grand-children will lag behind natives, it seems a safe bet that few will exceed them either, given the huge handicaps they inherit in childhood. Many immigrant children start very far behind in the competitive race. As a result many do not catch up, even after more than one full generation.

Demographic Rescue?

Nevertheless, immigration might reasonably be expected to bring *demographic* renewal. Immigrants are among the most adventurous of their fellow countrymen. Such risks are taken primarily by young adults. Thus, immigrants, particularly illegal immigrants, tend to be in their teens and twenties, below the current median age in the United States (about 36). Furthermore, most immigrants come from cultures with high birthrates, which can compensate for low fertility rates among natives. Indeed, this is one of the premises of Joel Kotkin's book *The Next Hundred Million: America at 2050:* The United States will be one of the very few developed countries whose population will continue to grow. Whereas Europe is expected to shrink by about 15% by the middle of the century, even at historically high levels of immigration, the United States will grow by about 30%, by 100 million people. (Demographers predict that both American and world populations will peak around midcentury and then decline gradually as births fail to keep up with deaths.)

Without question, immigration can retard the trend of declining fertility. But it cannot completely reverse it, because immigrants assimilate to native fertility behaviors also. Within one or two generations after most immigrants' arrival, their offspring are having children at about the same rate as natives. So unless rates of immigration remain high indefinitely, immigration will soften, but not arrest, demographic decline. The United States will be the developed county least affected by aging, but affected it will be. Comparatively speaking, America will have more of the underpinnings of future growth than other developed nations. But even the leaders in the early decades of the 21st century will not grow as fast as the laggards of the late 20th.

Overall

Most immigrants are risk takers, and every economy will need more of these. Some of the future immigrants to the United States will continue to be those with education and skills, who can create new economic opportunity in any hospitable climate. But a high portion will be poor peasants off the farm, with only a few years of schooling and no English. Many of these will become dependent on government subsidies. Those who remain self-sufficient will do so in low-wage jobs that offer little opportunity for advancement. Their numbers will continue to suppress wages for those with less than a college degree and encourage their employers to defer modernizing.

Many immigrant cohorts begin to adopt the behaviors—positive and negative—of their host country, or their children will. Unfortunately, this includes natives' fertility behaviors. So high birthrate immigrants are at most a very temporary and partial solution to America's declining fertility, and one that comes at a very high cost in poverty and dependency.

Chapter 7 Summary

- Since one of the main sources of the trends described herein is demographic, it is natural to consider America's traditional demographic solution: immigration.
- Recent American immigrants lack the dynamism of past generations. They are less educated (and therefore less able to succeed in a postindustrial knowledge economy). Many of the most promising immigrants return home when home offers greater long-term opportunity.
- Also, immigrants' demographic behavior (e.g., childbearing and family size) mimics natives in their new home quite quickly—within a generation.
- So immigration can—at best—slow, but not reverse, the trajectory outlined here.

PART II

Swimming Upstream Against the Strengthening Current

CHAPTER 8

Hedging Against Stagflation With Commodities, MLPs, REITs, and Preferred and High-Yield Stocks

Earlier chapters have argued that on America's present fiscal path—which has largely been set by decades of unaffordable commitments by politicians—and the world's demographic path—which is largely determined by the emancipation of women and rising incomes in more and more of the world—the U.S. economy is destined for stagnation, and the dollar's purchasing power will ebb away. This combination of anemic growth and inflation was termed "stagflation" in the 1970s, the last time we experienced anything like it.

Baby Boomers whose formative investing years came during the Great Moderation from 1983 through 2007, when both inflation and unemployment were low, are unprepared for an environment where both are high. If you do not expect to work in retirement, then unemployment won't directly affect you and may even present some indirect opportunities. But inflation wreaks havoc on retirees, and on anyone whose income is fixed. This chapter is intended to provide an outline of some of the steps you can take to soften the blow.

Stagnation and How to Defend Against It

As was demonstrated in earlier chapters, high tax rates—which are almost certainly in our future—lead to less investment, less innovation, less job creation, and more unemployment. Likewise, an aging population invents less and invests less. The long-term "trend" growth rate for the

U.S. economy (adjusted for inflation) is likely to decelerate from its past average of 3% per year to something closer to 1% to 1.5% per year. That may seem like a minor difference, but an economy that doubled in size in a generation will now need closer to three generations to grow as much.

This is bad news for anyone relying on economic activity for their daily income—that is, every wage and salaried private sector worker and every business owner. For retirees living off their savings, the effects will be less direct. They may exempt themselves from stagnation's direct effects by voluntarily choosing not to work, or by conceding the verdict of the marketplace if they are laid off.

They still are indirectly affected, however. If they are so fortunate as to receive a pension, those payments are ultimately dependent on the current revenues being generated by their former employer, who pays the pension: corporate sales for private sector employers and tax revenues for governments (which provide most surviving pensions in the United States). These will come under increasing pressure to reduce benefits to lessen the burden on those still working. So having a pension does not completely insulate you from the state of the economy.

Beyond pensions, most people will need considerable savings (i.e., investments) to fund their retirement. The value of retirees' corporate investments (stocks and bonds) depends directly on corporate earnings. Similarly, they may earn little on interest-bearing assets—CDs, bonds, and funds that invest in these—because slack investment demand and government monetary stimulus will drive down interest rates, as has occurred since 2008. Furthermore, retirees have, by definition, a much shorter investment time horizon (the number of years until they plan to liquidate and spend the investment) than, say, a 30-year-old, so an asset that loses value in stagnating times may not have enough years left to recover before you will need to liquidate it.

One area of opportunity in stagnant times is in consumption and investment in hard assets. In slow times, it seems everything is on sale at hefty discounts. Of course, a bargain alone is not a compelling reason to buy something you don't need. But if you planned to buy it anyway, why not take advantage now? Retirees who have done a good job of saving can make their savings go farther if they wait to make major purchases until stagnant times. This works best for any durable real property, such as autos, boats, and real estate.

Where to Invest in Stagnant Times

The conventional wisdom is to move more of your investments overseas during times of slow growth at home. But as the recent recession demonstrated with a vengeance, the national economies of the world are not as "decoupled" from one another as portfolio managers had thought. The recession that began in 2007 originated in the United States (in the housing sector specifically), but almost instantaneously infected other countries, first as foreign banks suffered huge losses in the U.S. housing market and then as Americans bought fewer imports from foreign exporters. So overseas investments are no guarantee of immunity from American stagnation. But they are a critical component of your portfolio to hedge against the decline in the dollar, as discussed below.

Within your domestic investments, during slow economic times, concentrate on "defensive" sectors: those in which consumer spending tends to hold up better than in other sectors. Traditional defensive sectors include consumer staples, health care, and low-priced retailers, including budget restaurants. Walmart and McDonald's both well outperformed their sectors during the recession. In contrast, sellers of big-ticket goods or services, like autos and airlines, tend to see their sales fall farther than the average sector in a recession.

Why such defensive sectors? Stagnant/deflationary times by definition mean that demand is less than available supply. Firms compete to survive by lowering their prices. Voilà: deflation. As firms earn less per unit sold, they cut back on employment, which means that some workers lose their jobs, and their families have less money to spend. They will shop less and when they do, generally buy less expensive brands for what goods they need. We recently saw this dynamic in late 2008 and early 2009. In a deflationary environment, the brands that are the quality low-cost producers will usually gain market share (sales) and be able to hold the line best against falling prices. (This is known as "pricing power," available when a brand is so strong it dominates its market, as do Walmart and McDonald's.)

True deflation is a very scary prospect economically, as anyone from Japan can attest. In 1989, the country entered a postbubble recession that eerily foreshadowed the global recession that began almost 20 years later. Japanese firms cut prices to try to retain customers (who had lost their jobs or feared the same), but the customers would have none of it.

They saw prices falling and deferred making major purchases—after all, they expected that Lexus they had their eye on to be cheaper 3 months in the future.[1] Japan's economy has been in a de facto recession for most of 2 decades. Avoiding this nightmare animated U.S government officials, starting in late 2008, to err on the side of stimulating the economy to excess.

Above all else, cash—or more precisely, highly liquid interest-bearing instruments like those held in money market funds—will allow you to preserve your capital while waiting for a recovery and maintain the liquidity you will need to be ready to pounce on bargains. Stocks may well drop in price (because stagnation depresses company earnings) until they trade at 6 or 7 times earnings or pay dividends of 5% or 6% of their share price, better than even long-term bonds. Many stocks fell to these levels in late 2008 and early 2009. You'll need cash at the ready to take advantage of such fire-sale prices. It can be very frustrating to see great investment bargains all around you but not have the funds to take advantage.

The *Wall Street Journal* published sample portfolio allocations for a long-term investor for each of three kinds of economies: *deflation-centric*, what I've called "stagnant"; *inflation-centric*, which will be discussed below; and *Goldilocks economy*, moderate unemployment and inflation, like most of the past 25 years during the Great Moderation.[2] Each allocation exploits the assumed state of the economy but also builds an "insurance" element in case the economy changes. For the deflation-centric economy, the asset allocation shown in Table 8.1 was recommended.

There are any number of low-cost mutual funds and exchange-traded funds (ETFs) in each of these categories. For bondholdings, you are best

Table 8.1. Sample Asset Allocation for Deflationary (Stagnant) Times

Core holdings	
Long-term treasury securities	35%
Cash (e.g., money market funds)	20%
Municipal bonds	15%
Insurance against return of inflation	
Treasury inflation protection securities (TIPS)	5%
Commodity exchange-traded funds (ETFs)	15%
U.S. domestic equities	10%

Source: Opdyke (2009), p. B1.

off purchasing individual issues, "laddered" (i.e., with staggered maturity dates), and hold them until they mature. That way you protect yourself against interest rate risk. Each bond's price floats, inversely related to the level of interest rates, so if you plan to sell the bond before maturity you face the prospect that rates may have risen since you bought it, driving down the price of your bond. Waiting to maturity ensures that you receive face value. As noted earlier, rising interest rates are almost certain over the next few decades. For treasury inflation-protected securities (TIPS) or I-bond savings bonds, whose rates are adjusted for inflation (unlike traditional bonds, whose rates are fixed), the inflation premium is paid at maturity.

While there will almost certainly be periods of recession (stagnation) in the next few decades, the primary and enduring threat will be from inflation.

Inflation: Its Causes and Its Cures

As the cliché goes, inflation is "too much money chasing too few goods." All prices react to the interaction of supply and demand. If there is too much supply, firms will lower their prices to attract more buyers (i.e., raise demand). Conversely, if there isn't enough supply to meet demand (a.k.a. "too much demand"), the opposite will happen: buyers will bid up prices, known in the aggregate as inflation. Those "buyers" can also be buyers of labor—such as employers, who increase wages in a labor shortage (such as a strong economy) to secure a share of scarce workers. Employers then to try pass their higher labor costs onto consumers through higher product prices. If they have pricing power—that is, if their competitors don't undercut them—they may succeed.

In the recent past, inflation has been purely a hypothetical concern. The recessionary economy was so stagnant that there was no risk of "too much demand," except for brief moments in isolated products such as certain new cars (inflated by the "cash for clunkers" subsidy in 2009) or starter homes (temporarily stimulated by the first-time home buyer credit). Such isolated instances need not lead to inflation, because it takes hold only when prices rise for a wide range of broadly purchased goods and services.

But when the economy is firing on all cylinders, inflation is a constant prospect. In a time of strong growth, consumers and businesses with ever more money in their pockets will spend or invest it. Although suppliers will try to expand their capacity fast enough to keep pace with growing buyer interest, demand may well outstrip supply (because more supply takes time to bring online), leading to a virtual bidding war. When the "product" being bid on is an asset like a stock, bond, or house, this kind of inflation is known as a bull market. But when prices rise on a variety of consumer products or services, the consumer price index (CPI) will climb.[3]

While it is accurate to say that inflation occurs when broad demand exceeds supply, that "excess demand" always has the same original cause: too much money—that is, excessive growth in the money supply. When the central bank prints too much money, its value responds just as any oversupplied commodity: its price drops. Its purchasing power over goods and services is reduced. Nobel prize–winning economist Milton Friedman coined the phrase "Inflation is always and everywhere a *monetary* phenomenon"[4] (emphasis added). While its immediate cause may appear to be greedy plutocrats, labor unions, or Arab sheiks, the price increases they extract could not be maintained if the money supply wasn't too large for the supply of goods and services available.

Notwithstanding the deflationary conditions at the end of the decade of the 2000s, inflation will be a far more common and ubiquitous challenge to Boomers over the next few decades than will recession. The U.S. government has committed roughly $100 trillion more to investors and entitlement recipients than it can be reasonably expected to be able to pay. Most of these commitments stem from Social Security and Medicare,[5] but these will be added to a national debt of more than $20 trillion by 2020 that has grown because of continued borrowing to pay for current expenses, such as military spending and most recently antirecessionary stimulus. Cumulative liabilities—including hidden but very real liabilities like entitlements—add up to an amount equivalent to about seven times present gross domestic product (GDP) and ten times the current national debt. In other words, for every dollar we owe that we know about, we owe 10 dollars more off the books. The explicit debt alone is on its way to reach a level of over 100% of GDP very soon, according to the Congressional Budget Office.[6]

Very high levels of government debt pose several major problems. Chapter 4 focused on those that will suppress economic activity and therefore stock prices. This chapter will emphasize the inflationary consequences.

Government—politicians—will accept only so much reduction in economic activity, or reductions in private sector investment that are crowded out because government is competing with companies for a finite pool of capital. (Over a long period, that pool will shrink, for the demographic reasons described in earlier chapters.) Higher taxes will be imposed in order to service the debt, but this will only magnify the economic problem. At some point, probably in a future deep recession (when tax revenues are especially low and welfare and unemployment payments especially high), consideration will be given to defaulting on the debt.

Default—the refusal to make interest and principal payments to service a debt—was a step taken by a number of Latin American nations in the 1980s, Russia in 1998, and Argentina again in 2002. In Greece's modern history, it has spent more time in default than in good standing. Often the defaulter is posturing to coerce creditors into relaxing the terms of the loan. Argentina's default and subsequent workout negotiations lowered their outstanding principal to a small fraction of face value, which was "paid off" with more bonds. Lenders accepted this as better than getting nothing at all. In the late 1990s, Western lenders preemptively negotiated forgiveness of the debts of some African countries that had no realistic prospect of repayment.

For a developing country the price of default—or negotiated reduction in principal owed—is dear: a terrible bond rating and pariah status in the credit markets. For such economically small countries, the wider effects on the international economy can be controlled. The danger would be much greater if a large country defaults. Russia's default in 1998 brought down a major Wall Street hedge fund, Long Term Capital Management (LTCM), whose collapse would have taken with it many other institutions but for intervention by the New York Fed. The stakes were such that *Time* magazine put the men who arranged LTCM's bailout (Treasury Secretary Robert Rubin, Deputy Secretary Lawrence Summers, and Fed Chairman Alan Greenspan) on its cover as "The Committee to Save the World."

The 1998 crisis, like the debt crises in several Asian countries a year earlier, would be minor next to the fallout from a rich country default. This is not farfetched: most rich countries have higher government debt loads relative to GDP than does the United States (although we are catching up rapidly), and most face much faster aging of their populations that will exacerbate their debt problems, as chapter 3 described. The prospect of default in a very small European country—Greece—brought forth a trillion-dollar bailout by the European Union and the International Monetary Fund.

A default by the U.S. government would have incalculable and devastating effects, for two reasons. Because the United States is the world's largest economy and has been so for generations, its debt is held very widely. U.S. treasuries make up nearly half of worldwide reserves held by central banks. A U.S. default would sink the balance sheets of dozens of countries and thousands of banks, mutual funds, pension plans (including the Social Security Trust Fund), and hedge funds. It would be analogous to, but vastly more severe than, the meltdown of 2008, which was caused by higher than expected mortgage defaults that sank mortgage-backed securities (MBS) and the institutions that held them.

The greatest blows would come to the United States, of course. Any hint of a possible default would cause investors to dump treasuries in a rush to other currencies or to commodities. Since U.S. treasuries are denominated in dollars, this would mean a rush out of the dollar also. This would be a mirror image of what happened in late 2008 and early 2009, and again in 2010, when the "flight to quality"—when not just MBS, but nearly all assets, were dumped in favor of the presumed safety of treasuries—drove treasury prices and the dollar to new highs. Subsequent more skittish investor sentiment about the U.S. government's ability to service its debt led in 2009 to a rolling sell-off of treasuries and a sharp slide by the dollar. While at this writing investors have not yet panicked, they are clearly becoming more worried. They have good reason.

Why Inflation?

If default is unthinkable and increased taxes are only a partial and costly solution, there remains only one option for our financial leaders: "monetize" the debt. Printing extra money for the government's use will at first seem a wholly desirable act. It can moderate a recession, as in and after

2001 (and continued far too long, producing the 2000–2006 housing bubble) and again in 2008 and afterward. This has been the policy of the Fed since late 2008, borne of desperation. Running the printing presses means more money will be spent or invested by consumers and investors, raising prices in retail and asset markets, respectively. Higher prices will encourage firms to reopen production lines and hire back workers. A little inflation will even be considered desirable, if the alternative was deflation (see Japan, page 97). At first.

However, if growth in the money supply isn't slowed, over time workers will see higher prices and demand higher wages they would not have dreamed of when the economy was slow and they were facing layoffs. Employers now facing higher input costs, including labor, will raise their prices. And an inflationary cycle will be underway. As actors in the economy see rising prices everywhere, they will try to anticipate future inflation by demanding higher wages, or prices, for what they sell. They will assume continued high inflation. To be prudent, they will probably expect it will accelerate. An upward spiral of the inflation cycle will be on. The only way we know to break the cycle is a very deep recession—deep enough to cause firms and workers to have to compete again based on (lower) price. This means a sharp reversal to money supply growth. Fed Chairman Paul Volcker did this to break the back of the late 1970s inflation, raising interest rates well into the double digits, and choking off borrowing and investing. This caused the 1981–1982 recession, which set the record for postwar unemployment until late 2009.

Theoretically, an independent central bank whose charter includes responsibility for price stability (i.e., low inflation)—normally, the core function of a central bank—will modulate the money supply to allow some economic growth but not too much. The Fed's problem is that repeated congresses and presidents have fiscally overstimulated the economy. That is, they have accelerated economic growth by overspending and running deficits. The Fed attempts to compensate for congressional profligacy, but unlike most other central banks, its mission is not only price stability. It is also charged to "maintain full employment." Coupled with the fact that Fed governors are political appointees (albeit with long terms), the Fed has a natural bias in favor of accommodating more economic growth and therefore some inflation, as was painfully illustrated by its behavior in the late 1960s and '70s, when it grew the money supply too fast for too long and sparked the kind of inflationary spiral described here.

Monetization of the federal debt would work as follows. As the Treasury Department issues more bonds (i.e., borrows more money) from investors, the Federal Reserve prints funds to compensate for investors' funds going out of circulation to buy those bonds (or the Fed may buy those bonds directly, as it did in 2009–2011). Voilà: issuing bonds need not reduce the money supply as it normally does; it can increase it and allow the economy to continue to grow—*in nominal terms*. In "real," constant purchasing power terms, the oversupply of money beyond what the economy needs at the time will devalue each dollar (i.e., accelerate inflation).

But what is bad for those on fixed incomes is good for those who owe fixed liabilities—such as debtors, including the U.S. government. Their interest and principal payments will now be made in depreciated currency.

In sum, the Fed may very well aid and abet a Treasury monetization plan to reduce the unpayable national debt, which is currently rising by more than $1 trillion per year. The price will be significantly higher inflation for as long as the monetization plan is in force (years, probably decades).

The scale of the challenge our government faces is such that it is extremely unlikely to solve with tax increases alone, or monetization alone: both—in liberal doses—will be necessary. For this reason, the fundamental forecast for the next few decades (that is, the horizon of interest to Boomers) is slower growth (due to higher taxes and aging populations) and higher inflation (due to debt monetization).

Hedging Against Inflation

In 2009 after a recession-induced drop in its price, gold came roaring back, crossing the $1,000 per ounce threshold in late summer. Investors both wizened and amateurish were bidding up the price in anticipation of the events described above. In other words, gold was a very fashionable inflation hedge, after most of 2 decades on the sidelines.

But is gold effective, and is it the best hedge?

No asset class, except possibly residential real estate, stirs up passions like gold does. "Gold bugs" have a permanent commitment to the metal, which was little rewarded for almost 30 years. Now gold has finally blown past its 1980 peak and is becoming a cocktail party investment again. But many investing pros point out that between 1980 and the early years of this decade, the price of gold dropped by roughly 75%. They question whether gold is a viable investment, or fool's gold.

Let's examine the arguments against gold. It is bulky and expensive to store. It generates no organic earnings. Some countries regulate or outlaw private gold holdings (as the United States did during and after the Great Depression), obliging an investor to store their gold holdings secretly, or overseas.

Not surprisingly, financial institutions have found ways around most of these problems. Gold ETFs such as the SPDR gold trust (GLD) sell shares (typically denominated in tenths of an ounce of gold), allowing investors to own "virtual gold," without concern for storage. GLD, for example, stores its gold in a vault in New York City. The Perth Mint, an arm of the government of Western Australia, offers gold certificates corresponding to holdings in their vaults there. And in times of market volatility, investors can sell "covered calls" (options that permit the buyer to "call"—buy—gold at a specified price) on their holdings to earn some income, with the risk the option will be exercised by the buyer and their holdings will be "called away."

The strongest argument against holding gold per se is that its price is not as negatively correlated with the dollar as conventional wisdom implies. "Correlation" refers to the pattern of movements of prices of two different assets. If they are perfectly correlated—that is, go up and down together in lockstep—they would have a correlation of 1.0. If they move in opposite directions (i.e., are perfectly negatively correlated), they would have a correlation of –1.0. Since in the real world such relationships are never perfect, a "good" inflation hedge should have a correlation of, say, –0.7 against the dollar or against U.S. consumer prices. Gold's correlation with most U.S. stock indices is low, but *positive* (not negative).[7] According to the financial website Darwin's Finance, gold's correlation with the dollar has been highly negative (about –0.6) for most of 2007 and 2008, but that relationship broke down in late 2008 as investors "fled to quality" in dollar-denominated treasuries.

The broader point is that gold is hardly a surefire inflation hedge. Correlations vary widely over long periods, even switching signs. For example, in the first half of the decade, gold's correlation with oil was very weak (0.13), but in the following 6 months, it grew fivefold to be strongly positive (0.63). And in 2008, almost all well-known relationships went haywire as institutional investors were forced to sell everything to meet redemption demands. As gallows humor at the time put it, "In a meltdown the only thing that rises is correlations." In other words, in late 2008 and early 2009, the price of every other asset class crashed as panicked investors sold them off to move to liquidity and presumed "quality" in U.S. cash and treasuries. Classes of assets that normally moved in different directions suddenly moved in the same direction—down—and were, by definition, highly correlated.

Erste Bank (Vienna) recently analyzed gold's performance compared with the CPI over a number of years. They found that gold outperformed the CPI in all periods, including deflationary ones, except very moderate inflation (1% to 3% per year, as during the Great Moderation). The greater the departure from moderation, the greater was gold's relative performance.[8]

A reasonable synthesis of the debate about the wisdom of gold as an investment seems to be that it is an excellent safe haven in troubled times—inflation or deflation, but especially inflation. Gold's correlation with alternative investments tends to be high in troubled economic times and weak in good times. The very successful "Goldilocks economy" during the Great Moderation from 1982 to 2007 created benign conditions that let other asset classes far outstrip gold. But as this book stresses, a favorable investment climate is far less likely for the next few decades.

Furthermore, as noted in earlier chapters, the dollar's problems, and dollar inflation, are hardly unique. Most rich countries hold very high levels of debt—many higher than the United States—and some may be tempted to monetize their own debts. It is a systemic problem of all "fiat" currencies (currencies backed only by a government promise to pay, not by a commodity in limited supply like gold).

A well-regarded financial newsletter expressed the current contrarian view of gold's efficacy as an inflation hedge quite well:

Anyone buying gold now thinking they're buying something of increasing intrinsic value somehow is fooling themselves. Gold is actually flat or declining in terms of other currencies and just because you may live in the US, do you want to continue to plow your money into a flat useless asset? If you feel the currency will continue to depreciate, there are more effective means to invest in that trend or even through the use of leveraged ETFs but I don't think they make good investments for the typical retail investor— they're really there for traders to exploit a near term trend and then get out.[9]

Hedging against a declining dollar (and consequent rising prices) can have a more direct benefit if the hedge pertains to a commodity that you use regularly. For example, you can hedge against rising food prices by buying an agricultural ETF like CROP or MOO. The same applies to energy ETFs to hedge the rising price of oil. As the writer noted, "It seems to make a heck of a lot more sense to me to either play currency ETFs or hedge energy and food prices than to buy gold."

A superior way to use precious metals as an inflation hedge is to own *mining stocks* instead of the metal directly. Miners typically see their profits rise by a multiple of the price of the metal they extract, for the simple reason that their costs to mine are fairly fixed, so when prices rise, their costs do not (or not nearly as much), so profits rise by a multiple of the increase in the price of the metal. For example, if a given mine spends $800 per ounce to mine gold when it is selling at $1,000 per ounce, it earns a 20% margin. If gold rises to $1,500 per ounce and the mine's costs stay essentially the same, margins will rise to 53% ($700 profit per ounce divided by $1,500 revenue per ounce). Mining analysts call this effect "leverage" relative to the price of the metal.

In practice, leverage may not be quite so high, because if the price of gold is rising due to inflation, some of the mine's costs (e.g., energy costs) will rise, too. But in general, an efficient mine's profits will increase by a multiple of the rise (in percentage terms) in price of the metal it extracts.

Mining companies are generally grouped into three categories:

- *Majors.* International firms with multi-billion-dollar market caps (e.g., Barrick) who exploit mature veins and have achieved strong economies of scale (efficiencies). They may be geographically diversified and inevitably take some political risk because many of their deposits are not in the most savory countries.

- *Juniors.* Smaller firms that often explore for new deposits and then exploit their finds. These are by definition riskier; in some cases, the results of a single venture can make or break the company. They usually are also riskier because they are smaller and far less geographically diversified. But, of course, the rewards can also be greater.

- *Royalty holders.* Buy the rights to a portion of the haul from a given mine (known as royalties) and sell it in the marketplace. Such firms take essentially zero risk and require relatively little capital, since they avoid capital-intensive exploration and extraction. Consequently, their stocks also tend to have lower returns (but are less volatile.)

Exchange-traded funds (ETFs) exist for the first two segments of this industry. GDX is the large gold miners ETF; it allows investors exposure to gold without sacrificing liquidity or taking on a storage obligation. GDXJ is the junior miners ETF. As of press time, there is not yet a royalty ETF (although as Wall Street continues to capitalize on gold fever, it may not be far away). Several companies specialize in royalties, such as (the aptly named) International Royalty (ROY), which at the time of this writing was being acquired by a major (Royal Gold). ETFs or sector-specific mutual funds have the advantage of diversification: You need not research and track individual companies; you can merely buy the whole mining sector.

For the most part, holding mining stocks (individually or in ETFs or mutual funds) is a superior way to use precious metals to hedge against inflation for two main reasons. First, these companies have implicit leverage against the price of gold: when its price escalates, their profits will rise faster. Second and even more important, they have earnings, which produce organic growth, even if the price of gold doesn't budge.

Gold isn't the only precious metal, of course. As of this writing, silver seems especially attractive because it is priced quite low relative to gold, compared with historical averages. There are silver mining stocks and silver ETFs (including SLV, the analogy to GLD) available to the retail investor. However, I recommend against coins, because much of their price is based on the scarcity of a particular issue over and above its bullion value. Coins can be a fine investment—or you can grossly overpay. I would only recommend them to true connoisseurs who can appraise scarcity themselves.

Other Commodities

As the author previously cited notes, "If you have your heart set on buying a commodity that is increasing in value due to a weakening US dollar, why not consider buying one that actually impacts your daily life?"[10] You consume food every day and oil every time you drive. These prices can be expected to rise as the dollar weakens. For a recent example, remember the 100% or more increase in these commodities' prices during the first half of 2008. Here again, you can invest in ETFs that track commodities indexes. Or better still, you can invest in producers of these commodities, which have the same advantages outlined for gold miners: leverage of the price of the underlying commodity, and earnings (a.k.a. organic growth). In agriculture, there are at this writing about six generic agricultural commodity ETFs. If you disproportionately consume a single product (as I do coffee and cocoa), there are commodity-specific ETFs as well. If you are bearish on any given commodity, or agricultural commodities in general, there are also "inverse" ETFs that rise when the commodity price falls (as it usually does in a recession, such as in late 2008 and 2009).[11]

But again, I personally strongly prefer to invest, not speculate. That is, I want to put my money into assets that organically generate growth, not simply bet on price moves. So for an agricultural play, I would prefer agribusiness stocks or those of suppliers to them. Three examples of well-regarded suppliers are Monsanto (MON), Potash (POT), and Mosaic (MOS). Some "sector" mutual funds also specialize in these areas. In the energy area, master limited partnerships (MLPs) have special tax advantages—they pay no corporate income tax as long as they pay their shareholders at least 90% of their earnings each year. Real Estate Investment Trusts, or REITs, discussed below, have a similar tax status.

To exploit the rise in oil prices, the industry can be segmented similarly: extractors (discussed above), major multinational players (now including Chinese companies), juniors (sometimes called wildcatters), and suppliers (e.g., of drilling services or equipment).

Legendary investor Jim Rogers, cofounder with George Soros of the Quantum Fund, has been very public in his enthusiasm for commodities, with an emphasis on agriculture and water. The fundamentals are on his side: As formerly poor Third World nations rise to middle-income status, they act more like rich-world consumers—including, at the most basic level, consuming more calories, particularly from meat. Economic growth near double digits in China (25% of the world population) and India (nearly 20% of the planet) is bringing sustained growth in demand for a wide range of commodities and raw materials, including food. Demand is so strong that many agricultural experts fear it will outrun the supply of arable land in the next few decades. Also, the increases in yields that the Green Revolution produced for 40 years appear to be plateauing. With shortages will come much higher food prices, guaranteed.

Real Estate–Related Hedges: REITs

Conventional wisdom holds that real estate is a good inflation hedge, but the supporting evidence is unconvincing. In addition, there are good reasons to be bearish on real estate over the long term. In the next few years, considerable overbuilt inventories will still exist in much of the country, speculation by vultures notwithstanding. In the longer term, demographics will dominate. The successor generation (born between roughly 1965 and 1982, better known as Generation X) is smaller in number, earning less and building smaller families than the Boomers. Many McMansions will be shunned by buyers for decades to come.

Of course, these are generalizations; real estate conditions vary widely across different local markets. For example, areas that restrict building (such as the coastal areas of the Western states) build a floor under prices. That is why in California, for example, house prices did not fall much in coastal zip codes but crashed in inland areas.

But, again, the United States is not the last word. Countries with fast-growing population will need housing; those with stable populations but fast-growing economies will need factories, office buildings, and infrastructure. Again, the best inflation hedges are stocks in those firms that feed this growing demand overseas, or mutual funds or ETFs that hold their shares. Investing in this arena has the added advantage that the firms' earnings will be in foreign currencies, which will often have better prospects than the dollar. (And if you convert your gains into dollars, a falling dollar will magnify them.)

An excellent way to invest in real estate (residential or commercial) is through REITs, which pay no corporate income tax. REITs often have the advantages of a hybrid fixed income/equity instrument, such as preferred stocks, discussed below. Newer, often nontraded REITs, which are often placed privately (i.e., are not traded on exchanges, at least initially), are often less saddled with underperforming "legacy properties," so their high yields are more secure. They often enjoy greater prospects for capital gains, because more of their properties were purchased at low postbust prices. But they also are less liquid; do not consider private REITs unless you are prepared for a long holding period and a slow disposal, say, 7 years and 6 months, respectively.

Stocks and Bonds in General

Bonds generally are poor investments in an inflationary environment. If their coupon was set under better conditions, interest rates have almost certainly risen far beyond the coupon rate, which means the price of the bond will fall. (Bond prices move inversely with interest rates, so that the coupon rate, which does not change, produces a market yield. If rates rise from 5% to 10% due to inflation, a bond paying a $50 annual coupon will fall in price from $1,000 to $500 so that its yield rises from 5% to 10% to conform to the market.) The longer the duration (years to maturity) of the bond, the farther its price will drop as inflation accelerates. In a time of rising inflation, your fixed income investments should have short maturities so that you can reinvest them at the (rising) market yield as they mature.

Stockbrokers argue that equities (stocks) would be a good investment in an inflationary environment. This is only partly true and needs explanation. Growing nominal earnings, and associated dividends, can in principle provide some compensation for inflation. But many firms' earnings will not grow much. Whatever boost in revenues they may see from inflation will be eaten away by commensurately rising costs. Stocks' valuations, measured by price to earnings (P/E) ratios, hit historic lows in the high inflation of late 1970s, even lower than in the late 2008 market crash.

In general, stocks are not a good investment under inflationary circumstances, with two great exceptions:

1. *Foreign stocks.* Foreign companies whose revenue stream is in a stronger currency than the dollar may not face inflation in their home country (although many countries' fortunes are tied to the dollar, officially or de facto). Gains that you repatriate into dollars will be magnified by the decline in the exchange rate. This also applies to U.S.-based multinationals, in proportion to their revenues that stem from overseas business.

2. *Dominant companies.* Companies that dominate their market space often have "pricing power": the ability to essentially dictate their price to customers. They may hold the line on inflation to gain market share or purchase such large quantities from suppliers that they can dictate their input prices. Examples of "world dominators" include Intel in microprocessors, McDonald's in fast food, and Walmart in retail. Signs that a particular company has dominator potential include whether their gross margins are rising (input costs are dropping); whether their sales are growing faster than the industry (i.e., their market share is rising), especially under difficult industry conditions; or whether they are able to increase their prices faster than their competitors can.

Common stocks, like many other asset classes, perform best when both inflation and unemployment are low. They may provide some inflation protection when prices begin rising, but inflation can quickly outstrip earnings growth, leaving stocks in the dust. Partial exceptions are foreign stocks (if their home currency is not depreciating) and stocks in dominant companies.

Other Dividends: MLPs, BDCs, REITs, and Utilities

Dividends—the portion of earnings that companies pay each year to stockholders—can be a partial hedge against inflation. A dividend yield equal to or higher than the inflation rate means that your investment is at least holding steady in purchasing power. But as inflation rises, such high yield stocks may be harder to find (unless you happened to be lucky enough to buy them near a market bottom when their yields are highest).

Also, many world dominator stocks pay a fairly modest dividend, for good reason: They can provide stockholders a better return by reinvesting those funds in the business and increasing the company's dominance. In addition, some companies pay too much of their earnings out in dividends (Eastman Kodak is a recent example), leaving insufficient funds for reinvestment or emergencies. A high dividend yield cannot be the sole criterion.

The payout rate is a simple proxy for a dividend's sustainability. This is the share of a company's earnings paid out in dividends. Aside from special cases such as REITs and MLPs that are legally required to maintain a high payout rate, for most companies investors are reassured if the payout rate is not too high—say, below 60%. That provides some safety margin to protect the dividend in the event of surprises.

There are a number of lists of "dividend growers," "dividend achievers," and the like, and even one company whose very business model from the time of its founding has pursued a growing dividend: REIT Realty Income Corp. (NYSE symbol O). Several financial websites maintain such lists (try searching on "dividends"), and most mutual fund firms have at least one fund that invests in promising dividend-paying companies. A number of academic studies have shown that the majority of the historical cumulative return of broad stock indexes, such as the S&P 500, has come from dividends, not from capital gains. Reinvesting dividends is an excellent way to grow an asset manyfold over a long period.

A similar equity-like asset is a corporation's convertible preferred stock. Preferred stocks receive a fixed dividend, making them like bonds—but usually at a higher yield than the common stock dividend (because preferred shares do not participate in the upside as the company grows). They share with bonds "preferred" creditor status, meaning they are ahead of common stock owners in line if the company goes into liquidation. But many have a useful common-stock feature: They can be converted to common at a specified price. An investor can buy a convertible preferred, collect the (generous) dividend, and wait for the share price to rise to the conversion price, at which time they usually have the option of converting to common stock or retaining the preferred shares. (In other words, convertible preferreds are most attractive when they are available at a price below the conversion price—often $25 per share.) Because most preferred shares pay a higher dividend yield than the underlying common stock, this can often be a superior way to use dividends as an inflation cushion.

How Much to Hedge?

How much of your savings should be invested in commodity-specific hedges? At a minimum, each commodity-specific hedge, representing specific line items in your budget, should equate to the percentage that each line item represents. For example, according to the Bureau of Labor Statistics (BLS), a typical American household spends 15.8% of their budget on food and beverages (8.2% at home; 7.6% at restaurants), 5.4% on energy at home (electricity and natural gas), and 3.2% on motor fuel (mostly gasoline).

In retirement, these items may take up a different share of your budget because work-related expenses will reduce or be eliminated, and you may have more time to pursue your interests (which can cost money; for example, travel). In addition, some "maintenance" expenditures will loom larger as you, personally, need more maintenance. This is discussed below.

Inflation is a central concern for retirees for three main reasons. First, those retirees on a "fixed income" such as a pension receive the same income every year, so their purchasing power will erode as prices rise. Second, retirees with considerable savings will likewise see its value ebb. Much of that savings will be invested in fixed income investments (e.g., bonds), that is, loaned to a borrower who will pay you back in depreciated currency. Your real return (the nominal rate on your bonds less inflation) may not be very much at all; it may well be negative, especially if inflation is accelerating. That is, you could lose purchasing power even if nominally you were still making money.

Finally, your expenditures will change. Some changes will be quite deliberate; for instance, you will have lower dry-cleaning bills and higher travel costs (if you wish). But some are unavoidable. Seniors spend escalating amounts on health care as they age, and health care has inflated at several times the headline consumer price index for decades.

More generally, seniors are especially susceptible to what economist William Baumol once termed "the cost disease of the service sector." As we age, we spend less of our budget on goods—because most of us have more "stuff" than we need already—and a larger share on services, such as restaurant meals, and household services, such as gardening and health care. Baumol recognized that while technological advances have allowed many goods to fall in price (think of most consumer electronics), because productivity in their industries rises every year, this is not true for many services. Barbers cannot speed up (much) the rate at which they cut hair. No one has yet invented a machine that will cut your grass at a price cheaper than a teenager. And health care has been nearly immune to the productivity improvements that have transformed so many other industries.

The "cost disease of the service sector" strikes retirees right in their wallets. The BLS has constructed an experimental consumer price index for the elderly, known as CPI-E.[12] It weights most personal services more heavily than in the better-known CPI-U (all urban workers) to reflect the larger share of the budget of elderly consumers spent on these services. For example, health care is weighted more than 50% higher in CPI-E (10.81%) than in CPI-U (6.35%). Housing also gets a higher weight (47.51% vs. 42.24%). Overall, CPI-E has risen faster than the headline CPI-U in 24 of the past 25 years, by an average of 0.24%. So because of differences in what they buy—more services, fewer goods—retirees face higher inflation than do working people. Over the course of a 30-year retirement, that difference will erode the purchasing power of your fixed income by an extra 7%—several years' worth of investment gains. This is in addition to the loss of purchasing power due to general inflation, which I have argued will probably accelerate. Retirees are significantly more vulnerable to inflation than those still working.

I believe that higher inflation will be a fact of life for anyone who is paid and invests in dollars for most of the next few decades (after the economy shakes off the recent recession). There will be episodes of disinflation or deflation in the future, of course, because the business cycle has not been abolished (and some of the policy responses to the recent financial meltdown make future cycles more likely and more severe). In the *Wall Street Journal's* terms, I will invest 75% for an inflationary environment, 20% for a deflationary environment, and perhaps 5% for a Goldilocks economy.

Chapter 8 Summary

- The future outlined here calls for a fairly defensive investment strategy. It emphasizes: (a) diversifying out of the United States and the dollar; (b) selecting securities that can provide a solid income stream, even in stagnant times; and (c) investing in companies with pricing power in a period of inflation.

- Commodities—for example, agricultural products, oil, precious metals—tend to become safe havens from inflation. But buying, say, gold or silver ingots is pure speculation on an upward trend in prices. Better to invest in related companies that have intrinsic earnings, such as gold or silver mines.

- Income-oriented equity investments such as REITs, MLPs, and preferred or utility stocks tend to fall less in bear markets, but at a price of reduced upside in bull markets. They are essentially hybrids between pure equity and pure income plays. Privately held REITs tend to be newer and less burdened with poorly performing legacy properties but also are less liquid and unsuitable for any but a long investing horizon.

- Retirees tend to be particularly exposed to inflation, both because their incomes are often fixed and because they spend more on higher-inflation services. Investing in higher-yielding stocks, which can sustain and grow their dividends, offers an attractive means to preserve your spending power in an inflationary environment.

- This suggests investing in companies with stable earnings that have the confidence in their financial condition to consistently expand their dividends. Such firms often dominate their markets.

Appendix to Chapter 8:
Sample Portfolios for "Inflation-Centric" and "Goldilocks ('Just Right') Economy"

Inflation-centric (i.e., inflation of more than about 4% per year)

Core holdings	
Commodity ETFs	25%
Cash	15%
Inflation protection securities (TIPS)	15%
REITs	10%
U.S. domestic equities	15%
Foreign equities	5%
Insurance against return of deflation	
Municipal bonds	10%
U.S. treasuries (mainly short term)	5%
U.S. domestic equities	10%

Source: Opdyke (2009), p. B1.

Goldilocks economy *(as existed during the Great Moderation: low inflation and low unemployment)*

Core holdings	
U.S. domestic equities	20%
Foreign equities	20%
Bonds	30%
Insurance against return of inflation	
U.S. treasuries (long term)	10%
Cash	10%
Commodity ETFs	10%

CHAPTER 9

Stiffing the Tax Man
With Roth IRAs

Note that all dollar amounts quoted in this chapter are only approximate, quite deliberately. First, I am not a tax adviser. You should treat the ideas in this book as educational, but they cannot, by definition, apply to each individual's specific circumstances. Rely on your accountant, financial planner, or tax preparer for advice on your particular situation. Second, because of inflation, evolving regulations, and Congress's unquenchable desire to diddle with the tax code (a.k.a. earn campaign contributions from tax lobbyists), specific thresholds change annually. So treat all amounts mentioned in this chapter as rough guides only.

Conventional retirement planning assumes that in retirement workers will be in a lower tax bracket than when they were working. But as the previous chapters have demonstrated, *none* of us will be in a lower bracket in 2020 than we are in 2010. This turns traditional retirement planning on its head: No longer should you *defer* taxes until retirement—as traditional IRAs and 401(k)s do. You are better off paying taxes at historically low rates *now—especially if you still have losses from 2008*—and letting your savings grow *tax free*.

Happily, there is a vehicle that allows for this: the Roth retirement account. It exists in IRA form, and, since 2006, in some employers' 401(k)s. Roths are a mirror image of traditional tax-advantaged retirement plans. Under the traditional plans, your contributions to a retirement account are tax deductible, and the taxes on their growth are deferred until you take "distributions" after age 59½. With a Roth, the opposite is true: You pay taxes when you make your original contributions, then they grow tax free, including when you withdraw funds in retirement. Although our esteemed Congress did not intend it so, Roths are perfect investment vehicles for workers to build their nest egg safe from the Internal Revenue Service.

All in all, this is a once in a lifetime opportunity to cut your lifetime tax bill and eliminate income taxes on your savings after you retire. But it is has considerable up-front costs, so it isn't for everyone.

"Traditional" 401(k)s and IRAs

With the slow decline of defined benefit plans that cover private sector employees in the late 1970s, Congress began attempting to encourage through the tax code greater individual savings to prepare for retirement. 401(k) plans, so named because they are authorized by Section 401(k) of the Internal Revenue Code, originally resulted from lobbying by large companies on behalf of senior executives who wished to shelter more of their income from taxes. The political price was that such plans were required to be open to all employees. These are known as "defined contribution" plans, as distinct from the "defined benefit" plans of traditional pensions. Many companies offered to match employee contributions up to a limit, effectively doubling their value. Contributing to your 401(k) to take advantage of your employer's match was a no-brainer—while that match lasted.

Private sector 401(k) plans were popular (although a distressing fraction of the workforce still does not contribute). They spawned analogs in other sections of the tax code, such as 403(b)s for nonprofits, and 457 plans. Individual retirement accounts, or IRAs, are equivalents available to any individual, including the self-employed and others who do not have a 401(k) plan available to them.

These arrangements are not investments, but a tax-advantaged shell within which investments can be housed. Over the years, the range of permissible investments has broadened to include most liquid assets and less liquid ones such as real estate.

Every personal finance author encourages readers to maximize contributions to these vehicles, up to the limit set by the IRS. For most employer plans, the limit in 2010 is $16,500 per contributor, with several thousand additional dollars possible for those older than 50 years to "catch up." Limits for IRAs are much lower: about $5,000, with a further $1,000 "catch up" addition possible for those older than 50 years.

Of course, eligibility isn't universal. Some employers don't offer a defined contribution plan. And the income ceilings for permitting contributions to IRAs are fairly low, around $50,000 per year.

These so-called traditional savings vehicles are so popular with financial experts for two basic reasons. First, they have substantial tax benefits: Your contributions are deductible from your current income, thereby lowering your current tax bill. More important, the balance in the account grows with taxes deferred until you begin taking distributions (withdrawing the funds to live on), which can occur no earlier than age 59½ years and no later than age 70 years (except for a few special circumstances, such as buying a first home or paying for college). You don't pay taxes on those gains until you take those contributions, thus the term "tax deferred."

Tax deferral is considered attractive because of the power of compounding. Say your $10,000 IRA is invested in corporate bonds that yield 6%, and you reinvest the coupon payments. Assume for the sake of this example that your total income tax rate (federal, state, and local) is 33%. If you invested in a taxable bond account, your after-tax rate of return would be 4%, not 6% (4 is two thirds of 6). After 20 years, your account would have grown to only 88% of the same investment inside an IRA shell.

What causes this magic? In the taxable account, one third of the gains each year get siphoned away by the IRS. That's why in Table 9.1 the "before tax" and "after tax" amounts for the taxable investment are identical—taxes were paid all along the 20 years, even if you reinvested the bond coupon. In the IRA, that siphoning is deferred until distribution time (assumed in this case to occur 20 years after when the original account balance was $10,000). Keeping the base of assets as large as possible—that is, not skimming off a portion for taxes each year—allows the power of compounding to do its utmost. That enhanced compounding is a countervailing force stronger than taxes—strong enough in this

Table 9.1. Ending Size After 20 Years of a $10,000 Starting Amount

Tax treatment	Growth rate	Amount at 20 years	
		Before tax	After tax
Taxable	4%	$21,911.23	$21,911.23
Tax-deferred (e.g., IRA)	6%	$32,071.35	$24,787.81

example that the IRA is 13% larger than the taxable account, even after paying the deferred taxes.

But the second strong reason for "traditional" retirement vehicles will not be true in the future. Traditional vehicles are desirable under the assumption that *you will be in a lower tax bracket when you stop working* than when you worked, and contributed, to these vehicles. The logic is that you will need somewhat less income in retirement than when working to maintain the same lifestyle (same level of consumption). Less income may mean a lower tax bracket. Why not defer some of your income until the day it will be taxed less?

The idea that you will need less income is premised on several assumptions that were reasonable in the past but are no longer always valid. First, when you no longer work, you no longer pay payroll taxes. Second, if your job required a certain standard of attire, such as suits and ties, those expenses will be greatly reduced. (You've probably seen the sweatshirt that says, "I'm retired. This is as dressed up as I get.") No more dry-cleaning bills, likewise no more commuting costs. Similarly, you may have owned the same home for long enough to have paid off your mortgage. Presto: lower housing costs. For decades, financial planners assumed that retirees could maintain the same lifestyle as at their last job on 70% to 80% of their working income.

Like many simplifying assumptions, it sounds reasonable, but probably isn't. First, the whole point of retirement is to use all the new time available for whatever pursuits turn you on. Chances are that each pursuit costs money. (For example, a week traveling costs far more than a week at home.) You may continue to work, at least part time, in "retirement," so those employment-related costs may not disappear entirely. You may also have other claims on your income in retirement, such as a second set of young children (in a remarriage), or so-called adult children that still need financial support. And how many people remain in the same house for 30 years? Chances are your career required you to move around a lot, so you will still carry a mortgage.

Furthermore, as noted in the previous chapter, many of the goods and (especially) services older people consume disproportionately rise in price faster than the consumer price index, a market basket that purports to capture spending by a "typical" urban consumer.[1] The cost of services often rises faster than the cost of goods, because many service industries cannot achieve the rates of productivity growth possible in manufacturing or agriculture. This has been lamentably true in health care, where prices have risen 3 or 4 times the CPI's rate for decades. Of course, older patients consume more health care than most working individuals.

Most important, *you may not be in a lower tax bracket in retirement*. As the earlier chapters have made clear, *it is much more likely that you will be in a higher bracket in the future*—because we all will be.

This turns traditional retirement planning on its head. Why deliver your savings, gift-wrapped, to Uncle Sam when you need them most? Why not instead pay the taxes due *now* when tax rates are at historic lows, and let your savings grow *tax free*?

Wouldn't that be nice? Well, it's not a fantasy. Congress created Roth savings vehicles in the mid-1980s and widened their availability in 2006.

Roth Accounts: Why They Are Attractive Now

Senator William Roth of Delaware is an unsung hero who helped to create the Great Moderation of the two-and-half decades between the early 1980s and the mid-2000s. During this exceptional period in history, inflation was moderate, unemployment was low (rising only modestly for brief intervals in the 1990–1991 and 2001 recessions), and productivity grew strongly, especially after 1995. Much of this is a product of the Kemp-Roth tax cuts of the early 1980s, authored by Roth and Congressman Jack Kemp and signed into law by Ronald Reagan in 1981.

Roth is less known for another great gift to thrifty Americans: Roth tax-advantaged savings vehicles. Roths (such as Roth IRAs) receive after tax contributions—that is, they are not tax-deductible like traditional vehicles; they have already been taxed. Thereafter the account grows tax free for life. There is no tax liability even beyond the grave: You can pass assets inside Roths onto your heirs free of income taxes (but not free of estate taxes).

If you believe that your income tax rate will be higher in retirement than at present—as this book emphatically argues—it is in your interest to place much of your retirement savings in Roth vehicles.

Both IRAs and 401(k)s exist in Roth versions. Roth IRAs have existed for decades; Roth 401(k)s are much more recent. Individuals can open a

Roth IRA, subject to income limits; but their employer must choose to offer a Roth 401(k).

Downsides

Roth vehicles have much greater flexibility than traditional tax-advantaged vehicles, so there is really only one downside: You have to pay taxes when you contribute (i.e., your contributions are all in "after tax" dollars).

If you are an "eat dessert first" kind of person and prefer deferring pain (taxes) as long as possible, this may not suit you. But bear in mind the later pain associated with paying taxes on distributions from a traditional IRA/401(k) may well be double—or more—the pain you would bear today.

How Much Can You Contribute to Roth Vehicles?

In round numbers—because tax law changes may make more specific numbers out of date before this book is published—individual earners can contribute just over $20,000 per year to a Roth 401(k) and $5,000 to a Roth IRA, plus $2,000 and $1,000 respective "catch-up" additions possible for those older than 50 years. IRA contributions are subject to an income limit of about $50,000; 401(k) contributions are not limited by income.

This suggests that if your employer offers 401(k)-type plans but no Roth 401(k), as has been allowed since 2006, you should lobby your human resources department to create one. I did so with my employer (the University of Oregon), who quickly realized that it would help them retain financially savvy employees.

How Much Should You Convert From a Traditional to a Roth Vehicle?

New contributions are one thing, but what about older workers—for example, Baby Boomers in their fifties and sixties—who may already have contributed to traditional vehicles for decades? Even after the bear market that began in 2007, you may still have considerable balances there. Through 2009, an income ceiling (at roughly $100,000) limited your eligibility to convert. But all that changes in 2010.

Until 2010, Roth IRAs were only available to taxpayers earning below an adjusted gross income in the mid-$100,000 range (the legislated income ceiling). But under current law you have a unique, and possibly only temporary, opportunity to convert your traditional IRAs to Roths, regardless of your level of income. Under current law, the conversion window opens on January 2, 2010. At present, this window will be open perpetually, but for reasons argued below, I am not so confident of that. So the opportunity may be fleeting.

Mechanics of Conversion to Roth

Conversion of a traditional retirement account to a Roth equivalent is only possible if the traditional account is an IRA. If most of your tax-advantaged retirement savings is in one or more employer plans, 401(k)s, 403(b)s, 457s, and so forth, you will need to "rollover" those proceeds into an IRA. Consult your tax adviser and representatives of the current and planned custodians of the account on procedures. But in general it is fairly painless: Ask the planned new custodian for an "IRA rollover kit," complete the forms, and follow the instructions to transmit them. (You will probably need to send copies to both the sending and the receiving custodians.) Financial institutions commonly administer IRAs, so you can leave your account with the same custodian if you choose.

Once an account is in IRA form, conversion to Roth is only a matter of completing the custodian's conversion form—and paying the required taxes. While contributions to an IRA must be made be the time you file your taxes each year, conversions are considered effective in the year they occur. IRS Publication 590 ("Individual Retirement Arrangements") includes the details. Smart savers converted some of their qualified funds to Roths in 2010 to take advantage of the chance to spread their tax liability over 2011 and 2012. But few political insiders expect the Bush tax cuts, which were extended for two years in late 2010, to survive much longer, especially for those earning more than about $200,000 per year. The prudent course is to convert as much as possible while the legal window is still open.

Wall Street stands to gain greatly from Roth conversions, so many wealth management firms have created online calculators to help you frame the conversion choice. In general, the longer the period until you plan to take distributions, and the greater the increase in your income taxes you expect by then, the more compelling is the argument for conversion.

This is a clean decision if you can pay the taxes from another source (i.e., if you need not reduce the retirement account balance to pay the taxes). After all, this maximizes the amount that grows tax free. If you must liquidate some retirement savings to pay the conversion taxes, that presents a countervailing argument: Will the decline in the asset's value (due to taxes paid in 2010) be greater than the taxes saved in, say, 2020? Online calculators can help you make this decision, but bear in mind that the results will only be as accurate as your assumptions (e.g., about future tax rates). Other chapters of this book have argued that your income taxes could double, or more, over the next 15 to 20 years.

Silver Lining: Should You Spread the Conversion Taxes Over 2 Years (2011 and 2012)?

Many investors have thus far balked at this opportunity because conversion of a traditional IRA to a Roth means paying the taxes you didn't pay when you made your initial contributions. USAA surveyed 1,259 Baby Boomers with traditional IRAs and found that 73% of them do not plan to convert to Roth IRAs.[2]

Here the economy has handed us a gift of sorts. Chances are you took considerable losses during the bear market that began in late 2007 (if you didn't, you should be writing your own book). Those tax losses can nullify much (perhaps all) of your investment gains in the converted IRAs. And chances are, the investments in those IRAs lost money, too, so you may owe no taxes on the conversion at all.

You could also accelerate charitable donations you planned to make anyway sometime in the future to offset some of the "income" the IRS will deem you to have received when you convert. All the normal rules about the deductibility of charitable gifts apply.

There's a further advantage, only available in the next few years: If you still owe taxes when you convert traditional IRAs to Roth IRAs, the tax law allows you to defer your tax payments briefly and spread them equally over two years: in 2011 and 2012. This was especially attractive when the tax rate on capital gains was scheduled to rise in 2011 (but currently deferred until 2013). So if you are one of the rare ones who do have capital gains on your traditional retirement accounts, you should convert them while tax rates remain uniquely low.

Note that while it is possible to pay the taxes owed for conversion out of the account being converted most financial advisers do not recommend it. It shrinks the base from which those assets can hereafter grow tax free.

What if the Law Is Changed?

The coincidence that a deep bear market has coincided with a historic opportunity to contribute to Roth savings vehicles, or convert traditional vehicles to Roths, is a delicious irony. (These provisions passed in 2006 in part because Congress wanted to encourage Baby Boomers to accelerate tax payments forward from the years when they will retire. Taxes have been deferred until the taxpayer takes distributions.) But with the onset of a deep recession and consequent decline in asset prices, those tax payments will be tens of billions lower than at the market peak.

Congress could pass amendments to the tax law (which it does with depressing regularity) to close the conversion window. I don't consider this likely for the reason noted: It will guarantee that those tax revenues are not received until retirees begin taking distributions from their traditional retirement accounts. Congress and the president are desperate for revenue, now.

Why take a chance? Better to exploit what may be a fleeting opportunity while the value of your retirement assets—and therefore the taxes owed to convert them—is at a recent low.

One more speculative possibility is that Congress, or your state legislature, may create some other type of tax to reduce the government's reliance on individual income taxes. California, for example, relies for more than half of its total revenues on income taxes. Half of those come from only a few wealthy earners. This makes revenues extremely volatile, causing booms and busts. An advisory panel has recommended a European-style value-added tax (VAT). The Treasury Department has also studied VATs, and Congress (particularly House Democratic leader and former Speaker Nancy Pelosi) is showing increasing interest due to their congenital inability to cut spending.

If a VAT also means European-style effective tax rates, this book has demonstrated that the United States will experience a European-style economy: a generous safety net but slow growth and high unemployment. If this unfortunate future occurs—as this book argues is almost certain—a VAT may partly substitute for income tax increases. This would reduce the tax savings from conversion to Roths, but it would be unlikely to eliminate them entirely. Some increase in income taxes seems unavoidable, and all current political signs confirm this. Progressive income taxation is a deeply held value for most Democrats.

A greater risk is that Congress may renege on the tax-free treatment of Roth accounts. Quite frankly, one of my goals for this book is to encourage so many Boomers to invest so much in Roth accounts—in new contributions or in conversions—that an invincible political constituency forms to preempt any such legislative mischief. But to hedge against this eventuality, it's probably best not to put all your eggs in one tax basket. Put the majority, but not the entirety, of your retirement savings in Roth vehicles.

Do-Overs

One special attraction of conversions to Roth IRAs is that you can change your mind. If, after making a conversion, you decide it all was a mistake— say, Congress finds a $50 trillion pot of gold somewhere and doesn't need to raise income tax rates after all—you can undertake a "recharacterization" to convert the Roth IRA back to a traditional IRA. Again, see your tax adviser for the mechanics. So even if the predictions in this book prove to be wildly off the mark, you need not live with any errors.

Future Contributions to Roth Vehicles

This chapter has been directed primarily to Baby Boomers who have had decades to build up assets in traditional retirement savings accounts such as IRAs, 401(k)s, and so on, and who can gain greatly from converting those accounts. But what about those who are still saving for retirement— younger Boomers and succeeding generations?

First, within the limits of what the IRS allows (which is determined by your income level), maximize your contributions to Roth vehicles. For Roth IRAs, you can contribute $5,000 per earner per year, $6,000 if they are older than 50 years. For employers' Roth 401(k) plans, you can contribute just over $20,000 per earner per year, with a small augmentation for those older than 50 years. Eligibility to contribute to IRAs phases out at a fairly modest income level (roughly $50,000); eligibility to contribute to an employer Roth 401(k) is universal, if the employer offers this option.

Conversion is not restricted to only 2010, at least under current law. It will be possible indefinitely. As long as Congress leaves the conversion window open, any traditional IRA can be converted to a Roth IRA. So if you choose, you can add to your existing traditional IRA every January 1 and convert it to a Roth IRA on January 2.

Conclusion

Undoubtedly, Congress would never have made this opportunity available had it known that asset prices would crash and the government would no longer harvest a windfall from Roth IRA conversions. It is quite possible that Congress may rescind this opportunity as part of a desperate effort to plug future federal deficits. If you expect to be at all dependent on your investments after 2015 or so, it is in your interest to maximize your new contributions to Roth accounts, and convert a large fraction of your traditional retirement funds into Roth IRAs. Your tax adviser can show you how. For some traditional retirement accounts that are not IRAs, such as 401(k)s, 403(b)s, or 457s, you'll first need to "roll them over" into traditional IRAs as a precursor step. Again, your tax adviser can explain the mechanics, and your investment custodian (mutual fund or brokerage firm) can execute the rollovers or conversions.

How much of your retirement funds should you convert to Roths? It depends on how confident you are of the scenarios described in this book. Personally, I expect to convert well over half of my traditional retirement accounts to Roths. I'll preserve a small portion in case I am wrong about my tax predictions (although I am extremely confident in them). Diversification is a wise policy, including for long-term tax planning.

All in all, this is a once-in-a-lifetime opportunity to cut your lifetime tax bill and eliminate income taxes on your savings after you retire.

Key Steps You Should Take

1. Review all the assets that you plan to rely on once you are no longer working, and identify a target percentage you wish to be in Roth form (I suggest 50% to 75%).
2. Request rollover kits for those accounts that are not already in traditional IRAs from the custodians of each account; complete the forms and send them to the custodians.
3. Once all assets you wish to convert are in traditional IRAs, request Roth conversion forms from the custodians. Ask them to estimate your tax liability (generally it is simply your tax rate times the value of the account, since you did not pay taxes on those contributions when you made them).
4. Reserve the requisite amount for taxes in a readily liquifiable form (e.g., a money market account), or consider spreading that liability over 2011 and 2012 (but note that tax rates may rise by then).
5. Complete and send the conversion forms.
6. If your income makes you ineligible to contribute directly to Roth IRAs, contribute the maximum allowed to a traditional IRA, then immediately convert it to a Roth IRA.
7. Enjoy tax-free growth in these assets hereafter, passing them on in your estate tax free if you choose.

Chapter 9 Summary

- Traditional tax-efficient retirement investing exploits the deferral of taxes possible in "traditional" retirement accounts such as IRAs or 401(k)s. In traditional accounts, contributions are tax deductible, and no tax is paid until distributions are taken, which can begin no earlier than age 59½ and no later than 70½.
- The implicit assumption underlying such accounts is that most retirees will be in a lower tax bracket in retirement than they were while working, so deferring taxation takes advantage of

the lower bracket and the value of a longer time period for compounding.

- But over the next few dozen years, tax brackets are likely to escalate—significantly. The late 2000s may prove to have the lowest tax rates in modern history.
- Therefore, it would be better to pay taxes on earned income now and have those earnings grow tax free into retirement. A Roth account allows for this.
- There are income limits on eligibility to contribute to Roth accounts, but starting in 2010, no restrictions on converting traditional retirement accounts into Roths.
- Roth conversion is worthwhile if your investing horizon is reasonably long—say, 10 years—so that your assets have time to grow to replace the taxes you pay upon conversion.

CHAPTER 10

Corporate Strategy Applications

The preceding chapters make the case that the Great Moderation of declining inflation and interest rates is over and so is the 25-year-long bull market in most asset prices. There will probably be temporary upward corrections, but corporations no longer have macroeconomic tailwinds at their backs. Investors will, therefore, need to diversify their portfolios much more, including reducing their reliance on the dollar, or any developed economy's paper currency. The immutable logic of demographics and debt leave little room for doubt.

This sea change in the economic environment has implications far beyond asset markets and individual retirement planning. You can plan for the day when you will no longer work, but the owners of your company (perhaps including yourself) expect its economic life to persist in perpetuity. They will need to plan corporate strategy in this new and more challenging environment. This chapter briefly outlines a few implications for strategy of this new reality. Other applications can be found in a number of teaching cases. Relevant cases are listed in an appendix, keyed to each chapter of this book.

Entering or Expanding in International Markets

Investment by Western multinationals—and in the past few decades, Asian and now Latin American multinationals—has stimulated the rising prospects for billions of the formerly poor in China, India, and many other formerly low-income countries. As their economies have prospered, these nations are no longer only sources of cheap labor; they are fast-growing markets for Western goods and services. For example, many iconic American brands such as McDonald's, Starbucks, or Walmart employ strategies that assume their home markets are nearly saturated, so future growth will come overseas. (In fact, several of these companies expanded too fast overseas and were caught by surprise when the Great Recession hit.)

The new future makes it even more imperative that your company relies less on developed economies, which have made entitlement promises that are unsustainable in the face of demographic realities, and instead rely much more on well-managed and still-growing developing economies. But there are several important caveats:

- *Central bank independence and prudence.* The political incentives to overprint currency are almost unstoppable. As noted earlier, excess money creation *temporarily* brings prosperity and happy voters. Serious inflation comes later and will accelerate if overprinting doesn't cease.
- Thus, independence of the monetary stewards—that is, the central bank—from direct politics is widely viewed as key to maintaining the value of the currency. Several countries (e.g., Japan and Great Britain) realized this and spun their central banks off from the national government. However, recently a few have moved in the other direction, with the presidents of Mexico and Argentina firing their central bank heads, usually for failing to cooperate enough with deficit financing (i.e., refusing to buy as much government debt as was on offer).
- Since any operations your company has in a country will earn revenues (and pay local expenses) in the local currency, your fortunes are hostage to the prudence of the local central bank, just as your U.S. domestic operations are dependent on the Federal Reserve. So assessing the commitment of the nation's central bank to a stable currency is an important criterion for choosing overseas markets to enter, whether "greenfielding" or by acquisition. If entry into a given country is unavoidable— say, to preempt a competitor—a clear-eyed assessment of likely inflation is essential to estimating the real return on your corporate investment.
- Information sources for such an assessment include the International Monetary Fund, any local inflation hawks (equivalents

of the Rep. Ron Paul or the National Inflation Association in the United States), and periodicals that focus on the intersection of business and politics, such as *The Wall Street Journal*, *The Economist*, or the *Financial Times*. Warning signs of a loss of anti-inflation zeal (or other types of financial mismanagement) will probably be visible in statistics about capital flight out of the country, such as those published by international bodies (e.g., the IMF, the World Bank, or the United Nations).

Product Mix

Many of the broad forces affecting marketing in the developed world will be repeated in middle-income countries as they become more prosperous and age in the process. Products considered luxuries by the poor become necessities as they advance into the middle class. Many features of middle-class life in the West are still new in much of the emerging world: for example, clean water or cheap, flexible transportation. For example, bicycle sales are replaced by motorcycles and then by small automobiles. If your firm relies mainly on a "commodity" strategy (what Michael Porter terms "cost leadership"),[1] you may find many of your core customers prospering out of your market space and seeking more differentiated and higher-priced products. On the other hand, successful differentiators can exploit a rapidly growing market among the new middle class overseas.

At the same time, any firm that offers services that older consumers buy can enjoy rapid market growth in these newly emerging economies. The same demographic forces—populations are aging as economies prosper, women are emancipated and bear fewer children—that will shrink capital availability will also expand demand for such services. Health care appears particularly attractive, both because older customers consume it disproportionately and because middle-income customers of any age only recently have been able to afford it.

Government and Public Relations

Businesses have a stake in the public finances of the countries in which they operate, because government spending, taxation, borrowing, and money creation will affect several corporate disciplines directly. *Controllers* will need to forecast changes in taxation—mostly upward—as demographic forces drive government budgets. *Treasurers and chief financial officers (CFOs)* can use information about government finances to project how much higher interest rates will be driven by government crowding out of private borrowing, or by capital flight by worried investors. *Sales and marketing* personnel will need to calibrate their market forecasts to the competence of the government's management of its finances and the larger economy. Finally, *CFOs and boards* can use the comparative state of public finance in several countries to prioritize investments among them.

Cash Management

All firms need to keep some "cash" (liquid investments) available to smooth spending and hedge against minor surprises. The themes in this book can help the CFO or other person who deploys retained earnings into short-term investments. A rising inflation/rising interest rate environment implies keeping investments short term so their income does not get eroded by inflation. CFOs may be tempted to reach for yield, but that almost always requires sacrificing liquidity. This can be particularly hazardous in a rising inflation or slowing revenue world since negative cash flow surprises will far outnumber positive ones.

These examples are intended to pique your imagination in developing ideas for how the new macroeconomic reality will affect your own specific responsibilities. Further illustrations are available in teaching cases, listed in the teaching cases appendix.

Chapter 10 Summary

- An understanding of long-term trends can assist corporate managers (whose investments of corporate funds often have multidecade horizons) as well as individuals.
- Corporate applications of the ideas in this book include corporate development, including acquisitions in other industries or nations, allocating capital to different product lines, managing relations with host governments and publics, and managing retained earnings in a volatile inflationary environment.
- Pertinent teaching cases are listed in the case study appendix.

CODA

Your Money, Your Future—Your Vote

I'll close on a personal note. This book has been about self-interest: protecting your investments, and your company's, from the depredations planned in Washington and other capitals. But you can help not only yourself but also generations to follow by voting with an eye to the interests of future generations. It's patently obvious that our politicians are willing to sacrifice that future to win votes today. This is immorality, plain and simple. Our moral imperative, as the beneficiaries of the strongest era of prosperity in world history, is to choose leaders who will be the stewards of that gift for our children and grandchildren.

So don't vote your pocketbook, vote your children's. Use your new economic literacy to choose leaders that honor our implicit social contract with the next generation.

APPENDIX A

Why the Yuan Affects You

A Primer on How International Economics Shapes Investment Valuations

This book has been written to help average Baby Boomers planning for retirement to anticipate negative trends to protect their savings. It assumes little background knowledge in economics, finance, or investments. However, some readers may need an introduction to these topics. This appendix, and the one following, are for you. More experienced readers may find them a useful refresher.

What Drives the Dollar's Value?

The value (purchasing power) of a unit of currency is driven by the magnitudes of its supply and its demand.

Demand for the dollar is driven by transactions and investments. Consumers use the dollars they receive in payment (e.g., in wages for the work they do) and spend those dollars on the goods and services they purchase. Say a given dollar received by a wageworker is spent at a restaurant. The restaurant owner will spend the same dollar for supplies, such as tablecloths. The tablecloth supplier (say, Sysco) will spend that dollar to pay its delivery truck drivers, who will spend their wages, and so forth. The same dollar will course through the economy several times before it finds a resting place in investments. The rate at which it circulates is known as the "velocity of money," or "money multiplier." Money velocities have generally been rising over the past few decades, as technology allows funds to be transferred faster and faster, but they fell sharply in late 2008.

The *supply* of a currency is controlled by that nation's central bank (the Federal Reserve for the United States, in partnership with the U.S. Treasury Department). Only they can legally issue new currency. If the supply of currency expands too slowly and monetary velocity does not accelerate to compensate, it can restrict (slow down) the growth of an economy. Tight money will cause interest rates to rise (because those with money to lend will be scarce, so they can command a higher price to rent out their money). This will slow lending and the investments in added capacity business would make with that borrowed money. Consumers will borrow less and therefore spend less. Too-slow growth in the supply of money can bring on a recession. In the early 1930s, the Fed's too-slow money growth turned a burst bubble into a decade-long recession. Milton Friedman won a Nobel Prize in part for his research that proved this.

If too-slow money supply growth can slow an economy, too-fast growth—a much more common problem—can have the opposite effect. Credit is readily available at low interest rates, which may be negative in real inflation-adjusted terms. Businesses and consumers will spend and invest freely. Businesses will need to hire more workers; so eventually, available workers will be in short supply, and businesses will have to raise wages to attract new employees. They will pass the higher wage costs onto customers through higher prices. Thus, inflation will be accelerated by an overheated economy, all catalyzed by excess monetary growth. For this reason, Friedman wrote that "inflation is always and everywhere a monetary phenomenon." Inflation can only exist if the money supply grows faster than the supply of goods and services that money can buy.

Central banks have an insidious incentive to expand the supply of money too fast. Politicians see the benefits of faster economic growth immediately, especially at election time. The inflationary side effects can take years to develop, and more years to become embedded in everyone's expectations. Thus politically controlled central banks have a built-in incentive to debase the currency by printing too much of it. Happily, a growing number of central banks around the world have become independent of their governments, so theoretically they can resist these temptations. However, the reliance placed on central banks around the world in the crisis of 2008 and thereafter to flood the financial system with liquidity—that is, print money to compensate for a sudden precipitous drop in velocity—have brought loud calls for greater transparency and accountability, including Rep. Ron Paul's call to "end the Fed," strongly supported by the Tea Party. In at least three cases (Mexico, Japan, and Argentina), the central bank head was fired by the country's president. It remains to be seen whether transparency and accountability are possible without also reducing independence.

The Foreign Barometer

Currencies are traded in foreign exchange markets. Foreigners may need to trade their own currencies for dollars to buy our exports or to buy American assets for investment purposes. Thus, every day there is a "poll" of the world's appraisal of the dollar's value (and that of every other traded currency). That appraisal reflects a variety or factors, including the attractiveness of dollar-denominated assets as investments, foreigners' confidence in the United States as an investment climate, and desired exchange rates. Any net buying of dollars by foreigners—say, to have them available to buy treasury bonds—will raise the dollar's price. The dollar will fall if there is net selling.

In the past decade, there have been immense (hundreds of billions) net purchases of dollars by foreigners. Beyond normal investing motives, several Asian central banks have sold their own currencies and purchased dollars, thus elevating the dollar's value and suppressing their own currencies. Why? Because this helps these export-dependent economies export more: Their goods are less expensive in foreign currency, and competing U.S. goods are more expensive. China and Japan in particular have used dollar purchases to suppress their own exchange rates and as a side effect raised the value of the dollar.

Nevertheless, the dollar's value has been in a long-term swoon for the second half of the 2000s decade. Explaining why means introducing international trade into the picture.

How High-Spending Americans Drive Down the Dollar

Generally, importers of products in other countries need to convert their home currency into whatever currency the good is priced. But Americans have enjoyed a special status since after World War II, because the dollar has been the world's de facto reserve currency (i.e., the default currency for many international transactions). For example, oil is traded in dollars. This eliminates the need to convert dollars into another currency to import oil.

The widely accepted reserve status of the U.S. dollar has enabled Americans' propensity to buy imports. We buy close to one trillion dollars more goods from foreign countries than foreigners buy from America. This is not so surprising, because many poor and middle-income countries price their goods cheaply to stimulate exports and so expand their economies, and the richest large country in the world is a natural market for those exports. Commentators have often termed the U.S. "the importer of last resort."

What happens to all the dollars Americans send overseas to buy imports? Some of them are spent locally in the exporting countries, but some—nearly a trillion dollars per year, in fact—are "recycled" to the United States into investments in American assets. This occurs for two main reasons. First, the very economic conditions that allow Americans the prosperity to spend so freely also make the United States an attractive destination for investment. In particular, a large part of foreign investment has gone to purchase U.S. treasury securities, seen as among the safest investments available. Second, exporting countries realize that their own economies depend on the continued ability of U.S. consumers to buy what they sell, so it is in their interest to support the U.S. economy through investment. This has led to a very codependent relationship: an unholy alliance between profligate U.S. consumers and export-dependent developing economies.

The net outflow of dollars from the United States to the rest of the world has flooded the world's markets with U.S. currency. Like any other commodity, a surplus of dollars drives its price down. The dollar has been in a long-term decline for most of the past 6 years, with the exception of the panic of late 2008 when investors rushed to dollars seeking the presumed safe haven of U.S. treasuries.

Crosscurrents

This codependent situation may change, however. First, as foreigners realize that they have invested heavily in assets denominated in a declining currency, they will diversify into investments in more stable currencies.

Officials in Brazil, Russia, and China have all argued that the world's reserve currency should be a "basket" of several currencies, not only the dollar. And China, which until recently purchased hundreds of billions of U.S. treasuries each year for its reserves, is now purchasing fewer dollar assets and more hard assets such as commodity supplies (e.g., oil leases in Africa and Iraq). Such developments cut into the demand for the dollar and accelerate its fall.

Second, in time there will be far less foreign investment in the United States, because there will be less foreign investment, period. This will occur for demographic reasons. As populations age, they save less and spend down accumulated savings from prior years. All developed economies, and most developing ones, are aging, so there will be fewer savings to deploy, including into American investments. This, too, will reduce foreign demand for dollars.

Finally, many exporting countries' governments recognize the dangers in the "imbalances" described previously (a chronic importer enabling export-dependence by other countries). They have spoken publicly about increasing domestic consumption (so that some of their "exports" are consumed locally rather than by the United States). Of course, in the long run this will happen naturally as aging populations save less and consume more anyway. Similarly, American savings rates began rebounding in 2009 as overindebted families relearned the virtues of thrift. Both instances—more consumption by exporters, less by Americans—were natural responses to changed economic conditions during the recession. The open question is what the new "normal" will be after the recession fades.

The Money Supply

Hard Versus Fiat Money

For most of recorded history, the bits of material we call "money" had intrinsic value; that is, it was made of material that was valued for its own sake. Most commonly that material was gold or silver. Such money is referred to as "hard money"; it did not require any "backing," because it had value by itself.

Over time, however, in nation after nation, the mints that produced new coins began diluting the bullion within by adding base metals. This reduced the coin's intrinsic value, also known as "debasing the currency." The first recorded example was in 2nd-century Rome, so this practice has a long tradition.

First in China around the year 1000, and later in almost every other country, governments began printing paper currency backed by bullion. The idea was that coins were heavy and inconvenient; why not carry bits of paper that could be presented to a bank to receive coins in exchange? Transactions could be solely with paper, and coins (or bullion itself) needed be moved only from one vault to the next. This, too, is a kind of hard money. In the United States the best examples were Federal Reserve notes, convertible into gold by the bearer by presenting them at any bank. Such notes were fully backed by gold.

Under a gold standard, the supply of money (bank notes) can't grow faster than the supply of gold owned by the central bank. This severely limits the ability of government to stimulate an economy during a recession. That's why Franklin D. Roosevelt ended gold-on-demand for U.S. residents in 1933: the limited supply of money was aggravating the recession, and he needed the supply to expand faster and cause some inflation (i.e., counteract then-extant deflation). The United States left the gold standard entirely in 1971. Thus, the era of fiat money began.

Fiat money is backed by nothing but a promise that the government can provide something (usually unspecified) of value to anyone who offers dollars to it. In other words, the money's value is based solely on the government's "fiat." The problem with fiat money is the mirror image of Roosevelt's problem in 1933: The only constraint on the growth in the money supply is self-restraint by the Federal Reserve. When that restraint fails, as it did from the late 1960s through the 1970s, money supply can grow too fast and depreciate the dollar through excess. In other words, too much money creation leads to inflation. In foreign markets, it leads to a decline in the dollar's exchange rate versus countries whose money supplies are growing more slowly.

The Secret: Few Politicians Really Support a Strong Dollar

All American politicians profess support for a "strong dollar," meaning stable or rising exchange rates. But in fact very few really do. The reason is that in the short run there are great benefits from a weakening dollar. First, U.S. exports become cheaper, so more are sold. These generate exporting jobs, many of which are members of politically powerful trade unions. Second, through exports and other means, the economy will be stimulated, lowering unemployment and making voters happy (so they reelect the politicians). The problem of embedded inflation is longer term, after the politician may well be out of office.

A true "strong dollar" policy would involve tightening the money supply until the dollar rose on foreign exchange markets. But that would have the opposite effect of the previous paragraph, which few politicians can stomach.

Taming the Inflation Beast

Nations that have grown their money supply too fast experience inflation. If the excess growth continues for long, that inflation will accelerate. In the extreme, hyperinflation—inflation rates of hundreds of percent per year or more—will ensue. For very recent examples, look at the experiences of Venezuela or Zimbabwe. Both financed very large government deficits by printing money, flooding markets with paper that rapidly became worthless. Shortages of basic necessities appeared because suppliers had no incentive to produce goods that would be bought with rapidly depreciating currency.

There is no painless way to reset everyone's expectations about future prices. The only known successful approach is very costly: a sharp recession. Workers will stop demanding wage increases when unemployment is rising. Firms that see their wage costs stabilize will expect more moderate price increases. (They may have to cut prices if economic activity slows enough to leave their products unsold.)

The Federal Reserve led by Paul Volcker was forced to administer this bitter medicine in 1979, after more than a decade of accelerating inflation. Double-digit inflation rates had become "normal" and were built into everyone's plans. The Fed raised interest rates very sharply—the prime rate exceeded 20% in 1981—which caused lending to shut down and therefore hiring, too. The ensuing recession was the deepest since World War II up to that point. But inflation fell from roughly 12% to 1% within a few years. The recent recession was not engineered by the Fed (it occurred because a speculative bubble burst), but a similar though less dramatic story played out: A consumer price index that grew at more than 5% in 2007–2008 fell into negative territory during the worst parts of the recession in 2008 and 2009.

Fed officials in 2008–2009 saw the urgent problem as deflation, not inflation, and flooded the financial sector with "liquidity" (money). This arrested what would otherwise have been Great Depression 2.0, leaving only a very bad recession. Deflation became very moderate inflation (roughly 1% to 2% per year). This averted the kind of deflationary downward spiral that cost Japan at least 20 years of economic vitality from 1990. In such a spiral, businesses facing anemic demand compete by cutting their prices, which requires them to lay off or not hire more workers. Those idle workers can't buy very much, and those still employed see falling prices and defer purchases in the knowledge that the item they want will be cheaper next year. Demand falls further and extends the recession, so the downward spiral continues.

Fed Chairman Bernanke, a scholar of America's Great Depression in the 1930s, believes that the greater sin in combating recession is to do too little, not too much. This philosophy was also behind the $787 billion fiscal stimulus passed in February 2009 as the American Reinvestment and Recovery Act. The failed example of Japan would seem to support this view. Bernanke believes that as the economy recovers the Fed can engage in an "exit strategy": It will reverse its extreme expansion of the money supply, mainly by selling the treasury and mortgage-backed bonds it bought in the hundreds of billions in 2008 and 2009. (Selling bonds soaks up currency of the buyers of those bonds, thereby shrinking the money supply. Central banks sometime use this technique to defend their currency by absorbing the effects of excess money printing; this is called "sterilization.") As of this writing in early 2010, it remains to be seen whether the Fed can be as nimble in withdrawing stimulus as it was in injecting it. The political incentives all encourage waiting too long. Arguably, the Fed did so after the 2001 recession, which helped cause the housing bubble.

The Future Is Now

Although Bernanke is quite right that inflation is likely still several years in the future, this distant threat has not prevented investors from dumping the dollar in anticipation. Why such rash actions now in concern about a problem in 2015?

Investors make money if they have foresight about a future development not apparent to the seller of the asset. As knowledge of that development spreads, the asset's buyer loses their advantage. Therefore, when an investor believes he has identified a development that is not widely known, it is in his interest to act quickly, before that information is "priced into" the asset. This is why markets can move so quickly on important news.

As increasing numbers of investors—foreign and domestic—recognize the trends outlined in this book, they are perceiving the value of diversifying out of the dollar. They will get the best price possible (say, on Brazilian stocks) if they act before other investors can bid that asset's price higher. Thus, investing is always based not only on current conditions but also on the future that investors anticipate, and try to exploit.

Conclusion

That's international economics in a very few pages. I've avoided jargon as much as possible, but many commonly used specialist terms are included in the Glossary.

In sum, a country's currency is a commodity just like wheat, and its price (the value, or purchasing power, of that currency) is likewise determined in the marketplace. That marketplace can include foreigners as well as residents. If there is greater demand for that currency than supply available, its price (value) will rise; and it will fall if the supply is too large compared with demand. A rise in purchasing power is deflation; a fall is inflation. Once either one becomes embedded (i.e., widely expected), it is impossible to exorcise without dramatic and very costly steps.

The United States has enjoyed a special privilege for the past 60-odd years because the dollar has been the default currency in many international transactions, and dollar-denominated assets are held by countries in their reserves (roughly two thirds of all reserves worldwide). This has allowed Americans to buy imports without the costs of converting dollars to other currencies (thus encouraging more imports, which is quite all right to the exporters). It has also encouraged export-dependent countries to recycle their export earnings into dollar assets, both for their investment merits and to depress their own currencies to make their exports cheaper. This led in the mid-2000s to an insidious "imbalance" and codependence: Americans overconsuming imports, and countries like China relying on that overconsumption to maintain domestic peace through exports to drive fast economic growth.

The late 2000s recession temporarily interrupted this codependence as American households devoted themselves to spending less and improving their overindebted balance sheets. Time will tell whether this nod toward greater "balance" is a temporary artifact of the recession or a new normal. This book argues that several of the underpinnings of the Great Moderation of 1983–2007—high Chinese savings from the codependence and a youngish population—will not hold true in the next 25 years.

Foreign investors are learning the lesson of the recession: It is imprudent to depend so heavily on one customer—America—or one currency—the dollar. We are already seeing plenty of examples of diversification out of dollars. Reduced demand for dollars is causing it to slip in currency markets. This book's main advice is that you should diversify, too.

APPENDIX B

Retirement Investing 101

An Introduction

This volume was designed for readers with little background in investing, but it does assume basic knowledge, along the lines of the typical reader of *Money* magazine. If you aren't there yet, this chapter can fill you in. More experienced readers may also find it a helpful refresher.

Why Save for Retirement?

Most of us earn a living through a salary that (hopefully) grows over the years. But most people do not wish to work until they die. The years after the period of their lives in which they worked full time are conventionally called "retirement," although today many "retirees" continue to work, at least part time.

Most of us do not wish to greatly reduce our standard of living in retirement. Economists characterize the "replacement ratio" as the income a family will need in retirement as a proportion of their highest income while working. As noted in chapter 5, those who are content with a modest lifestyle may get by with 60% or 70% of their peak income, because many employment-related expenses will cease. Someone for whom retirement is a chance to live their dream—for example, of indulging in some long-deferred and expensive pastime like travel—may need 125% of their peak working income.

Won't Social Security Fund My Retirement?

Social Security was primarily designed to lift the indigent elderly out of poverty. Its checks provide basic subsistence but not much more.

Payments, which are based on your age at retirement and your payroll tax contributions while working, rarely exceed $30,000 per year for a couple (less for an individual). Payments will be lower if you retire before the official age (currently about 67, escalating each year), or if you earned a low income while working. For some who aspire to a relatively affluent retirement lifestyle—and who doesn't?—*Social Security payments will only provide a small fraction (20% or 30%) of the income you will require.*

Where Will the Rest Come From?

Unless you also will receive pension income (and the fraction of workers that can expect it has declined by 80% in the past 30 years), the rest of your income in retirement will need to come from savings you accumulated while working.

Here's an illustration. Say that the Social Security Administration has advised you (through its annual statements sent late each year) that you and your spouse can expect to receive $25,000 in payments each year after your planned retirement date. Assume that you wish to have a total income in retirement of $55,000—roughly the median household income in the United States. You would need to use savings to generate the missing $30,000 per year.

Many financial planners use as a rule of thumb the "4% rule": To ensure that your investments last as long as you live, you should not spend an amount that is more than 4% of their starting value when you first begin to draw them down. That implies that you will need to have accumulated investments 25 times that $30,000, or $750,000. (It's 25 times because 100% divided by 4% equals 25.)

The 4% is a common rule of thumb, but like all such rules, it captures "average" conditions—that is, the average of the past few decades, when asset markets have mostly been rising. It assumes that your remaining portfolio will grow faster than 4%, with the residual going to compensate for (assumed fairly modest) inflation. Planners have not yet adjusted this rule for the historic crash in asset prices during 2007–2009, or for the possibility of higher inflation in the future. To be more conservative, you may wish to set lower withdrawal rates, such as 3% or 2.5%, but then you will need to increase your investment target proportionately. For example, a 3% withdrawal rate would require accumulated investments of 33 (not 25) times $30,000, or in round numbers $1 million.

But I Can't Possibly Save That Much!

Few Boomers feel they have saved enough toward retirement, and most are right. Many personal finance advisers exhort higher savings, and they are right to do so. But beyond trying to make up for lost time, you have an additional option: Work longer. This can be full-time or part-time work. Delaying your complete withdrawal from the world of work has several salutary consequences: First, you extend the number of years you can accumulate savings; second, you reduce the number of years when you will need to tap into those savings. Finally, many gerontological studies have demonstrated the value to health and well-being of keeping mentally active; work is a great way to do so and get paid besides.

Savings Versus Investments

Financial writers often conflate these two terms, because they have the same economic effect. But let's be more precise.

Savings is the portion of your disposable income that you do not consume. You probably deposit it in a bank, at least temporarily: think "savings" account. Statisticians track the overall national savings rate—that's the percentage of disposable income that is not consumed. In the early postwar decades, the savings rate exceeded 10%, while by the middle of the last decade it was negative—the nation as a whole spent more than it earned. Households, governments, and nations can do this by borrowing the difference—as long as lenders will allow it.

People commonly keep those savings that they need to access quickly in a liquid form, such as a checking, savings, or money market account. If such accounts are held by an FDIC-insured bank, those deposits are guaranteed by a government-financed insurance program up to $250,000 per account. However, because they carry so little risk, they also offer very little return: today, money market accounts offer interest rates in the range of hundredths of one percent.

Redeploying savings from highly liquid, low-return accounts into less liquid, higher-return assets is known as *investing*, and the assets purchased are *investments*. Investment scholars have found that there is a stark trade-off between investments' safety and their return. "Safety" is measured as the inverse of variability in the asset's price (i.e., assets whose prices are stable are safer) and "return" by the excess returned to an investor over and above the purchase price of their investment. This negative correlation between safety and return—usually expressed as a positive correlation between "risk" and return—is an axiom of finance, and it makes intuitive sense: If you wish to earn a higher return, you will have to pay something for it, such as accepting greater ups and downs (volatility) in the price of the asset.

This chapter will outline the major alternative assets you can invest in and vehicles within which you can make those investments.

Classes of Assets

Financial institutions are endlessly creative in inventing new kinds of assets, so any attempt at a complete list will quickly become obsolete. This list is restricted to relatively easy-to-understand asset types for investing beginners. Financial writers advise strongly against buying anything you don't understand.

Fixed Income

Fixed income investments represent loans from you to the issuer of the asset. They are, essentially, IOUs from the issuer to pay you for the temporary use of your money. These go under a variety of names, depending on the issuer and the length of time for which they are borrowing your money: For instance, the U.S. Treasury Department issues bills, notes, and bonds for maturities (length of time borrowed) of, respectively, less than 90 days, 91 to 365 days, and more than 1 year.

Bank certificates of deposit (CDs) are a fixed income instrument. When you buy a CD, you are ceding to the bank use of your funds for a fixed period (say, 6 months). The bank will compensate you by paying you a percentage of your investment in addition to returning your original investment to you. CDs are very safe (if issued by an FDIC member bank), but very illiquid (hard to sell) up until the maturity date (the date when the bank returns your funds plus interest).

Many corporations and governments issue bonds. In general, the farther in the future the maturity of the bond, the higher the interest rate. Investors demand added compensation to tie up their money longer. (You'll see this relationship referred to in the business press as the "yield curve": how bonds' yields rise with longer maturities. Changes in the slope of the yield curve—the difference between rates on long-term versus short-term bonds—can be an important economic indicator.) Unlike bank CDs, however, you can back out of a bond deal by selling your bond on the secondary market. But the bond may have changed value since you purchased it.

Each bond commits to paying a coupon; bonds are compared by expressing those coupons as a percentage *yield.* Say you purchase a $1,000 bond with a $50 coupon; that's a 5% yield.

Now, say that interest rates rise to 10%. The bond's coupon doesn't change—it is still $50—but the bond's price will drop until its $50 coupon again reflects a market interest rate. In this case, the bond's price would fall from $1,000 to $500, making the $50 coupon 10% of the bond's value. Thus, bond prices always move inversely with interest rates: Bonds' prices rise when interest rates fall, and vice versa.

Fixed Incomes and Inflation

An interest rate can be broken into two components: a real return of purchasing power to the investor (often known as the "real interest rate"), and an inflation premium to cover the effects of inflation. If the consumer price index is rising 5% per year and your bond pays 8%, only 3% is real return.

As inflation accelerates, investors demand an escalating inflation premium to compensate. As a result, bonds that were issued before the inflation increase will fall in price. For example, a bond that pays 2% per year when inflation was zero will fall in price after 8% inflation so that it now pays a 10% rate: A $1,000 bond with a $20 coupon will fall to $200. Ouch!

Long-term lenders—that is, holders of long-term bonds—can be ravaged by accelerating inflation. First, their bonds will fall sharply in price. Second, their coupon payments, and the return of their capital when the bond matures, will be made in inflation-depreciated dollars. All this is reversed if inflation abates, known as disinflation, and even more so if prices actually decline (i.e., deflation), as can happen during a deep recession.

Financial planners advise fixed income investors to create a "ladder" of bonds—to stagger maturities so that different bonds mature in sequence. As the shortest-maturity bond matures, you invest its proceeds into a new long-term bond, and so forth over time. This reduces "interest rate risk"—plunges in the price of your bonds when interest rates rise—because successive bonds will mature and can be reinvested at the new rates. You will spread out the cost of your bonds so that you aren't buying at a bond price peak (a low interest rate). (Under deflationary conditions like recent years, the new rates will probably be lower, not higher.) Investment specialists therefore advise fixed income investors who see inflation on the horizon to concentrate their bond investments in short maturities so their prices are not greatly affected by rising rates.

As of this writing in mid-2010, interest rates are about as low as they can possibly get, so arguably purchasers of bonds can only expect low or even negative returns for the near future.

Fixed Incomes' Role in Your Portfolio

Fixed incomes are the ballast that keeps the ship on an even keel. Since they reduce portfolio volatility, they become more and more important to investors as their investing time horizon (the time until they need to access the investment) dwindles. Young investors (in their 20s and 30s) can afford to take risks, since they have a multidecade horizon until they will need their investments for retirement. The opposite is true for those in or near retirement. A very simple rule of thumb is the percentage of your portfolio in fixed incomes should roughly equal your age. Stocks—whose long-run return, but also their volatility, has been higher—should have a declining place in your portfolio over time, but never disappear entirely, to provide some growth to protect against inflation. Stocks' share of your portfolio should equal roughly 100 minus your age.

A contrary view is that this asset allocation, as well as the "buy and hold" philosophy of stock ownership, is an artifact of the disinflation that was a hallmark of the Great Moderation. Over the 25 years from 1982 to 2007 equities were in a long-term bull market, punctuated by only a few, brief bear market interruptions. Naturally, a generous allocation to equities, "bought and held," was a very successful strategy for millions of investors. But it has produced great disappointment in the past few years. While it is too early to be very specific, it seems likely that in time the conventional wisdom will recommend a smaller allocation to stocks than that cited earlier, for a shorter holding period than "forever." As several analysts have put it, "stocks will be for renting, not for buying." (But see the earlier comment about the low returns being currently offered by most bonds.)

Bond Issuers

All bonds face interest rate risk, with that risk rising for bonds of longer maturity. But different types of bonds face different default risks (the risk that the principal won't be paid back). The rating agencies Standard & Poor's, Moody's, and Fitch rate most fixed income securities to help investors choose the level of default risk they are willing to accept (and the interest rate they will receive in return). These ratings are hardly infallible; when default rates on mortgage-backed securities (see below) exceeded the raters' expectations, the market for these securities collapsed, taking banks that owned them along for the ride down.

U.S. treasuries are the presumptive "risk free" investment for default risk, since if the federal government defaults, other issuers will be in far worse shape. (But this book argues that a default by the U.S. government is becoming less far-fetched.) In late 2008 and early 2009, treasury rates plunged and prices skyrocketed, because investors panicked about default risks in many other investments and fled to the safety of treasuries. A variety of government-sponsored enterprises (GSEs), such as Fannie Mae and Freddie Mac, also issue *agency* bonds, at rates not much above treasuries because of the market's presumption that the treasury will bail them out if necessary (as occurred in late 2008 for Fannie and Freddie). Being the lowest risk, treasuries offer the lowest return. Many other types of bonds described below and on the following page are measured by their "spread" versus treasuries (i.e., the additional interest they pay compared to treasuries).

Corporates are borrowing by companies; these can be long-term bonds or very short-term commercial paper. (Most money market funds invest in such short-term corporate instruments; they ran into trouble when the commercial paper market froze up in late 2008.)

Many corporate bonds rely on payments out of the general revenues of the issuing company. Others are tied to payment streams from particular revenue sources. Mortgage-backed securities (MBS), for instance, rely on a package of mortgages that the original lenders have sold into the bond market (i.e., combined into a security, or *securitized*). Banks likewise issue securitized bonds backed by receipts from the credit cards they issue or from auto loan payments. All of these revenue streams become shakier during an economic downturn, because many borrowers have lost their jobs and can no longer keep up their payments.

Corporate bonds can be highly rated along a quality continuum from very high—a strong, stable revenue stream—to below investment grade (a.k.a. "junk"). Junk bonds must offer a higher interest rate to compensate buyers for higher default risk. In general, the premium paid by junk bonds over lower-risk equivalents (the spread) is substantially higher than is the increment of default risk. But this is not always true when defaults are rising, as in a recession.

Municipal bonds ("munis") are issued by states and local jurisdictions. They are attractive to investors because the federal government, and many state governments, subsidize interest payments by making them tax deductible. Investors pay no federal taxes on muni interest payments, and no state tax on most bonds issued in the state where they reside. Like junk bonds, munis' interest premium (spread) over riskless equivalents is usually substantially greater than the incremental default risk. Again, this relationship may break down, or magnify, during a recession when tax revenues dry up and localities are at the greatest risk of defaulting.

Who Should Invest in Fixed Incomes?

Again, fixed incomes should have a place in almost everyone's investments, one that expands as your time horizon gets shorter (i.e., it gets nearer to the date when you need the money). Those in high tax brackets will find munis especially attractive.

In addition, the lower your tolerance for risk—the more the thought of investment losses may keep you up at night—the higher should be your percentage in fixed income investments.

If you have a long time horizon—say, you are saving for your new-born's college education, or for your retirement decades from now—you should invest in a "ladder" of bonds of staggered maturities out to the end of your horizon (say 20 years hence). The more concerned you are about prospective inflation—and this book gives you reason—the greater should be the proportion in short maturities, so that you can reinvest them as interest rates rise.

A Special Inflation Hedge: Foreign Bonds

Investing in foreign bonds, issued by corporations or governments, has a special advantage if the dollar is declining (as this book argues will continue). Your coupon payments will be in foreign currency; when you repatriate them to the United States, the declining dollar will magnify those payments. However, most developed countries, and some developing nations, are at risk of monetizing their debts, too.

Once accounting by foreign companies and governments was highly opaque, so the quality of their bonds was uncertain. Today, the major rating agencies evaluate foreign issues with similar scrutiny as they do domestic issues. (You may or may not find this reassuring.) Many foreign bonds from both developed and emerging countries can be purchased through U.S. brokers.

Equities (Stocks)

Owners of bonds do not own a piece of the firm that issued the bond. They have no *equity* interest in the firm; on the other hand, their bond payments are secure and must be paid ahead of dividend payments to stockholders. Equity owners are in the opposite situation: They are paid last, but they enjoy all of the upside if the firm does well. These higher-return/higher-risk characteristics are the source for much of the romance of the stock market.

Like bonds, stocks exist because a firm needed capital and offered a piece of paper (partial ownership) to the investor who provides it. A company divides its total value into shares—say, one million shares—then sells them on the open market to acquire its capital. An "IPO" is an initial public offering of stock. Thereafter, original owners may sell their stock on the secondary market, such as the New York Stock Exchange (NYSE) or American Stock Exchange (AMEX). There are also many regional and foreign stock exchanges.

Stocks offer advantages to those who can take additional risk—say, young adults who don't need the money for decades. Because the companies that issue stock operate in competitive industries, they are obliged to constantly find ways to make their product or service better, faster, or cheaper. As they succeed, they will acquire added customers and grow their business. Only their stockholders (not their bondholders) will see the direct results of that growth.

A share of stock is priced to capture its slice of the company's future earnings. So share prices change because (a) the number of shares outstanding changes, as when a company buys some of its stock back; (b) earnings forecasts change; (c) the rate at which future earnings are capitalized into the stock price—sometimes known as the company's "risk premium"—changes; or (d) the risk premium for the entire market changes, because of negative news. In late 2008, stock prices plunged nearly 40% because investors suddenly were much less willing to accept risk, so they fled stocks for treasuries.

A simple summary measure of a stock's valuation is the ratio of the price of a share to the earnings on which it has a claim (a.k.a. earnings per share). This is known as the price to earnings, or P/E, ratio. When investors are wildly optimistic, P/Es can become stratospheric, where it takes $40 or more to have a claim on a stream of one dollar per year in earnings. (Several recent Internet company IPOs are at this writing at the nosebleed level.) The reverse occurs when investors are deeply pessimistic: P/Es fell below 10 during the late 2008 market panic and are low for some "value" stocks today.

As noted earlier, inflation can suppress stock prices, because revenue growth subsides due to consumers' eroding purchasing power and because rising costs eat into corporate profits. In the last period of significant inflation in the United States in the late 1970s, P/E ratios plunged from 16 (near the historical average) to 8. Stock prices fell even faster, since earnings (against which the P/E multiple is applied) fell also.

Investment advisers who were shaped by the period of the Great Moderation (and who forget the 1970s) argue for stocks as an inflation hedge. This seems only true for relatively low levels of inflation (say 1% to 3%); above this level, inflation can be very bad for stocks. Yet as noted in chapter 8, several types of companies can do very well in an inflationary environment.

The Efficient Market?

Forty years ago economists developed the "efficient market hypothesis," which asserted that in a liquid market (as markets for U.S. stocks definitely are) all relevant information must be revealed, so stock prices already reflect that information. In other words, it is extremely unlikely that anyone other than a company insider would possess information that would allow them to "beat the market." (The SEC scrutinizes insider transactions quite closely.)

But a casual observation of major moves in the market would suggest that markets overreact to both good news and bad news. Stock prices overshoot upward on good news and overshoot downward on bad news. The very dramatic decline in P/Es in late 2008 far exceeded what was necessary to adjust stock valuations to the new realities (lower or negative earnings) of the recession. Many argue the same was true for the sharp rally after March 2009.

Large Cap Versus Small Cap

Companies are often categorized by size. One measure of size is simply the annual revenue they generate. Another sizing approach is market capitalization (a.k.a. "market cap"). Market cap is the value the stock markets place on a company, captured by multiplying its share price by the number of shares outstanding. Large-cap stocks are those of companies whose market cap exceeds a threshold, such as $10 billion, with small cap and "microcap" stocks associated with smaller companies.

As companies progress through the stages of their lifestyle, typically their growth slows (the company "matures"). Therefore, large-cap stocks are usually much less volatile than small caps. After a bear market, small caps often lead, until their prices overshoot reasonable valuations, and the rally becomes dominated by large caps. Over long periods, small caps as a group have seen greater increases in price but much more volatility.

Sectors

Stocks can also be classified by their industry sector. Each sector has a different trajectory; for example, electronics (tech) stocks did very well at the birth of the Internet but crashed hard when that speculative bubble burst in early 2000. In a recession, stocks from industries dependent on big-ticket consumer purchases, such as automobiles, luxury goods, or vacation travel, do poorly, since such discretionary items are the first to be sacrificed. By contrast, staples and "value" items, and the retailers which sell them, generally gain market share as consumers move down market in a recession. Their stocks fare relatively well.

Some investment experts advise concentrating your stock portfolio in companies whose products you know well and value. But bear in mind that tastes and circumstances change, so leading sectors rotate over time.

If you are concerned about inflation, you will wish to overweight (put a disproportionately large amount of) your investments into sectors that do well in inflationary environments. Commodities—the basic materials that go into finished goods—are often viewed as inflation hedges, because temporary shortages of some commodities can lead to bidding wars that raise their prices. If the commodity is used in a wide range of goods or services, like oil or electricity are, its price increases can spread into general inflation.

Until recently, individual investors had a difficult time investing in commodities. But today there are a variety of commodity-specific and multicommodity exchange traded funds (ETFs) and mutual funds available, some with very low costs. As noted in chapter 8, I generally prefer to buy shares in commodity suppliers because they have organic earnings, rather than the commodities themselves, which are a simple bet on price moves.

Growth Versus Value

Another common distinction is between "growth" stocks—fast-growing companies, which often have high P/Es—and "value" stocks—stocks considered underpriced. Many value stocks derive their value from a relatively generous dividend. At a time when the dividend paid by an average share of common stock is less than 2%, some stocks can offer 5%, 6%, and even 10%. These are commonly very stable businesses, where their stability can stem from their competitive position or from industry regulation. Only such stability can enable the consistent payment (or better still, growing payment) of a substantial dividend. The iconic dividend stock is an electric utility, whose stability stems from its regulated local monopoly position.

Conservative investors favor dividend-generating stocks because "dividends don't lie": Companies can manipulate their earnings (legally or not), but dividend payments require actual cash out the door. However, a few companies will maintain a high dividend long past the point of affordability. Dividend specialists recommend that you consider a company's payout rate—what share of earnings is being paid out to shareholders in dividends. Too high a rate is unsustainable and can be a warning sign of future cuts in the dividend. Some recommend excluding stocks whose payout rate is greater than 70%. A really conservative rule might be 50%.

Several academic studies have demonstrated that the large majority of total returns stocks have earned come from dividends.

Several investment sites publish lists of companies that have a long-term record of growing their dividends. Try Googling "dividend achievers" or "dividend aristocrats" for examples. Also, there are several dividend-oriented mutual funds, which you can find at the website of your preferred fund family.

Some companies offer discounted dividend reinvestment plans (known as "DRIPs") to existing shareholders (usually you can join a DRIP after you own as little as one share). These offer three advantages. First, reinvesting dividends helps you accumulate shares faster—you will have the magic of compounding in your favor. Second, many companies offer a small discount (e.g., 5%) of the market price of shares purchased through dividend reinvestment. It is always nice when you can buy $100 bills for $90 or $95. Finally, direct purchases from the company usually avoid brokerage charges, although there may be a small handling fee.

Who Should Invest in Stocks?

Stocks are too volatile for short-term investing. Restrict your stockholdings to those funds you do not need for a number of years. (Daytraders need not apply.) As this implies, the fraction of your portfolio in stocks should decline as you near retirement (or another major event when you will need the money) and your horizon gets shorter. By the same token, you should keep some of your portfolio in stocks even in retirement, to protect against inflation—but you must choose stocks that can withstand inflation, as discussed in chapter 5.

The standard rule of thumb is that a long-term investor should have a share of their portfolio in stocks equal to 100 minus their age. This assumes "average" tolerance for risk. If you are more conservative, reduce that share by 10% or 15%.

If you find the prospect of owning any stocks too risky for your tastes, bear in mind that planners maintain that stocks have the best long-run track record (i.e., highest return) of any widely available asset class. (However, see the "Buy and Hold Versus Active Trading?" section on the next page.) You can leaven stocks' high volatility by reducing their share of your portfolio and raising the fixed income share by an equal amount.

Because of this volatility, investment specialists suggest having no more than a few percent of your portfolio in any given security (stock or bond). This *very definitely* includes the stock of your employer, often available as an investment option in company 401(k)s. You are already 100% dependent on that firm for your current income.

A nice compromise between risk and return is to concentrate your stock investments in high (but not too high) dividend-paying companies. If you think the company remains a good bet, reinvest your dividends to enjoy compounding.

Dollar Cost Averaging

Numerous academic studies have found that essentially no one can "time" the market (i.e., have the foresight to know when the lows and highs are, so that they buy near the low and sell near the high). Therefore, financial planners recommend systematic purchases of investments on a regular schedule (for example, by reinvesting dividends when a company pays them). When prices are low, a given purchase amount will buy more shares; the opposite is true when prices are high. The average cost of your purchases is what matters, and systematic investing will bring that average cost down. This approach is known as "dollar cost averaging."

Rebalancing

Say your desired allocation of your investments between stocks and bonds is 60% stocks, 40% bonds (this would be about right for a 40-year-old). A year after you make the allocation, the stock market shoots upward but bond prices don't budge. A year later your portfolio's total value might be allocated, say, 70% stocks and 30% bonds. You should "rebalance": return the portfolio to your desired weights by selling some of your stocks and investing the proceeds in bonds. You will, by default, have sold stocks near their high and bought bonds near their low. You didn't "time" the market, but you achieved some of the benefits of successful timing. Many Boomers (including me) suffered avoidable losses in the recent market crash because they had failed to rebalance as they aged.

Buy and Hold Versus Active Trading?

As noted, many academic studies have demonstrated that most of us are lousy market timers. We poorly choose the times for us to "buy low" and "sell high." This includes mutual fund managers: see the "active versus passive" discussion in the following section. So the conventional wisdom was to choose stocks carefully and hold them for a very long time. (Warren Buffett's ideal holding period is "forever.")

However, this advice is a creature of the Great Moderation, when stocks had sustained earnings growth and low volatility. Those conditions haven't applied since about the middle of 2007 and, arguably, since 2000. But should you be frequently trading? Many studies have shown that heavy traders spend far more on commissions than any added return. And as noted, few of us can successfully "time" the market.

Market watchers believe that the ideal holding period for most stocks has declined due to increased volatility. As several analysts put it, "Stocks are now for renting, not for owning." Certainly, a specific sector or category of asset can enjoy a bull market where prices can overshoot fundamentals, after which investors will switch to another less popular sector/class. If you wish to devote considerable time to investing, you may be able to switch your investments among sectors at roughly the right time, but bear in mind the odds are well against you. Presumably, you don't wish your investing activities to consume very much of your time. Your investments should allow you to enjoy life, not become your life.

Vehicles to Hold These Assets

Financial planners preach the virtues of diversification. Mixing stocks and fixed income securities in a portfolio is the most common approach to diversification.

But how can you do this if you have only a limited amount to invest?

Wall Street is happy to oblige. This section will outline the main types of diversified investment vehicles available to retail investors. Most of these aren't assets like those listed in previous sections; rather, they are baskets within which such assets are placed.

Mutual Funds

In a mutual fund investors pool their monies together to purchase a range of assets. The total value of the fund is divided into shares, with each investor owning shares based on the dollar amount invested. If you invest $1,000 in a fund with, say, $1 billion in holdings, you have purchased one-one millionth of the value of that fund. The arithmetic is exactly the same as for purchasing a share of a company's stock. But because you've combined your money with many other investors, you all have collectively achieved far greater diversification than any of you could manage individually.

Most funds are governed by a general investment policy that specifies the types of securities in which they invest. There are, therefore, stock funds, bond funds, and "balanced" funds (which invest in both stocks and bonds). "Target date" funds are a special subset of balanced funds, discussed next. There are funds that specialize in particular regions or even particular countries, and funds that specialize in industrial sectors.

The greatest debate about mutual funds relates to "actively" versus "passively" managed funds. In the first few decades of the industry's existence, most funds were run by managers who actively chose and traded the securities in their portfolios. By the 1970s, it was apparent that very few of these "active" funds performed better than simply buying the universe of all stocks or the stocks that comprised an index that mimicked the broader market. In response, "passive" funds were born that simply buy and hold the index.

The Vanguard Group pioneered index funds, and Vanguard founder John Bogle remains indexing's most eloquent proponent. Bogle believes that the added cost of active management is rarely justified, so Vanguard's core passive products compete on the basis of efficiency, not investment performance (since they aspire only to match their index). Vanguard investors, who call themselves "Bogleheads," prize its funds' low costs. Typical actively managed funds can charge investors 1.5% to 2.5% of the value of their investment each year, but Vanguard's costs run in the few tenths of 1%. Academic research generally supports Bogle's view.

There are tens of thousands of mutual funds, with a wealth of information available from clearinghouses like Morningstar to help investors choose among them. Besides being classified based on their underlying investments, funds differ in their sales charge (known as the "load") and the annual cost to manage the fund (known as the "expense ratio"). I generally favor no-load funds that also have low expense ratios (less than 0.5% of assets per year or so), because there is little evidence that paying a load or higher expenses translates to higher returns. Although most finance professors will argue in favor of indexing and against active management, that hasn't stopped the active segment of the industry from commanding considerable market share.

Target date funds are mutual funds that invest in both stocks and bonds, on a long-term schedule where the fraction of its portfolio in stocks declines over the years while that in bonds rises, leading to the target date (usually the shareholder's approximate retirement date). In essence, the fund automatically rebalances so that the shareholder need not. Each proportion (stocks vs. bonds) is determined by the fund's manager, so they may not be the same across funds for a common target year. In the bear market, many target date funds were discovered to hold a larger share of their portfolio in stocks than they implied in their advertising.

More generally, many funds, including some target date funds, suffer from "style drift": the tendency of the manager to shift resources into asset classes that are performing well, even if they are outside the fund's investment policies. Some mutual fund raters check for style drift but most do not.

ETFs

Exchange-traded funds (ETFs) were pioneered in the 1990s as a variant on indexed mutual funds: low-cost, passively managed collections of stocks, usually similar to index funds but even more efficient. Over the years, ETFs have proliferated to mimic most segments of the mutual fund industry. Commodity ETFs can be a promising component of an inflation-hedged portfolio, as are precious metals ETFs.

I prefer ETFs that own the stocks of commodity producers because those producers are implicitly leveraged against their product's price; that is, their earnings rise at a multiple of the rise in the price of the underlying commodity. Also, they have organic earnings, unlike the commodity itself, which has only price change. See chapter 8 for an explanation.

REITs, MLPs, BDCs, and Utilities

Real Estate Investment Trusts (REITs) are essentially real estate–oriented mutual funds, purchasing not stocks but income-producing properties (apartment buildings, groups of houses, office buildings, shopping malls, etc.). They receive favorable tax treatment—being exempt from corporate tax—as long as they distribute at least 90% of their earnings to shareholders (i.e., have at least a 90% dividend payout rate). REITs can provide an attractive stream of dividends, but they can also be hostage to the real estate cycle, which can be quite sharp (as events of 2007–2010 have illustrated). Also, most REIT dividends do not qualify for the reduced 15% tax rate on "qualified" dividends, as do dividends on common stocks. Chapter 8 noted that many newer nontraded REITs have the advantage of a portfolio of properties purchased at low postbust prices. But their private placement means they lack liquidity: Investors often must commit to a holding period of five years or longer.

MLPs (master limited partnerships) are likewise quasi-mutual funds that buy energy infrastructure projects (most commonly, oil or natural gas pipelines). They have very similar advantages and disadvantages to REITs, except that their fortunes are dependent on energy cycles. Many MLPs actually benefit from low energy prices, since the MLP does not own the fuel; it only earns a fee per unit for transporting it. Low prices encourage increased demand, which means more volume to transport.

Utilities are often mentioned in the same breath with MLPs. These electricity or natural gas producers are highly regulated, so their earnings are fairly stable and grow slowly (unless in a fast-growing region). Consequently, most utilities attract capital by paying a large share of the earnings in dividends. Utilities are classic "widows and orphans" stocks—they generate income, but with a more modest upside.

Business development corporations (BDCs) are a special class of small business lender that is exempt from corporate taxes if it pays out a large share of its earnings, like REITs and MLPs. This exemption from corporate taxes allows for a generous payout ratio and high dividends. BDCs, like the other types of investments discussed in this section, depend heavily on borrowed money, so they tend to be highly interest sensitive.

Tax-Favored Plans: IRAs and 401(k)s

IRA and 401(k)s are legal baskets into which investments can be housed to gain favorable tax treatment. IRAs can be set up by individuals with a financial institution as custodian. 401(k)s are established by employers on behalf of their employees, with employees arranging to have a portion of each paycheck deposited into the 401(k). While 401(k)s are the most common type of employer plan, there are other types that are also identified by the section of the tax code that governs them: 403(b)s for employees of nonprofit ventures, 457s, and so forth. If taxpayers hold assets inside these shells, taxes on the growth in those assets is deferred until the taxpayer begins to draw them down (take "distributions" in IRS-speak). This is advantageous because investment growth is not diluted by taxes until distributions are taken, so more dollars can compound. For most tax-deferred plans, distributions cannot occur before age 59½ (with a handful of exceptions) and must begin by age 70.

Virtually any sort of liquid asset, and many illiquid assets (such as real estate), can be held inside a tax-deferred plan. Generally, the taxpayer must secure the services of a custodian (usually a financial institution) to handle compliance issues to preserve the favorable tax treatment.

Roth accounts are a variation of tax-favored shells. They are a mirror image of the "traditional" tax-deferred account. With a Roth, the taxpayer's contribution to the account is not deductible (as in a traditional account). Instead taxes are paid (i.e., the contributions are "after-tax," not "pre-tax"), but thereafter all investment growth is *tax-free*. Distributions cannot be taken until 59, but they are not mandated to commence at any time thereafter. Roths are discussed at great length in chapter 9, which makes the argument that foreseeable higher tax rates in the future make Roths quite attractive.

Hybrids of Fixed Incomes and Equities

In between stocks' high risk/high returns and bonds' lower risk/lower returns are a class of hybrid products. New ones are constantly being invented, so this section cannot be comprehensive. It will focus on one type—preferred stocks—as fairly representative of the larger group.

Besides "common" stock, companies may issue "preferred" shares, so called because their holders are "preferred" in a liquidation over common shareholders. Preferred shares are issued to pay a dividend that is expressed as an interest rate, like the yield on a bond, so they are often treated as close to fixed income securities. But preferreds have two advantages:

- Preferred shareholders are stockholders, not creditors, so they take more risk than holders of a corporation's bonds. (That is, in a liquidation, they fall in line behind bondholders, but ahead of common stockholders.) Consequently, they receive a higher rate than bondholders—and a much higher dividend rate than common stockholders.
- Many preferred shares are convertible to common shares if the common shares rise to a specified price. Therefore, preferred shares can have some upside (and, after conversion, all the upside and downside of common shares).

Therefore, preferreds have several of the advantages of other classes of assets (bonds and stocks) with few of the disadvantages. A company's preferreds typically trade under the same ticker symbol as its common shares, with a suffix indicating the particular preferred issue (different issues have different dividend rates).

Such hybrids permit investors to approximate the returns of common stock, with fewer risks.

What Should Your Goal Be?

Again, a 3% to 4% withdrawal rate commencing in retirement is a widely accepted way to ensure that your money lasts at least as long as you do. To hedge against inflation, you may wish to make it even lower, say, 2%, but that will mean you will need to accumulate 50 times your annual needs (vs. 25 times under a 4% withdrawal rate).

Until recently, many investors' goal was to swing for the fences—to stay heavily in stocks and aim for as much return as they could get. The crash of 2008 demonstrated the severe risks of such a strategy. Financial planners today are offering different advice: Determine what you need for retirement income, and invest in the least risky way that can get you there. Your portfolio should always include some stocks, but no more than you need to compensate for past insufficient saving and for inflation. If you are in the rare position of having enough saved already, invest quite conservatively. Being able to sleep at night with confidence is worth far more than a few tens of thousands of added dollars.

Many Boomers are taking extra risk to make up for recent losses and for insufficient savings earlier. You may feel you have no choice, but bear in mind that you may just dig your hole deeper.

For More Information

The resources chapter lists a number of valuable sources of information on retirement planning and investing.

Glossary

This listing is not comprehensive, but it addresses many of the most common unfamiliar terms in international economics and investments. The interpretations given here are very much my own.

(Arithmetical) Average rate of return: An asset's **return on investment** averaged over multiple periods. If the S&P 500 returned 10% 3 years ago, 7% 2 years ago, and 1% last year, the average annual rate of return over the three years is (10 + 7 + 1 = 18) ÷ 3 = 6% per year. Strictly speaking, this is an arithmetic average: summing the returns and dividing the sum by the number of years. A superior approach that accounts for the effects of compounding is a geometric average, the **compound annual growth rate (CAGR).**

Balance of payments (see also **trade balance**): The difference between the total funds leaving a country in a given year (e.g., to buy imports) and those flowing into the country (e.g., from foreigners buying our exports). For several decades the United States has imported several hundred billion dollars more than the total value of its exports; that is, it has run a **trade deficit.** Technically, the balance of payments has two components: trade flows (captured by the trade balance) as well as capital flows (i.e., investment flows). But many commentators do not distinguish between the trade balance and the balance of payments.

Bear market: A sustained period in which the general direction of the price of a class of assets is downward. For contrast, see **correction, rally,** and **bull market.**

Beta: A measure of a financial instrument's (like a stock's) **volatility** relative to the broader universe of similar instruments. For example, a stock's beta is the ratio of its standard deviation to the standard deviation of a broad stock index such as the S&P 500. A beta of less than 1.0 is associated with a low volatility stock such as an electric utility. A beta of above 1.0 might mean a small-cap or growth stock, where investors overreact to both good and bad news. A beta of 1.0 implies a stock with volatility equal to the index.

Bond: An **investment** that pays the buyer a stream of coupon payments at a specified interest rate. Also known as a "fixed income" investment. The price of bonds moves inversely with their interest rate.

Bond vigilantes: A term coined to refer to investors who are quick to sell an institution's bonds if they believe the issuer is running excessive deficits and taking on too much debt. The resulting rise in interest rates will magnify the issuer's **debt service** burden and impair its financial condition further, creating a self-fulfilling prophecy. The Clinton administration's 1993 deficit reduction plan was heavily influenced by a desire to preempt bond vigilantes.

Borrowing: Essentially, renting someone else's money with the promise to pay it back later. The added rental costs are known as "interest." Accumulated balances from borrowing are also known as **debt**. Borrowing is quite rational if the funds are used to purchase an asset whose value grows at a higher rate than the interest rate charged on the borrowing. Households, corporations, and nations who spend more than their income—that is, who run a **deficit**—may borrow to cover that difference. But the less assured repayment is, the higher will be the interest rate lenders will demand to finance that borrowing. Both the U.S. private sector (i.e., households) and the government sector borrowed heavily in the 2000s decade, driving debt levels to historic highs.

Bull market: A sustained period of upward movement in the price of an asset class. Bull markets can be punctuated by **corrections**.

Capital account: Analogous to the trade account that computes the **trade balance,** this applies to flows on investment capital in and out of a country. For the past two decades, the United States has received far more capital investment than U.S. investors have made overseas. This will likely soon reverse as more Americans invest overseas and more foreigners diversify away from the dollar.

Capital gain: The part of an asset's **total return** that occurs because of changes in its price, as opposed to from **dividend** payments. Capital gains are sometimes taxed at more favorable (lower) rates than is ordinary income such as wage income.

Central bank: The only authority in a country with the legal right to issue currency. Central banks therefore have some control over the supply of money. Most nations' central banks have as their primary mission preservation of the value of the currency in order to maintain price stability. In the United States, the Federal Reserve has the additional goal of maintaining full employment of the workforce. These goals can come into conflict; see **inflation**.

Compound annual growth rate (CAGR): Annual growth based on the geometric average, not the arithmetic average. Using the example from "average rate of return," the CAGR would be [(1.10) × (1.07) × (1.01) = 1.1877] raised to the one-third power (to reflect 3 years of compounding = 1.05933, or a 5.933% CAGR). In this example, the result is very close to the arithmetic mean of 6%, but with larger growth rates or more years, the arithmetic and geometric means can diverge significantly. CAGRs are the superior way to compute an asset's long-term **return on investment (ROI)**. For a simple way to roughly compute CAGRs in your head, see also the **Rule of 72**.

Compounding: The exponential effect of persistent growth. One hundred dollars deposited into a mutual fund that grows at a 5% rate of compounding will be worth $105 at the end of the first year, $110.25 after the second year, $121.62 after the fifth year, and $155.13 after the 10th year. Higher rates will compound even faster. Compounding can make the job of saving a given amount much easier if the saver starts early enough, because its effects are magnified over time.

Consumer price index (CPI): Monthly tabulation by the Bureau of Labor Statistics of the prices paid by consumers for a representative set of goods and services. BLS produces several CPIs for different consumer groups. A rise in the CPI is known as consumer **inflation**.

Correction: An interruption in a **bull market** or **rally** in which an asset's class's prices fall (by convention, by at least 10%). **Bull** and **bear markets** need not reflect a uniform rise or fall in asset prices; they can be interrupted by corrections (downward) or **rallies** (upward).

Correlation: A measure of the relationship between two variables. In the context of investing, correlations are used to represent the degree to which asset class A (say, stocks) moves in tandem with asset class B (say, bonds). If A rises whenever B rises, the two assets have a high **positive correlation**. Investors seek to hold assets that move in opposite directions, that is, that have a high **negative correlation**, so that when A falls, B rises and compensates for (hedges against) the effects of the drop in A. This smooths out fluctuations in the combined portfolio value of A and B together. Correlations are measured on a scale from –1.0 (perfect negative correlation—A always rises when B falls, and vice versa) to 1.0 (perfect positive correlation). See also **decoupling**.

Cumulative rate of return: The accumulated returns achieved by an asset over a specified period. If $1,000 in 2005 grows to $2,000 by 2010, it achieved a 100% cumulative growth rate for those 5 years. Its **compound** *annual* **growth rate (CAGR)** would be 14.9% per year.

Debt: The stock of funds borrowed due to past **deficits**. Analysts often compare debt to ability to pay, such as a percentage of household income. For a national government, the equivalent measure is the ratio of debt to **gross domestic product**. The U.S. national debt has been as low as zero (after Andrew Jackson paid it off in the 1830s), and as high as more than 100% of GDP (after very large deficits were run to finance World War II). Current large deficits, financed through added debt, are projected to lead to a debt level above 100% of GDP by the end of this decade. Private debt also reached a recent peak in 2007, at 300% of total household income.

Debt service: Payments a debtor is obligated to make to meet obligations to creditors (lenders). In a home mortgage, for example, your monthly payment is composed of two parts: interest on the money you borrowed and principal (payment of a part of what you borrowed). Traditional mortgages are structured for a fixed payment, with the interest component falling and the principal component rising over time. Currently, despite a roughly $10 trillion national debt, federal debt service costs are not that large because interest rates are very low. But economists are concerned that over the next few years interest rates will rise and debt service costs will become the single-largest component of the federal budget, crowding out important programs or driving up taxes.

Decoupling: A widely discussed view in the months before the late 2000s recession that emerging markets' **correlations** with developed markets had declined; that is, markets had "decoupled." In the severe **bear market** of 2008, stock indexes in emerging markets generally fell faster than those in developed markets, but both fell sharply. Conversely, in the **bull market** of 2009, both rose sharply, but emerging markets rose faster. So it appears that any decoupling is at most only very partial.

Deficit: In general, the difference between income and outgo; when costs exceed revenue, the entity runs a deficit. The most commonly discussed deficit is the government's fiscal deficit: the difference between spending and tax revenue. This can be expressed in dollars or as a percentage of GDP. The opposite of a deficit is a **surplus**.

Defined benefit (DB): A traditional pension plan in which employees of a company receive a defined payment in retirement. Generally, the size of the payment depends on the number of years worked (with some minimum necessary to "vest," or be eligible to collect), the employee's salary while working, and their age at retirement. Unlike **defined contribution** plans, in defined benefit plans, employers take most of the risk if their investment returns fall short of what is necessary to pay pension commitments. Most such plans are at least partially "pay as you go" and rely on the incomes and productivity of current workers to pay for past workers' pensions.

Defined contribution (DC): A savings plan offered by many companies as an alternative to **defined benefit** pensions. 401(k)s, for example, are DC plans. Workers, not employers, take the risk that contributions will grow to sufficient size to fund their needs in retirement. Most private sector employers today only offer defined benefit plans, but proposals for a conversion from DB to DC plans in the public sector have met fierce resistance from public employee unions.

Deflation: The opposite of **inflation**. When deflation occurs, the **purchasing power** of a currency rises. Another way of saying the same thing: prices fall. Deflation is quite common in recessions, as firms compete with one another through lower prices. Deflation can also be self-reinforcing, as consumers may defer purchases until prices drop, which magnifies the deflationary recession. U.S. policy makers in 2008–2009 devoted unprecedented efforts to avoiding inflation, because they were forewarned by Japan's recent experience: It has been caught in a deflationary spiral for most of the past 20 years.

Deleveraging: See **leverage**.

Demographics: The study of whole populations and their characteristics, such as gender, age, income, education, and childbearing. Demographic forecasts tend to be more reliable over the long run than other types (such as economic or market forecasts) because an individual's demographic characteristics rarely change, except predictably through aging.

Devaluation: A decline in the value of a nation's currency. "Devaluation" connotes that this decline is the result of policy, implicit or explicit. Arguably, the implicit policy of the U.S. government has been to accede to the devaluation of the dollar in currency markets (see **dollar, defending the**). A **competitive devaluation** occurs when more than one nation attempts to stimulate growth or secure an advantage for its exports by devaluing its currency to make those exports cheaper.

Disinflation: Decelerating inflation. If the rate of growth in the CPI decelerates to below zero, **deflation** occurs.

Diversification: Avoiding putting all your "eggs" in only one "basket." Diversification of an individual's investment portfolio means holding several classes of assets (not only stocks or only bonds), as well as multiple securities in the class (e.g., owning stock shares in several different companies). Commercial transactions may diversify the currency used (e.g., including euros or yen as well as dollars). Diversification smooths out fluctuations in value—as long as the assets that are added fluctuate based on different causes than the original ones. See also **correlation**.

Dividend: A portion of a corporation's earnings paid to its stockholders. A company's "dividend payout rate" is that proportion. Stocks can be compared by their dividend yields (dollars of dividend per share divided by the purchase price of the share). Many academic studies have found that the vast majority of stocks' **total return** comes from dividends.

Dollar, defending the: If a nation's currency is declining in price—because more foreigners are selling than buying it in foreign exchange markets—its central bank can "defend" the currency by using **reserves** to purchase its currency in the markets. Although it is a ritual for American politicians to espouse a "strong dollar" policy, most have exercised a revealed policy of benign neglect—letting market forces dictate the value of the dollar without intervention by the Fed. Some export-dependent nations, such as Japan and China, have exercised a strong-dollar/weak-local-currency policy by buying up dollars and selling their own currency in exchange markets. By weakening their currency, their exports are less expensive to importing nations. By default, the United States has also practiced this strategy, although not strongly enough to counteract exporting nations' efforts to suppress their own currencies' values.

Economies of scale: Typically, as you gain experience at producing a product or service, quality improves and costs per unit fall. That is, you learn how to make it more efficiently. In other words, as you "scale up" production, you achieve "economies." This is one of the reasons that a new product must be priced substantially higher than the same product a year or two later: In the meantime, the manufacturer has achieved "scale" and learned to make it cheaper. Economies of scale drive many industries such as consumer electronics (think about the price of a plasma TV or DVD player in 2010 vs. in 2000), but are especially common for any digital content (e.g., a downloaded movie and MP3 file of a song), since the **marginal cost** of any digital product is essentially zero.

Elasticity: The responsiveness of a quantity to some other variable, expressed as a ratio. For example, the price elasticity of demand for a product reflects the change in the quantity of that product demanded as its price changes. It is expressed as a ratio, for example, the percent change in the volume of gasoline produced per 1% change in the price of a gallon of gas. Income elasticities similarly measure the response of demand to incomes: For example, the income elasticity of demand for luxury cars is measured by how much purchases of luxury cars rise as incomes rise (or fall as incomes fall). Generally, firms can raise prices on products with a low price elasticity of demand; that is, they have great **pricing power.** Low elasticity is also known as **inelastic demand,** meaning consumers are not very price sensitive.

Consumers may have a different (usually higher) elasticity in the long run versus the short run. If gasoline prices shoot upward, in the short run you can change your behavior only modestly, so the volume of gas you purchase will decline only modestly (meaning your demand can change little; it has low elasticity). But with more time you can make more significant changes in your behavior—for example, taking the bus where before you drove—that will reduce your gasoline volume much more. In econo-speak, your "long-run price elasticity of demand" is higher than your "short-run price elasticity of demand." This is almost always true, because greater adjustments are always possible in the long run.

Note that suppliers have an elasticity, too, which reflects their ability to increase production as prices rise. Many commodities need long periods to expand capacity. Producers rely on prices to signal whether they should hold production steady or change the volume produced. Rising prices mean there is a shortage—more production is needed. Falling prices mean the opposite.

Entitlements: Government safety net programs to which individuals are entitled, with few eligibility requirements. The largest and best-known entitlement programs are Social Security, an income program, paid to all those who have reached the official retirement age, and Medicare, a health insurance program also for seniors. Both are financed by pay-roll taxes paid equally by employees and employers. Because the tax is paid at a **flat tax** rate up to a designated level of income and not paid above that level, economists see the payroll tax as moderately **regres-sive.** Because payroll taxes are collected from current workers and paid out to current retirees, entitlement systems are presently running large **deficits** because the number of retirees is growing as Boomers enter their 60s, and the number of younger workers is growing much more slowly.

Equities: Common **stocks**, so called because their owner holds a share of the company's "stockholder's equity" (net worth).

ETFs: Exchange-traded funds; mutual fund-like investment pools that invest in a particular class of security, such as stocks of companies lo-cated in a particular country or a specific industrial sector. When they originated, ETFs were passively managed funds with commensurately low costs. As their numbers have proliferated, ETFs are becoming less diversified and more expensive.

Fertility: A demographic measure of childbearing propensity, to suggest whether a population will grow/get younger or age/shrink. Fertility is commonly defined as the number of children born to the average woman in her lifetime. A fertility rate of just over 2.0 (i.e., 2.05) is the "replacement rate": the threshold at which a population is stable (ignoring **migration**). Populations whose fertility is below the replace-ment rate will age and shrink; those above will get younger and grow.

Fiat currency: A national currency, usually made of paper, not backed by specific assets (where its value is supported by government "fiat"). In the late 20th century, fiat currencies replaced **hard money**, such as currencies on the **gold standard.** Under fiat money, the production of gold does not constrain the supply of money, so government can issue too much currency and bring on inflation.

Fiscal policy: Government policy related to taxation and spending, whose net effect is either a **surplus** or a **deficit.** Fiscal policy is the jurisdiction of the national government (i.e., the executive and legisla-tive branches).

Fixed costs: The costs a firm bears regardless of how many units it produces. Commonly fixed costs are borne before the first unit is manufactured, such as research and development or factory construction. Many digital products (music, recorded books, videos, movies) have high fixed costs but very low **marginal costs**.

Flat tax: A tax whose rate does not rise as the activity being taxed increases. (The amount paid will still rise because it is a constant percentage of a rising base.) In contrast, see **progressive taxation**.

Gold standard: A promise by a government to redeem paper currency for gold. This constrains the money supply to the supply of gold held by the central bank.

Great Moderation: The period of low inflation, low unemployment, and infrequent and mild recessions, generally dated from 1983 to 2007. Sometimes known as the "Goldilocks economy" (as in "not too hot; not too cold.") The premise of this book is that Boomers who make their retirement savings and investment plans based on the assumption that the future will be like this period are being far too optimistic: Demographic and fiscal trends make it very likely that the next 25 years will be much less benign than the past 25.

Gross domestic product (GDP): The total goods and services produced in an economy. The United States GDP, at nearly $15 trillion, is about 25% of world GDP. GDP per capita is a measure of the standard of living: a nation's GDP divided by the size of its population. U.S. GDP per capita is among the highest in the world. Gross national product (GNP) is GDP plus the net effect of the balance of payments (**surplus** or **deficit**).

Gross margin: One definition of margin also known as "profit." Gross margin is revenues minus only those costs directly related to the production of the company's product, such as raw materials. Net margin, or the "bottom line," also deducts company-wide costs such as overhead. Margins are often expressed as a percentage of company revenues to make them comparable across companies.

Hard money: More general expression of the **gold standard**, in which paper currency is backed by bullion (most commonly gold or silver).

Incidence of a tax: How tax collections are distributed over subpopulations. These subunits could be different income classes, ethnic groupings, geographic units, or industries.

Income distribution: The proportions of an economy that are poor, middle class, and rich. There are a variety of summary measures of income distribution, including the ratio of average incomes of the top 10% to the lowest 10%. After many decades of a flattening of its income distribution (i.e., fewer rich and poor, with more in the broad middle class), in recent decades the U.S. distribution has become somewhat less flat. This is another way of saying that income inequality has risen.

Income redistribution: Generally, any transfer by government of income from one group to another. But, as practiced, income redistribution policies take income from the prosperous and give to the poor, directly or indirectly. In the aggregate, American income policy is moderately redistributionist: **tax rates** rise for higher incomes (i.e., income tax rates are **progressive**), and a variety of benefit programs are available only to the indigent (paid for with taxes from the prosperous). Efforts are under way to make Social Security more generous to low-income beneficiaries. This would be implicitly redistributionist, because higher-income earners would see no benefit increase.

Inelastic demand: When volume purchased does not drop very much when prices are raised. This is another way of saying that consumers of the product are not very price sensitive.

Inflation: An increase in the general level of prices, usually measured by the consumer price index. Put another way, an indication that the supply of money is growing faster than demand for it (i.e., than overall economic activity). This oversupply of money causes it to decline in value. This is reflected in higher prices for the things money buys, that is, inflation. As Nobel Prize–winning economist Milton Friedman noted, "inflation is always and everywhere a *monetary* phenomenon" (emphasis added).

Investment: The purchase of assets to achieve greater returns than the cost of the asset. For an individual investor, the goal is a positive **return on investment (ROI)**—the excess received over the original investment amount. An investment is economically significant to an economy if it allows a larger amount of goods or services to be produced. Houses may be seen as an "investment" by a family but not to a larger economy, since they do not increase the economy's productive capacity.

Leverage: The use of other people's money to purchase an asset. An example is a homeowner who secures a mortgage from a bank to buy a house. Because the bank has loaned funds (as opposed to purchased an equity share of the house), the borrower experiences the full effect of price movements in the asset. When the asset's price is rising, the borrower enjoys the full gain; but the same is true if the asset price falls. The recent recession was largely caused because major banks had used massive leverage—sometimes borrowing more than $30 for every dollar of equity they had—to purchase mortgage-backed securities (MBSs). When the MBSs fell in price because of rising defaults, the banks suffered magnified losses because of the extent of their leverage. The late 2000s recession was long because households were obliged to **deleverage** (a.k.a. "unwind") their heavily indebted positions.

Margin: Also known as "profit." **Gross margin** deducts from revenues only direct costs of production, such as raw materials. Net margin deducts both direct costs and indirect costs, such as corporate overhead.

Marginal cost: The cost to produce one more unit. Many products have substantial fixed costs but very low marginal costs. (A movie is a good example: It may cost $200 million to produce but near zero to show to one more viewer.) Once firms have covered their **fixed costs,** they have every incentive to sell as many additional units as possible—if marginal costs are low, since almost all added revenue will translate into profits.

Marginal tax rate: The **tax rate** collected on your next dollar of income (i.e., "at the margin"). High marginal rates are believed to discourage the earning of additional income, because the earner keeps little of their new earnings.

Market cap: Short for "market capitalization" or the current value stock markets place on an entire company. If a company has one million shares outstanding that traded today at $6 per share, it has a market cap of $6 million. Companies are categorized as "large cap," "midcap," and "small cap." There is no standard definition of the breakpoints between the categories, but a rough rule of thumb is above $10 billion; $1 billion to 10 billion; and below $1 billion, respectively. "Microcaps," as the name implies, are even smaller than small caps with a market cap in the millions, not billions.

Market share: A company's (or country's) share of sales in a given market. If a company sells $10 billion into a $50 billion marketplace, it has a

20% market share. Corporate strategists loosely define a "dominant" company as one whose market share is at least half again that of its next largest competitor (e.g., 30% when Number 2 has a 20% share). If a company's revenues grow faster than the overall market (e.g., the company grows at 10% while the market has grown only 3%), it has by definition increased its market share.

Migration: The movement of people across national borders. Immigration represents inflow of population into a country; emigration is the outflow. Developed nations with low fertility rates need immigration to revitalize their populations. Migration flows increased markedly in the late 20th century and thereafter as transportation became less expensive and national policy restrictions were reduced. (For example, residents of the former Communist Bloc were now free to emigrate.) Emigration from underdeveloped countries is often welcomed by the sending country because emigrants may send part of their incomes home (known as "remittances"). Immigration is more controversial in receiving countries, which may have difficulty assimilating people of different cultures, languages, and education levels. (In-migration is a synonym for immigration.)

Monetary policy: Control of the money supply by the central bank to stimulate or restrict (slow down) economic activity. Increasing the supply of money stimulates the economy and thereby raises the price level (CPI); reducing the money supply does the opposite. Monetary policy is the jurisdiction of the central bank.

Negative correlation: See **correlation**.

Negative real interest rates: See **real interest rates**.

Negative savings rate: When a population spends more than its income in a given period. It finances the difference through a **deficit**, that is, through borrowing, which accumulates **debt**. The United States had a negative savings rate briefly in the middle of the past decade.

Nominal: In general, "nominal," such as a "nominal return on an investment," means not adjusted for inflation. **Real** reflects that adjustment. If your CD offers a 2% coupon but inflation is 3%, you've earned a +2% nominal return but a –1% real return.

Nominal interest rates: Rates quoted in the market, unadjusted for **inflation**. Nominal rates have two components: inflation (the change in the CPI) and the **real interest rate**.

Options: Contracts that give the purchaser the right to buy or sell an asset (such as 100 shares of stock) at a specified price. "Call" options give the right to buy, and "put" options give the right to sell. Someone might buy a call option if they believe the price of the stock will go higher than the strike price. Options have an expiration date, so if the stock does not rise above the strike price, the option will expire worthless (known as being "out of the money"), and the seller of the call will not be obliged to sell the shares (the shares will not be "called away"). A seller of a call option who owns the asset to be called is selling a "covered" call; if they do not own it, they've sold a "naked call." Covered options are far less risky than naked ones.

Ponzi scheme: Coined for the master swindler Charles Ponzi in the 1920s; refers to an investment arrangement in which part of the superior returns being offered to investors comes from a constant influx of new investors. When that supply dries up (usually in a **bear market**), commitments to incumbent investors cannot be maintained. A recent very large example was the fraudulent operation of Bernard Madoff. Most "pay as you go" retirement pensions are "Ponzi" because they rely on growing revenues, which is most unlikely if the supply of new workers is shrinking.

Positive correlation: See **correlation**.

Preferred stock: Shares in the equity in a company that also pay a coupon like a bond (unlike common stock, which may or may not pay a **dividend** at the discretion of the company's board of directors). Preferred shareholders are so called because in a liquidation their claim on the firm's assets is "preferred" (takes precedence) over that of common stock shareholders. Because they are a hybrid asset somewhere between common stocks and bonds, preferred shares are generally less volatile than common stock but also rise more slowly.

Pricing power: The ability of a firm to raise prices without seeing much decline in volume purchased. Firms tend to have pricing power if they operate under slight competition or if their product has very **inelastic demand**.

Productivity: The value of output produced per unit of input. The most common type is labor productivity: the value produced per hour worked. In general, living standards cannot rise unless productivity rises, usually through automation or through workforce education.

Progressive taxation: A tax structure in which the **tax rate** owed rises as income rises. For example, in 2009 low-income households owed 10% of their incomes in federal income taxes, while high-income households owed 35%. A **regressive tax** structure is the opposite: tax rates rise as incomes fall. Many sales taxes, even if nominally **flat**, are implicitly **regressive**, because rich people consume a declining share of their income as it rises. Supply-side economists argue that progressive tax structures discourage work effort, because an ever-rising share of the fruits of your labors are taken by the government. Supply-siders object especially to high tax rates (e.g., 50% or higher).

Purchasing power: The amount of goods and services that can be purchased by a unit of currency. If last year gasoline cost $2.00 per gallon and this year it costs $4.00 per gallon, the purchasing power of the dollar with respect to gasoline has fallen in half. (It requires twice as many dollars to buy a gallon of gas.) The overall price level for a representative consumer is captured in the **consumer price index.** "Purchasing power parity" adjusts currency exchange rates so that they reflect the amount needed to buy the same amount of a tradable commodity. *The Economist* occasionally publishes its Big Mac Index to estimate purchasing power parity, using the eponymous hamburger as a commodity available in many urban markets worldwide.

Rally: Temporary interruption in the downward movement of an asset class's prices. Rallies are the mirror image of **corrections**. It is not uncommon for **bull markets** to be punctuated by corrections and **bear markets** by rallies.

Real: Adjusted for inflation, by subtracting the inflation rate. See also **nominal**.

Real interest rates: Nominal interest rates adjusted for inflation (by subtracting it). If a certificate of deposit (CD) pays a 3% nominal rate, but inflation is 2%, investors receive only 1% of added **purchasing power** through interest payments. In other words, the CD's *real* interest rate is 1%. Real interest rates can be negative: If the same CD offers a nominal 3% and inflation is 5%, it pays a negative 2% real rate. Economists assess central bank **monetary policy** by computing real interest rates. Negative real rates are economically stimulative, while positive rates are restrictive. In 2009, the Fed kept short-term nominal rates near zero while inflation was between 1% and 2%. So real rates were roughly negative 1%, a stimulative policy. Investors' great concern in late 2009 and early 2010 was that the Fed would stimulate for too long.

Real rate of economic growth: The nominal rate of GDP growth adjusted for inflation; that is, by subtracting the inflation rate. This is the growth rate commonly reported in the media. The United States' long-term ("trend") rate of growth in the late 20th century was about 3%, but this book argues it will fall to 1% to 1.5% in the coming decades.

Regressive tax: A tax whose rate falls with higher incomes. In other words, low-income people pay a larger share of that income than do higher-income taxpayers. In most developed economies, income tax rates are the opposite: **progressive**. In between the two is a **flat tax**.

Reserve currency: The currency used most often to store value or to value trade across borders. For decades, the U.S. dollar has been the world's reserve currency, with most tradable commodities (such as oil) priced in dollars. About two thirds of the world's central bank reserves are in dollar-denominated assets. This reserve status has conferred major privileges on American importers, who can purchase imports without exchanging currencies.

Reserves (sometimes known as "foreign reserves"): Readily tradable assets held by central banks to support the currency it issues. In the past, as much as half the total central bank reserves in the world were denominated in dollars (e.g., U.S. treasury securities). Today, with growing skepticism about the sustainable value of the dollar, many central banks are diversifying their reserves into other assets, such as euros or gold.

Return on investment (ROI): The excess an investor receives over the amount he invested. In general, higher-risk investments must offer higher average returns to attract investment. In an efficient market, each investment's **risk-adjusted return** should be about the same.

Risk-adjusted return: An investment's return, adjusting for variability in that return, typically by dividing by its standard deviation. The Sharpe ratio (named for Nobelist William Sharpe) makes this computation.

Roth retirement account: Named after congressional author Senator William Roth, these accounts, which exist in 401(k) form through employer plans, and in IRAs for individuals, provide tax-free growth of retirement contributions. Unlike **traditional retirement accounts**, in which contributions are tax deductible and investment gains are tax deferred until "distributions" are taken (the assets are liquidated) in retirement, Roths are the mirror image. Contributions while working are after tax, but thereafter they grow tax free forever. Traditional plans make sense if you believe that your tax rate in retirement will be lower than while working. But as chapter 6 explains, it is much more likely that the opposite will be true: Tax rates in 2025 may be twice as much (or more) as in 2010. This makes Roth plans much more attractive.

Rule of 72: A simple rule of thumb that provides an approximation of the effects of compounding sufficient to double the value of an asset: If you know its average growth rate in percent, divide that number (omitting the percent sign) into the number 72 to get the number of periods needed for the asset to double in value. For example, an asset that grows at 6% per year will require 12 years (72 divided by 6) to double. At 8% per year, it will need nine years (72 divided by 8) to double. The Rule of 72 is not exact but is a reasonable approximation of the complicated math of compounding. It is also useful for increases of more than a factor of 2. For example, a factor of 8 increase is 2 to the third power, so the Rule of 72 could be applied 3 times over.

Savings: The portion of an individual's income that is not consumed. Savings are the source of all **investment**, so a nation with a low **savings rate** must either borrow from other sources or reduce investment.

Savings rate: The proportion of income that is saved (i.e., not consumed). This rate fell throughout the 2000s as households took on increasing debt. A **negative savings rate**—as occurred in the mid-2000s—means that households are on average spending more than they earn. This is only possible by selling assets or borrowing.

Short selling: Borrowing and selling an asset in anticipation that its price will drop so that you can buy it back at the new lower price to meet your obligation to your lender. Short selling of bonds by those concerned about a nation's fiscal policy can put great pressure on its bond prices or its currency. A technique often used by disgruntled **bond vigilantes**.

Sovereign debt: Debt issued by (i.e., money borrowed by) governments. In the United States, the federal government's sovereign debt is issued by the U.S. Treasury Department, so such bonds are known as "treasuries." In 2010, many governments that had borrowed heavily in 2008–2009 to combat the recession faced a sharp decline in investor confidence. At this writing, Greece is on the ropes, but several other countries may not be far behind.

Sovereign wealth funds: Investment funds maintained by the governments of countries that run budget **surpluses**, usually because the nation exports more than it imports (e.g., oil-exporting countries). These funds act much like other institutional investors, except that their client is, directly or indirectly, a national government. This leads to concerns that these funds' capital will be deployed in pursuit of foreign policy goals, not commercial goals.

Spread: The difference between interest rates of two different fixed-income instruments (e.g., corporate vs. treasury bonds). Used as an indicator of how investors view the comparative riskiness of the two instruments. In late 2008, spreads between most other types of bonds and treasuries widened greatly, as investors who were spooked by market turmoil rushed to the safety of treasuries, bidding down their yields and bidding up the yields of other issues. (Remember that bond yields vary inversely with bond prices.) See also **yield curve**.

Sterilization: When a central bank prevents its increase in the money supply from depreciating the value of the currency. Commonly this is done by simultaneously issuing currency and bonds, in the expectation that investors will buy the bonds and thereby take currency out of circulation.

Stocks: Claims on a portion of the assets of a company. Also known as **equities**, because common stock owners own a portion of the company's equity: its net worth. **Preferred stockholders** also own a share of company equity, but they take precedence over common stockholders if the company is liquidated (i.e., its assets are sold off).

Supply: One half of a market transaction. The "supply side"—firms—offers whatever product is being exchanged for money. The "demand side"—customers—pays money to buy the product. See also demand.

Supply shock: A sudden change in the availability or price of a product. An embargo by a trading partner (e.g., the OPEC oil embargo of the mid-1970s) is a negative supply shock: It curtails available supply, causing a shortage that drives up prices (tripling them in the case of oil at the time). Positive supply shocks, where available supplies suddenly rise, driving down prices, are possible, too. A common positive supply shock historically has been a bumper crop (i.e., a harvest much larger than expected) that can cause the price of that commodity to crash. In the 1990s and 2000s, the developed world enjoyed a mammoth supply shock as formerly socialist countries entered the world trading system, competing by offering lower prices. This deflationary force helped keep inflation in check during the **Great Moderation**.

Surplus: Excess of revenues over expenditures. When a family spends less than it earns, its surplus is better known as **savings.** When a national government does so, its surplus is used to pay down the national debt. For the United States, this last occurred in the late 1990s.

Tax base: The total amount of taxed activity. Most tax experts believe that tax policy should establish a broad base (i.e., exclude few activities from taxation), so as to have a low rate. This is to avoid noncompliance by those who believe they are being discriminated against, which is hard to argue if everyone is being taxed. Recent tax changes in the United States have done the opposite: They have narrowed the tax base by eliminating any income tax obligation for households with lower incomes (currently nearly 50% of all households). Also, any items excluded are implicitly subsidized (since no taxes are paid on them). Many economists believe that the unlimited mortgage deduction and exemption of up to $500,000 in gains on a house's appreciation encouraged overconsumption of housing, contributing to the 2000–2006 housing bubble.

Tax rate: The portion of an activity that is collected by the government.

Total return: The sum of an investor's returns stemming from **dividends** received, plus gains in the price of the asset (**capital gains**). Over the past 80 or more years, the total return of stocks has averaged in the high single digits in percent. But in the decade of the 2000s, stocks' total return was close to zero, because the decade was bookended by **bear markets**.

Trade balance and **trade deficit**: The difference between the value of exports and that of imports. A nation is in trade deficit if it imports more than it exports. For a generation export-dependent economies like China have recycled their export income into U.S. assets, keeping interest rates low to encourage continued U.S. imports.

Trade surplus: When the value of a nation's exports exceeds its imports. Nations that are heavily dependent on exports, such as China, seek to run a trade surplus by manipulating the value of their currency to make its exports cheaper and imports more expensive (see **dollar, defending the**).

Traditional retirement plans: Tax-advantaged vehicles, for example, 401(k)s or IRAs, into which workers can save for retirement. Workers contribute money that they deduct from their income, and then that money is not taxed until "distributions" are taken after age 59½ years. Such plans make sense if you believe you will be in a lower tax bracket when you retire than when you were working. But this book argues that all of us will be in higher brackets in 2025 than in 2010, so the opposite type of plan—a **Roth retirement account**—seems superior.

VAT (value added tax): Like a sales tax, except applied not only at the point of final sale but also at each stage of production. VATs are typically flat rate taxes applied throughout the value chain so that it cannot be avoided by clever transfer pricing. Most European countries and Canada rely on VATs for a large share of revenues. Some states and the congressional leadership are considering imposing a VAT as part of their desperate attempts to seek more tax revenue.

Velocity of money: The rate at which a given dollar circulates through the economy as it moves through the value chain. The sharp drop in bank lending in late 2008 (see **leverage** for more) caused the velocity of money to crash, catalyzing the recession.

Volatility: Variation in the price of an asset or in its growth rate. Investors, of course, are happy with volatility on the upside but less so with downside volatility. For stocks, the most common measure of volatility is **beta**.

Yield curve: The profile of interest rates offered by bonds of different maturities. Generally, investors demand higher yields to lend their money for longer periods, so the yield curve is upward sloping. An inversion of the yield curve—where short-maturity bonds offer higher yields than long maturities—has been an excellent predictor of recession, because it implies that investors expect rates to fall in the future. This usually happens when demand for capital dries up because firms see declining sales and no longer wish to make investments in adding productive capacity.

Resources

This section includes a sampling of documents and organizations that readers can access to learn more about the trends described in this book, the investment options available, and organizations devoted to arresting some of the malign developments described herein.

Agora Publishing

Agora, founded by Bill Bonner, is a holding company that owns a variety of investment and lifestyle-oriented publications. Its flagship is *The Daily Reckoning*, Bonner's witty perspective on financial developments, distributed free by e-mail. I subscribe to several Agora newsletters, and I've found them insightful and reasonably priced. But fair warning: Once you are on Agora's mailing list, expect regular solicitations for new subscriptions. http://www.agora-inc.com

American Enterprise Institute (AEI)

Right-of-center-leaning Washington think tank, home of Nicholas Eberstadt. AEI scholars like Peter Wallison were among the first to warn of the precarious condition of many government-sponsored enterprises (GSEs), including Fannie Mae. http://www.aei.org

Blogs

Of course, if you wish to be an economics and finance junkie and nothing less than hourly or daily updates will do, there are a variety of interesting blogs (weblogs) available on these subjects. Personally, I do not wish to have investing rule my life quite so much, so I rely on mainstream publications (which still take far too much time to digest). The **Daily Crux** (http://www.thedailycrux.com; see following) is a free e-mail clipping service that searches the Web twice a day for interesting stories and blog entries. For example, the Crux introduced me to Mish Shedlock's blog, on global economic trends, at http://globaleconomicanalysis.blogspot.com.

Board of Governors of the Federal Reserve System

The "Fed" is America's central bank. http://www.federalreserve.gov

Bureau of Labor Statistics (BLS)

A division of the U.S. Department of Labor, BLS is best known for reporting the unemployment rate. BLS also reports a variety of economic indicators, including the consumer price index (CPI), the basic measure of price levels. http://www.bls.gov

Brookings Institution

Left-of-center counterpart to AEI. Cofounder of the Tax Policy Institute (see following). http://www.brookings.edu

Bureau of Labor Statistics

The BLS, a bureau of the U.S. Department of Commerce, tabulates and reports a variety of statistics about the labor market, including the unemployment rate. The BLS also maintains the consumer price index (CPI), the best-known measure of price inflation. http://www.bls.gov

Center for Retirement Research at Boston College

This center "promote(s) research on retirement issues, to transmit new findings to the policy community and the public, to help train new scholars, and to broaden access to valuable data sources." Excellent source for studies about retirement trends and policies. http://crr.bc.edu/

Concord Coalition

This organization was founded in the early 1990s by former Senators Warren Rudman and Paul Tsongas. It is dedicated to educating Americans about the country's fiscal challenges. http://www.concordcoalition.org

Congressional Budget Office

Congress's adviser on budgetary issues, CBO annually produces a "baseline" forecast of the national budget, deficit, and debt under "current law"—that is, if the law is not changed. CBO also "scores"—estimates the budgetary impact for the next ten years—major legislation. http://www.cbo.gov

Council on Foreign Relations, Center for Geoeconomic Studies

Formally known as the Maurice Greenberg Center for Geoeconomic Studies, this arm of the Council on Foreign Relations analyzes trends in the international economy. http://www.cfr.org/thinktank/cgs/

The Economist magazine

The best general periodical covering the world economy and politics. http://www.economist.com/

Daily Crux

A free web clipping service for financial news, issued twice per day. Be advised that a large fraction of its clips are content from its publisher, Stansberry Research (an arm of Agora), often advertising its products. But since I am a satisfied Stansberry subscriber, I don't find it a significant problem. Sign up for twice-daily e-mail alerts, but be prepared for it to absorb a considerable chunk of your discretionary time. http://www.thedailycrux.com/

DefeatTheDebt.com

Advocacy and education group on issues related to the national debt. An arm of the Employment Policy Institute, a centrist think tank that studies employment issues that affect growth and prosperity. http://www.DefeatTheDebt.com

Economic Cycle Research Institute (ECRI)

ECRI monitors growth and inflation cycles for all major economies, regularly forecasting cycle turns for professional clients. A good place to learn about the dynamics and recurrent patterns in the business cycle. http://www.businesscycle.com/

Financial Times newspaper

Daily newspaper, published in London, on economic and financial news. Columnist Martin Wolf is a particularly sage commentator on international economics. Gideon Rachman is also highly recommended. http://www.ft.com

Government Accountability Office

GAO is Congress's financial watchdog. Then-comptroller general David Walker—now president of the **Peter G. Peterson Foundation**—conducted a "fiscal wake-up tour" in the mid-2000s to alert citizens to the dangers of mounting federal debt. http://www.gao.gov

International Monetary Fund

The IMF, founded at the 1944 Bretton Woods Conference that designed the world's postwar financial order, exists as a lender of last resort for nations in financial difficulty. Its rescue missions are often controversial among recipients of emergency loans, because the discipline the IMF demands as a condition of its loan often aggravates the recipient's condition in the short term. http://www.imf.org

Kiplinger's magazine

A competitor of *Money* magazine. For when you've passed through the introductory phase of personal financial planning. http://www.kiplinger.com/

MetLife Mature Market Institute (MMI)

MMI is MetLife's research organization, emphasizing the multidimensional and multigenerational issues of aging and longevity. http://www.metlife.com/mmi

Money magazine

A good layman's introduction to personal finance issues, including budgeting; saving for college, a home, or retirement; and investing. For a slightly more advanced version, see also *Kiplinger's*. http://money.cnn.com/pf/

National Bureau of Economic Research (NBER)

NBER is a loose collection of academics that sponsors research into a wide range of economic issues. NBER's newsletter highlights, in a reasonably accessible writing style, recent research results. http://www.nber.org

National Inflation Association

The NIA is a new organization "dedicated to preparing Americans for hyperinflation and helping Americans not only survive but also prosper in the upcoming hyperinflationary crisis." While many of its transmissions emphasize investment advice (for a fee), it is a valuable clearinghouse for information on how to protect against a phenomenon many Baby Boomers have not considered. There is some indication that NIA exists mainly to promote certain investments. Buyer beware. http://www.inflation.us

Organisation for Economic Co-operation and Development (OECD)

OECD brings together the governments of countries committed to democracy and to the market economy from around the world in support of economic growth and prosperity. Originally limited to only developed economies, over time OECD has broadened its focus to include financial stabilization (like the International Monetary Fund) and long-term growth (like the World Bank). http://www.oecd.org

Peter G. Peterson Foundation

Peterson, a former secretary of the treasury and founder of the Blackstone group, has been vocal about America's fiscal condition for decades, writing several best-selling books on fiscal threats. His eponymous foundation continues this campaign, including sponsorship of the 2008 hit movie, *I.O.U.S.A*. Many of the statistics cited in this volume come from the foundation. http://www.pgpf.org

Peterson Institute for International Economics

Peterson Institute for International Economics is also endowed by Peter G. Peterson and formerly known as the Institute for International Economics. IIE "is a private, nonprofit, nonpartisan research institution devoted to the study of international economic policy." http://www.iie.com

Population Reference Bureau (PRB)

The Population Reference Bureau provides information about population, health, and the environment. A good source of world demographic information. http://www.prb.org

RAND Corporation

RAND is the original "think tank," founded soon after World War II by the U.S. Air Force to maintain a cadre of civilian scientific advice that had been so useful in wartime. RAND has since diversified well beyond defense to include international demographics. *Full disclosure*: I am a graduate of RAND's PhD school. http://www.rand.org

Stansberry & Associates Research

Stansberry & Associates Research is a division of Agora that publishes a variety of investment newsletters. The *S&A Resources Report* by Matt Badiali focuses on commodities, with an emphasis on energy. Other newsletters have also dealt with looming fiscal challenges and the inflation that will result.

Tax Policy Center

A joint venture of the Urban Institute and the Brookings Institution, the Tax Policy Center "provides timely, accessible analysis and facts about tax policy to policymakers, journalists, citizens, and researchers." http://www.taxpolicycenter.org

Tea Party

The "Tea Party" is a spontaneous, loosely organized group of individuals concerned about taxes and government growth. Because of its informal nature, many views are attributed to the "Tea Party" that may be held by only a minority (or a handful of kooks).

United Nations Development Program (UNDP)

UNDP is the UN's global development network. It commissions the Human Development Report as well as global demographic forecasts that are the source of many of the projections in this volume. http://www.undp.org

Wall Street Journal newspaper

The *Wall Street Journal* is the best United States–based daily for business and economic news. Columnists David Wessel and Gerald Seib each cover aspects of economic policy. Wessel emphasizes the economics and

Seib the politics. Jason Zweig writes a fine personal finance/investing column. http://www.wsj.com

World Bank

Known formally as the International Bank of Reconstruction and Development, the World Bank originated at Bretton Woods to provide long-term financing to nations rebuilding after World War II. Today, the World Bank acts as a multilateral international aid facilitator and financier, with emphasis on aid to developing nations. http://www.worldbank.com

Business Teaching Cases Related to Book Chapters

Business or public policy instructors may wish to draw upon one or more of the many business school cases that relate to the themes of this book. A list of pertinent cases (available from Harvard Business School Publishing: http://www.hbsp.harvard.edu) is shown below.

Chapter 2

"Subprime Meltdown," J. J. Rotemberg, 708042-PDF-ENG

"Brazil Under Lula," A. Musacchio, 707031-PDF-ENG

"Singapore, Inc.," R. H. K. Vietor, E. J. Thompson, 703040-PDF-ENG

"The Credit Crisis of 2008: An Overview," V. G. Narayanan et al., 110048-PDF-ENG

"Roaring Out of Recession," R. Gulati et al., R1003C-PDF-ENG

"A Country Is Not a Company," P. Krugman, 14840-PBK-ENG

"The Big Three Performance Variables," A. R. Beckenstein, UV2719-PDF-ENG

"Restoring American Competitiveness," G. P. Pisano, R0907S-PDF-ENG

Chapter 3

"Japan: Deficits, Demography, and Deflation," R. H. K. Vietor, 706004-PDF-ENG

"U.S. Current Account Deficit," L. Alfaro et al., 706002-PDF-ENG

"Brazil: Leading the BRICs?" A. A. Daemmrich, A. Musacchio, 711024-PDF-ENG

"Malaysia: People First?" D. Comin, J. Abraham, 710033-PDF-ENG

Chapter 4

"World 3.0," P. Ghemawat, 12314-HBK-ENG

"European Union: The Road to Lisbon," G. Trumbull, D. Choi, 711032-PDF-ENG

"Angola and the Resource Curse," A. Musacchio et al., 711016-PDF-ENG

"East of Africa (and West of China)," M. Schuetz, C. Ramon-Berjano, HKU897-
   PDF-ENG
"China 'Unbalanced,'" D. Comin, R. H. K. Vietor, 711010-PDF-ENG
"Remaking Singapore," M. E. Porter et al., 710483-PDF-ENG
"Welcome to the False Recovery," E. Janszen, F1004B-PDF-ENG

Chapter 5

"Ben Bernanke: Person of the Year?" L. Lyer, M. C. Weinzierl, 710051-PDF-ENG
"Greenspan's Conundrum and Bernanke's Nightmare," F. Warnock, UV3951-
   PDF-ENG
"Geithner and Bernanke Amid the Global Financial Crisis," F. Warnock,
   UV3957-PDF-ENG
"Eurozone Rate Cuts in 2008," P. Rodriguez, UV2711-PDF-ENG

Chapter 6

"The Outlines of Your Generation," T. Erickson, 7785BC-PDF-ENG
"Managing Demographic Risk," R. Strack et al., R0802J-PDF-ENG

Chapter 7

No cases available, but see the works by Borjas and Vigdor cited in the references
   section.

Chapter 8

"The Hidden Risks in Emerging Markets," W. J. Henisz, B. A. Zelner, R1004H-
   PDF-ENG
"The Way to the India Way," P. Cappelli et al., 5814BC-PDF-ENG
"A Note on Long-Run Models of Economic Growth," P. Rodriguez, UV4282-
   PDF-ENG
"Colombia: Strong Fundamentals, Global Risk," A. Musacchio et al., 710012-
   PDF-ENG
"Economic Exposure," M. Lipson, UV2564-PDF-ENG
"Monsanto Company," M. Lipson, R. Green, UV2556-PDF-ENG
"China: Building 'Capitalism With Socialist Characteristics,'" J. Oi et al., 70641-
   PDF-ENG
"India on the Move," R. H. K. Vietor, E. J. Thompson, 703050-PDF-ENG

"Gold in 2011," R. Greenwood, B. Steiner, 211095-PDF-ENG
"A Cautionary Tale for Emerging Market Giants," J. S. Black, A. J. Morrison, R1009J-PDF-ENG

Chapter 9

No cases on Roth accounts exist, but a number of authors publish on tax issues. See Thomas in the references section, for example.

Chapter 10

"How BMW Is Defusing the Demographic Time Bomb," C. H. Loch et al., R1003H-PDF-ENG
"National Demographics & Lifestyles (B)," M. J. Roberts, 390006-PDF-ENG
"Government in Your Business," R. B. Reich, R0907L-PDF-ENG
"Are You Paying Too Much for That Acquisition?" R. G. Eccles et al., 99402-PDF-ENG
"Strategies That Fit Emerging Markets," T. Khanna et al., R0506C-PDF-ENG
"Principles of Microeconomics for Strategists," F. Oberholzer-Gee et al., 705801-HTM-ENG
"Standing on the Sun," C. Meyer, 14729-HBK-ENG
"The Promise and Peril of Russia's Resurgent State," R. Abdelal, R1001K-PDF-ENG
"Doing Business in a Postgrowth Society," J. G. Speth, F0909A-PDF-ENG
"Pursue Game-Changing Acquisitions and Partnerships: Making Strategic Deals in a Downturn," D. Harding, D. Rigby, 6676BC-PDF-ENG
"Determinants of Investment," A. R. Beckenstein, UV3933-PDF-ENG

Appendix A

"The Big Shift," J. Hagel et al., R0907Q-PDF-ENG
"The Euro in Crisis," G. Trumbull et al., 711049-PDF-ENG

Appendix B

"Managing Risk in an Unstable World," I. Bremmer, R0506B-PDF-ENG
"The Risk-Reward Framework at Morgan Stanley Research," S. Srinivasan, D. Lane, 111011-PDF-ENG
"Want People to Save? Force Them," D. Ariely, F1009G-PDF-ENG

Notes

Chapter 1

1. The "great moderation" of low inflation and low unemployment was the term coined by Federal Reserve chairman Ben Bernanke in 2004 for the period beginning in 1982.
2. Gibbon (1776).
3. Chua (2007).
4. Abkowitz (2009).

Chapter 2

1. Thirty-six months versus nine months for the nation; and a 5% drop in unemployment in California versus 1.25% for the nation.
2. Richardson (1997).
3. Schrag (2006).
4. In Romero (2005).
5. "Defined contribution" (DC) plans are exemplified by 401(k) plans: Employees contribute a portion of their wages (and matching employer contributions, if available) to an investment account they own personally and can invest as they choose. DC plans are portable; they can migrate with the employee if they change jobs. By contrast, traditional pension plans are "defined benefit" (DB): An investment company manages the contributions on behalf of members and guarantees a pension payment, whose size is based on the member's age at retirement, years of service, and final salary. Because DB payments are guaranteed, any shortfall in investment returns must be made up by larger employer contributions; conversely, in strong bull markets, employers can reduce their contributions and let investment gains make up the difference. In the late 1990s, CalPERS's investment returns were strong enough to allow the state to reduce its contributions, but the early 2000s bear market had the opposite effect: required state contributions rose very rapidly.
6. In November 2010, Jerry Brown was elected governor. He did not abjure tax increases but promised they would be subject to popular vote. His 2011–2012 budget was premised on the assumption that the 2009 temporary tax increases would be extended, that is, approved by voters.

Chapter 3

1. "Ponzi scheme" and other specialized terms are explained in the glossary.

2. Of course, most attempts to improve GM's fiscal position caused greater short-term problems. Its benefits structure assured that even layoffs would not reduce its liabilities as much as simple arithmetic would suggest. For example, plant closures added to the ranks of retirees (as those laid off who were near retirement age declared retirement).

3. "Entitlements" are government expenditures that go to all eligible recipients, regardless of their behavior, as long as the program is maintained. These are distinct from "discretionary" programs, where government can pay or not pay subject to its discretion. Social Security is an entitlement: Anyone over the official retirement age (currently about 67) is eligible to receive payments, although the amount of payment is somewhat affected by the recipient's earnings while working. An individual weapon system procurement is discretionary: The Pentagon can choose to cancel the purchase.

4. "Fiscal" stimulus refers to changes in government spending or taxation to put more money into the hands of households to spend or invest. This is the province of the executive and legislative branches. "Cash for clunkers" and the various homebuyers' credits are examples of fiscal stimulus. "Monetary" stimulus entails increasing the supply of money; it is carried out by the Federal Reserve system (with considerable involvement by the U.S. Treasury). The Fed's various lending programs to financial institutions (and others) in 2008–2009 expanded liquidity (i.e., the money supply), encouraging economic activity.

5. A common source for recurring annual deficit and debt projections is the Congressional Budget Office (CBO). These figures came from a report of the Peterson-Pew Commission on Budget Reform, Red Ink Rising: A Call to Action to Stem the Mounting Federal Debt. The Commission drew on CBO, General Accounting Office, and other forecasts.

6. Reinhart and Rogoff (2009a). See also Reinhart and Rogoff (2009c).

Chapter 4

1. Prestowitz (2005).

2. Harvard historian Niall Ferguson coined the term, connoting China and America's codependent relationship, in 2008. See, for example, Ferguson (2009b).

3. Chinese FDI to the U.S. in 2008 from Bureau of Economic Analysis (2008).

4. Setser (2009a).

5. Congressional Budget Office (2009).

6. OECD (2007–2008).

7. Vice Premier Wang Qishan said: "As a major reserve currency-issuing country in the world, the U.S. should balance and properly handle the impact of the dollar's supply," as quoted by Barkley and Solomon (2009).

8. Eberstadt (2006).

9. World Bank (2011).

10. Maps of India (n.d.).

11. Bloom et al. (2003).

12. Federal budget figures from U.S. Bureau of the Census (n.d.). Chency quote from Entous (2004) based on an account by former Treasury Secretary Paul O'Neill about a 2002 meeting.

13. Federal Reserve (n.d.), "Treasury Constant Maturities."

14. U.S. Bureau of the Census. (n.d.), *Statistical Abstract of the U.S.*, "International Investment Position by Type of Investment," http://www.census.gov/compendia/statab/tables/09s1249.xls.

15. Setser and Pandey (2009c), http://www.cfr.org/cgs. See also Setser and Pandey (2009b).

16. See, for example, Eunjung Cha (2009).

Chapter 5

1. Laffer et al. (2008), p. 37.

2. Laffer et al. (2008), p. 14.

3. Reinhart and Rogoff (2009c).

Chapter 6

1. Kennedy (1989).

2. Kotkin (2010a).

3. As of February 2010, combined government and private debt in the United States was a larger percentage of GDP—more than 300%—than for any other developed country. (Most developed countries have higher government debts but far less private debt than the United States.) The International Monetary Fund produces the most comprehensive comparative data on total national debts by country.

Chapter 7

1. Kotkin (2010).

2. Borjas (1991).

3. Borjas (1991).

4. See Romero (2007).

Chapter 8

1. Contrarians note that the deferred-consumption argument about deflation is specious. After all, annual double-digit declines in prices in consumer electronics and home computers did not encourage many consumers to delay purchases; they brought many more consumers into the market. However, whatever the mechanism, periodic deflation has unquestionably contributed to Japan's 2 decades of stagnation.

2. Opdyke (2009).

3. The CPI is based on a "basket" of goods and a few services in the proportions that the Bureau of Labor Statistics believes consumers purchase. Variants are the Core CPI (CPI omitting food and energy) and the PPI (equivalent to the PPI at the wholesale level). As will be argued, the CPI very likely understates inflation for older Americans.

4. Friedman (1992). It is believed he first coined this phrase in the late 1960s.

5. Trustees' reports for Social Security and Medicare. See Board of Trustees of the Federal Old-Age and Survivors Insurance and Federal Disability Insurance Trust Funds (2009), and Boards of Trustees of the Federal Hospital Insurance Trust Fund and the Federal Supplementary Medical Insurance Trust Fund (2009), respectively.

6. Congressional Budget Office (2009). CBO forecasts two scenarios: an "extended baseline" scenario of continued business as usual and an "alternative fiscal scenario" of greater restraint than in the past. This text assumes a near business-as-usual ("extended baseline") scenario. Even if Congress becomes much more frugal and follows the latter scenario, the debt-to-GDP ratio is projected to exceed 100%. It just takes longer: to 2038.

7. Peterson (n.d.).

8. Stoeferle (2010).

9. Darwin's Finance (n.d.).

10. Darwin's Finance (n.d.).

11. For a list of agricultural ETFS, see Stock-Encyclopedia.com, http://etf.stock-encyclopedia.com/category/agriculture-crop-price-etfs.html.

12. Stewart (2008), pp. 21–22.

Chapter 9

1. The Bureau of Labor Statistics (BLS) tabulates several consumer price indices. The best known is the CPI-U for all urban consumers; this is the one that gets the headlines. It also maintains the CPI-W for all urban wage and clerical workers. BLS has also produced an experimental version of the CPI that reflects different spending patterns by the elderly, termed CPI-E. For the 25 years

from 1982 to 2007, CPI-E cumulatively grew 9.8% faster than the headline rate, CPI-U, or 0.05% per year faster. See Stewart (2008).

2. *Financial Advisor* (2009).

Chapter 10

1. Porter (1985).

References

Abate, T. (2010, April 4). Equipment movers in demand as factories shut. *San Francisco Chronicle*.

Abkowitz, A. (2009, October 6). China buys the world. *BusinessWeek*.

Achenbach, J. (2009, December 8). In debate over nation's growing debt, a surplus of worry. *The Washington Post*.

Agricultural-Crop Price ETF List. (n.d.). In Stock-Encyclopedia.com. Retrieved from http://etf.stock-encyclopedia.com/category/agriculture-crop-price-etfs.html.

Andrews, E. L. (2009, November 23). Wave of debt payments facing U.S. government. *The New York Times*.

Applebaum, A. (2009, June 9). Where's the revolution? *The Washington Post*.

Arends, B. (2009, June 3). Is your portfolio ready for hyperinflation? *The Wall Street Journal*.

Armstrong, B. (2009, August 25). Income limits on Roth IRAs disappear next year. *Boston Herald*.

Arnold, D. A. (2008). *The great bust ahead*. Mill Valley, CA: Vorago.

Augustine, N., et al. (2010, February). *The trillion dollar gap: Underfunded state retirement systems and the roads to reform*. Pew Center on the States. Retrieved from downloads.pewcenteronthestates.org/The_Trillion_Dollar_Gap_final.pdf

Bacevich, A. J. (2008). *The limits of power*. New York, NY: Metropolitan Books.

Back, A. (2010, March 10). Beijing cools to gold, reassures on treasurys. *The Wall Street Journal*.

Banyan. (2009, May 9). A watched frog never boils. *The Economist*.

Barkley, T., & Solomon, D. (2009, July 29). Chinese convey concern on growing U.S. debt. *The Wall Street Journal*.

Barley, R. (2009, July 9). Treasury's perilous interest costs. *The Wall Street Journal*.

Barnes, F. (2010, July 12). Obama's entitlement opportunity. *The Wall Street Journal*.

Barone, M. (2010, April 16). Immigration reform: The new third rail. *Washington Examiner*.

Barr, A. (2010, April 8). Poll: 49% would reelect incumbent. *Politico*.

Batson, A. (2009, May 11). Long-term challenges test China's growth. *The Wall Street Journal*.

Bayh, E. (2010, March 13). Why Democrats must restrain spending. *The Wall Street Journal*.

Belkin, D. (2009, June 20). Boomers to this year's grads: We are really, really sorry.

Belsie, L. (2010, April). Growth in a time of debt. *NBER Digest.*

Bergsten, F. (2009, November/December). The dollar and the deficits. *Foreign Affairs.*

Bernanke, B. (2004, February 20). The great moderation. The Federal Reserve Board. Retrieved from http://www.federalreserve.gov/boarddocs/.../2004/20040220/default.htm

Bernanke, B. (2005, March 10). The global savings glut and the U.S. current account defi cit. The Federal Reserve Board. Retrieved from http://www .federalreserve .gov/ boarddocs/ speeches/ 2005/ 200503102/

Biggs, A. (2010a, April 6). *The market value of public-sector pension deficits.* AEI Retirement Policy Outlook, *1.* Retrieved from http://www.aei.org/outlook/100948

Biggs, A. (2010b, March 30). Overloaded with debts unseen. *The New York Times*/American Enterprise Institute.

Bischoff, B. (2009, June 1). Reversing a Roth IRA conversion. *The Wall Street Journal.*

Black, S. (n.d.). *What capital controls in the United States will look like.* Retrieved from http://www.sovereignman.com/finance/what-capital-controls-in-the -united-states-will-look-like/

Blackstone, B. (2010, May 15–16). Confidence wanes in bailout, austerity. *The Wall Street Journal.*

Blinder, A. S. (2009, June 21). Why inflation isn't the danger. *The New York Times.*

Blinder, A. S. (2010, May 20). Return of the bond market vigilantes. *The Wall Street Journal.*

Bloom, D., Canning, D., & Sevilla, J. (2003). *The demographic dividend.* Santa Monica, CA: RAND Corporation.

Bloomberg Businessweek. (2010a, January 25). Not-so-heavy metal.

Bloomberg Businessweek. (2010b, March 22 & 29). Stimulus spending: How to get more bang for the buck.

Bond, T., Kochugovindan, S., & Dicks, M. (2010, February). *Equity gilt study 2010.* Retrieved from Barclays Capital, http://www.barcap.com/egs/

Bonner, W. (2010, March 26). Chermany vs. Gremerica. *Daily Reckoning.*

Bonner, W., & Wiggin, A. (2006). *Empire of debt.* Hoboken, NJ: Wiley.

Bonner, W., & Wiggin, A. (2009). *Financial reckoning day: Fallout.* Hoboken, NJ: Wiley.

Borjas, G. J. (1991). *Friends or strangers: The impact of immigrants on the U.S. economy.* New York, NY: Basic Books.

Borjas, G. J. (2001). *Heaven's door: Immigration policy and the American economy.* Princeton, NJ: Princeton University Press.

Boskin, M. (2009, July 23). Obama needs a move to the middle. *The Wall Street Journal.*

Boskin, M. (2010, May 6). Time to junk the corporate tax. *The Wall Street Journal.*

Brock, H. (2009, May 18). *The end game draws nigh—the future evolution of the debt-to-GDP ratio, John Mauldin's "Outside the Box."* Retrieved from http://www.investorsinsight.com/blogs/john_mauldins_outside_the_box/archive/2009/05/18/the-end-game-draws-nigh-the-future-evolution-of-the-debt-to-gdp-ratio.aspx

Broder, D. (December 21, 2009). Debt at crisis. *The Topeka Capital-Journal.*

Brooks, A. C. (2010a, April 14). "Spreading the wealth" isn't fair. *The Wall Street Journal.*

Brooks, A. C. (2010b, June 8). Slouching towards Athens. *The Wall Street Journal.*

Browning, E. S. (2009, December 28). Adjusted for inflation, bad run looks worse. *The Wall Street Journal.*

Budaghyan, A. (2010, June 8). *How to play emerging market growth in the coming decade.* Montreal, Canada: BCA Research.

Buffett, W. E. (2009, August 19). The greenback effect. *The New York Times.*

Bureau of Economic Analysis, U.S. Dept. of Commerce. (2008). Retrieved from http://www.bea.gov/international/xls/CAP-08.xls

Bureau of Labor Statistics (2008, April). *Monthly labor review.* Washington, DC: U.S. Department of Labor.

Burman, L. E. (2006, May 22). Roth conversions as revenue raisers: Smoke and mirrors. *Tax Notes.*

Businessweek (2009, November 23). Why you'd better beware of "the big shift."

Bussewitz, C. (2010, April 5). Study: Calif. pensions underfunded by $500 billion. *San Francisco Chronicle.*

Buttonwood. (2009, May 16). Birth pains. *The Economist.*

Buttonwood. (2009, May 30). Not so risk-free. *The Economist.*

Capretta, J. C. (2009, Fall). The new middle class contract. *National Affairs.*

Card, D. (2010). *Immigration and inequality* (NBER Working Paper No. 14683). National Bureau of Economic Research.

Casey, D. (2009a). *End of the nation-state.* Casey Research.

Casey, D. (2009b). *Into the fourth turning: Interview with Neil Howe.* Casey Research.

Casey, D. (2009c, September 25). End of the dollar? It's happening. *Casey's Daily Dispatch.*

Congressional Budget Office. (2009, June). The long-term budget outlook. Retrieved from http://www.cbo.gov/ftpdocs/102xx/doc10297/06-25-LTBO.pdf

Cendrowski, S. (2009, October 26). Beware a gold bubble. *Fortune.*

Chang, E. (2010, February 25). Rogers: China will keep dumping U.S. treasuries. *MoneyNews.*

Charlemagne. (pseud.). (2010, May 10). Europe's 750 billion euro bazooka. *The Economist.*

Chon, G. (2010, February 10). States skip pension payments, delay day of reckoning. *The Wall Street Journal.*

Chu, D. (2010, July 13). U.S. stripped of AAA credit rating . . . by China?! *Zero Hedge.*

Chu, H. (2010, May 9). EU unveils $968-billion emergency bailout plan. *Los Angeles Times.*

Chua, A. (2007). *Day of empire.* New York, NY: Anchor Books.

Cline, A. (2010, March 11). Obama accepts Paul Ryan's premise. *The American Spectator.*

Cochrane, J. B. (2010, May 18). Greek myths and the Euro tragedy. *The Wall Street Journal.*

Cohn, L. (2010, April). It's not just gold that glitters. *Kiplinger's Personal Finance.*

Colvin, G. (2009, May 11). The government's new definition of rich. *Fortune.*

Congressional Budget Office. (2009, June). *The long-term budget outlook.*

Connolly, A. M. (2009). *Mining the retirement income market.* Deloitte LLP.

Cooper, J. (2007, February 13). The incumbent party. *The Wall Street Journal.*

Coy, P. (2010a, February 15). U.S. debt: It's not dark yet, but it's getting there. *Bloomberg Businessweek.*

Coy, P. (2010b, February 22). The bond vigilante who left Greece in ruins. *Bloomberg Businessweek.*

Coy, P. (2010, April 12). Inflation hawks show their talons. *Bloomberg Businessweek.*

Crawshaw, J. (2009, June 8). Bill Gross: GM failure a preview of our future economy. *Newsmax.*

Crowe, D. (2010, May 10). Currency woes dog Venezuelans after devaluation. *The Wall Street Journal.*

Cui, C. (2009, November 7). Central banks join a new gold rush. *The Wall Street Journal.*

Curan, R. (2010, April 5). Quirks of commodities funds. *The Wall Street Journal.*

Dalio, R., & Rotemberg, J. (2008, October 23). The next bubble that is now emerging. *Bridgewater Daily Observer.* Bridgewater Associates.

Dalio, R., Rotenberg, J., & Post, F. (2008, October 31). A template for understanding what's going on. *Bridgewater Daily Observer.* Bridgewater Associates.

Dalio, R., Rotenberg, J., & Post, F. (2009, September 9). Reflation. *Bridgewater Daily Observer.* Bridgewater Associates.

Damato, K. (2009, December 8). A very different animal. *The Wall Street Journal.*

Daniels, M. (2009, September 4). The coming reset in state government. *The Wall Street Journal.*

Darwall, R. (2010, June 29). Britain tries fiscal austerity. *The Wall Street Journal.*

Darwin's Finance. (n.d.). The gold-dollar correlation explained and why it broke down [Web log post]. Retrieved from http://www.darwinsfinance.com/gold-dollar-correlation/

Davey, M. (2010, March 27). States seeking cash hope to expand taxes to services. *Businesswire.*

De Borchgrave, A. (2009, August 6). Experts: Expect the worst for the economy. *Newsmax.*

Denning, L. (2009, December 11). Gold trades on luster and bluster. *The Wall Street Journal.*

Dinan, S. (2010, June 20). Rich got richer: Paid more taxes under Bush. *Washington Times.*

Doll, B. (2010, June 8). The bullish case for U.S. equities. *The Wall Street Journal.*

Donmoyer, R. J. (2009, December 21). How many ways can you tax the rich? *Businessweek.*

Dorning, M. (2010, March 15). Slashing the deficit without massive tax hikes. *Bloomberg Businessweek.*

Dougherty, S. (2009, August 26). *The metastasis of moral hazard and its effect on gold.* Kitco.

Dreman, D. (2009, September 7). Inflation's coming, hide here. *Forbes.*

Eberstadt, N. (2006, January). *Global population trends: Shaping the strategic future.* American Enterprise Institute.

The Economist. (2009a, May 16). Damage assessment.

The Economist. (2009b, June 6). America's fiscal Cassandra.

The Economist. (2009c, June 6). This way out.

The Economist. (2009d, June 11). Seeing red.

The Economist. (2009e, June 13). Chasing ghosts.

The Economist. (2009f, June 13). The big sweat.

The Economist. (2009g, June 13). The biggest bill in history.

The Economist. (2009h, October 22). Round and round it goes.

The Economist. (2009i, December 3). Default lines.

The Economist. (2010a, February 23). Golden years.

The Economist. (2010b, February 25). East or famine.

The Economist. (2010c, April 8). Europe's worrying gerontocrary.

The Economist. (2010d, April 8). The wax melts.

The Economist. (2010e, April 15). Three years to save the euro.

The Economist. (2010f, April 29). My word, your bonds.

The Economist. (2010g, May 5). The end of the party.

The Economist. (2010h, May 10). Rollercoaster.

The Economist. (2010i, May 27). Fear returns.

The Economist. (2010j, May 29). A sticky gas-pedal.

The Economist. (2010k, May 29). Rescuing the rescuers.

The Economist. (2010l, June 10). Socialist workers.

The Economist. (2010m, June 16). State of denial.

The Economist. (2010n, June 24). Is there life after debt?

The Economist. (2010o, July 6). After the gold rush.

Edelson, L.(2009). *Bernanke's secret debt solution to the global financial crisis.* Seattle, WA: Wisdom/Weiss Research.

Edwards, C. (2010, Winter). Public sector unions and the rising costs of employee compensation. *The Cato Journal.*

Eichengreen, B. (2009, September/October). The dollar dilemma. *Foreign Affairs.*

Eichengreen, B., & Irwin, D. (2009, October). *The slide to protectionism in the great depression: Who succumbed and why?* (NBER Working Paper No. 15142). National Bureau of Economic Research.

Entous, A. (2004, January 11). AOL News (Reuters).

Eunjung Cha, A. (2009, May 17). China gains key assets in spate of purchases: Oil, minerals are among acquisitions worldwide. *The Washington Post.*

Evans, K. (2010a, March 1). Frugality forecasts look at bit generous. *The Wall Street Journal.*

Evans, K. (2010b, April 6). The inflation chasm between fed, investors. *The Wall Street Journal.*

Evans, K. (2010c, April 14). Deflation diagnosis: Shelter skews the view. *The Wall Street Journal.*

Federal Reserve. (n.d.). Treasury constant maturities. Retrieved from http://www.federalreserve.gov/releases/h15/data/Annual/H15_TCMNOM_Y30.txt

Feldstein, M. (2009a, May). The return of saving. *Foreign Affairs.*

Feldstein, M. (2009b, June 28). The Fed must reassure markets on inflation. *Financial Times.*

Feldstein, M. (2009c, September 8). ObamaCare's crippling deficits. *The Wall Street Journal.*

Feldstein, M. (2009d, December 9). The dollar's fall reflects a new role for reserves. *Financial Times.*

Ferguson, B., & Nicholson, J. (2010, April 29). Senate budget raises questions if dividends rates will top 40 percent. Washington, DC: Bureau of National Affairs.

Ferguson, N. (2002). *Empire: The rise and demise of the British world order.* New York, NY: Basic Books/Perseus.

Ferguson, N. (2004). *Colossus: The rise and fall of the American empire*. New York, NY: Penguin.

Ferguson, N. (2008). *The ascent of money: A financial history of the world*. New York, NY: Penguin.

Ferguson, N. (2009a, November 28). An empire at risk. *Newsweek*.

Ferguson, N. (2009b, January/February). What Chimerica hath wrought. *The National Interest*.

Fernando, V. (2010, February 25). Goldman: Treasury yields will crash because inflation is dead and Bernanke's a dove. *Business Insider*. Retrieved from http://www.businessinsider.com

Ferrara, P. (2009a, March 4). Obama's fantasy budget. *American Spectator*.

Ferrara, P. (2009b, June 24). Washington's plot to explode your taxes. *American Spectator*.

Ferrara, P. (2009c, July 23). Obama is delaying the economic recovery. *American Spectator*.

Ferrara, P. (2010, March 10). The devil is in the deficits. *American Spectator*.

Fiat currency: Using the past to see into the future. (n.d.). *Daily Reckoning*.

Fieler, F. S., & Bell, J. (2010, May 7). The gold standard: The case for another look.

Financial Advisor. (2009, August 17). Boomers sticking with traditional IRAs. Retrieved from http://www.fa-mag.com/fa-news/4391-boomers-sticking-with-traditional-iras.html

Financial Times. (2009, May 7). Tackling Britain's fiscal debacle.

Fiscal Affairs Department. (2009, November 3). *The state of public finances cross country fiscal monitor: November 2009* (SPN/09/25). International Monetary Fund.

Forelle, C., & Walker, M. (2010, April 9). Greek bond crisis spreads. *The Wall Street Journal*.

Fortune. (2009, August 17). Whither Medicaid.

Fortune. (2010, February 8). Blackrock interview.

Fox, J. (2009, November 9). What's a banker worth? *Time*.

Friedman, G. (2009). *The next 100 years*. New York, NY: Doubleday.

Friedman, M. (1992). *Money mischief*. New York, NY: Harcourt Brace Jovanovich.

Friedman, M. (1994). *Money mischief: Episodes in monetary history*. San Francisco, CA: Mariner Books.

Fund, J. (2010, May 8–9). The next capital insurgency. *The Wall Street Journal*.

Gelb. L. H. (2009). *Power rules*. New York, NY: HarperCollins.

Generational Adviser. (2010, January 11). Half way between spendthrift and tightwad. Retrieved from http://generationaladvisor.com

Gibbon, E (1776). *Decline and fall of the Roman Empire*.

Gibson, Gary. (2009). *The 7 deadly ingredients for the coming U.S. hyperinflation . . . and how to protect your money.* Whiskey and Gunpowder. Retrieved from http://whiskeyandgunpowder.com/7-deadly-ingredients-for-the-coming-us-hyperinflation/

Gilbert, M. (2010, January 11). The Fed's next act could be its hardest. *Bloomberg.*

Gold Carry Trade Special Report. (n.d.). *Whiskey and gunpowder.*

Goldberg, J. (2010, April 9). Who'll do America's job? *New York Post.*

Golden years: Time spent in retirement has increased. (2010, February 23). *The Economist.*

Goldstone, J. (2010, January/February). The new population bomb. *Foreign Affairs.*

Gongloff, M. (2009a, June 30). Inflation fears seem to be, well, inflated. *The Wall Street Journal.*

Gongloff, M. (2009b, July 11). Fed's conundrum on treasury purchases. *The Wall Street Journal.*

Goodman, W., & Reynolds, G. (2009, December 9). PIMCO says "fear not" weak dollar will spur growth. *Bloomberg.* Retrieved from http://www.bloomberg.com/apps/news?pid=newsarchive&sid=a4ny.J5sdqak

Grant, J. (2009, December 5–6). Requiem for the dollar. *The Wall Street Journal.*

Greece is going to default (eventually). (2009, December 28). *Daily Dirtnap.*

Greek tragedy. (2010, February 22). *Bloomberg Businessweek.*

Greenhut, S. (2010, April 11). Pension crater much deeper. *Orange County Register.*

Greenspan, A. (2009, June 25). Inflation is the greater threat to a sustained recovery. *Financial Times.*

Greenspan, A. (2010, June 18). U.S. debt and the Greece analogy. *The Wall Street Journal.*

Gross, B. (2009, July). "Bon" or "non" appetit? *PIMCO Investment Outlook.*

Gupta, J. K. (2010, January 4). Gold is my favourite currency. *Business Standard* (India).

Harrington, K. (2010). *The financial politics of Peak Oil.* Clarium Capital Management.

Hatzius, J. (2009, June 13). GS US economics analyst: Is the Fed's big balance sheet on inflation risk? Goldman Sachs.

Hatzius, J., et al. (2009, June 7). Inflation—the only thing to fear is fear itself. Goldman Sachs.

Hayashi, Y. (2010, March 1). Japan scrambles to avoid being the next Greece. *The Wall Street Journal.*

Helman, R., Copeland, C., & VanDerHei, J. (2010, March 9). *Retirement confidence survey 2010.* Washington, DC: Employee Benefit Research Institute.

Henninger, D. (2010, May 13). The we're not Europe party. *The Wall Street Journal.*

Hill, E. (2006, December). *Cal facts: California's economy and budget in perspective.* Sacramento, CA: Legislative Analyst's Office.

Hill, L. E., et al. (2010, April). *Immigrant legalization: Assessing the labor market effects.* San Francisco, CA: Public Policy Institute of California.

Hilsenrath, J. (2009, June 22). Timing, tools of fed's exit strategy come into focus. *The Wall Street Journal.*

Hinds, M., & Steil, B. (2007, October 30). History's warning about the price of money. *Financial Times.*

Hoisington, V., & Hunt, L. (2009, fourth quarter). Quarterly review and outlook. Hoisington Investment Management Company.

Holland, R. (2010, February 9). Prepare now to escape Obama's retirement trap. *Whiskey and Gunpowder.*

How to play commodities. (2009, December 28, and 2010, January 4). *Bloomberg Businessweek.*

Huebscher, R. (2009, April 28). Gary Shilling: Economic forecast and current market opportunities. *Advisor Perspectives.*

Inflation Hedge. (2010, April). *Kiplinger's Personal Finance.*

Irwin, N. (2010, June 1). Despite U.S. deficit concerns, investors still pour money into treasury bonds. *The Washington Post.*

Javers, E. (2009, July 29). "G-2" highlights status of U.S., China. *Politico.*

Jeffries, A. (2009, July 1). Boomers and the bust. *Money.*

Jenkins, H. (2009, October 28). Washington's suicide mission. *The Wall Street Journal.*

Joffe, J. (2009, September/October). The default power. *Foreign Affairs.*

Johnson, P. (2009, April 13). Lessons for Obama from Britain. *Forbes.*

Johnson, R. W., & Mommaerts, C. (2010, February). *Will health care costs bankrupt aging boomers?* Urban Institute. Retrieved from http://www.retirementpolicy.org

Jolly, D., & Rampell, C. (2010, March 15). Moody's says U.S. debt could test triple-A rating. *The New York Times.*

Jones, F. (2009a, August 10). Buffet loads up on debt ahead of inflation. *Newsmax.*

Jones, F. (2009b, September 24). Chinese spending puts treasuries in danger. Newsmax. Retrieved from http://moneynews.newsmax.com

Kadish, L.(2009, October 13). Taking the national debt seriously. *The Wall Street Journal.*

Kalwarski, T. (2009, October 19). Betting on a big boom in natural gas. *Businessweek.*

Kalwarski, T. (2010, February 22). A wide world of crushing debt. *Bloomberg Businessweek.*

Karabell, Z. (2009a). *Superfusion.* New York, NY: Simon & Schuster.

Karabell, Z. (2009b, October 13). Deficits and the China challenge. *The Wall Street Journal.*

Karabell, Z. (2010, May 11). The world's dollar drug. *The Wall Street Journal.*

Kasler, D. (2010, April 4). Businesses scared off by California go global. *Sacramento Bee.*

Kasliwal, P. (2009, June 2). A tale of two bankruptcies. *Qatar Tribune.*

Katsenelson, V. (2009, August 25). Forget about the Chinese stock market: Whole Chinese economy is a bubble waiting to burst. *Business Insider.*

Kennedy, P. M. (1989). *The rise and fall of the great powers.* New York, NY: Vintage Books/Random House.

Kessler, A. (2010, February 4). Bernanke's exit strategy: Tighter reserve requirements. *The Wall Street Journal.*

Khalilzad, Z., et al. (1999). *The United States and a rising China* (MR-1082-AF). Santa Monica, CA: RAND Corporation.

Kimes, N. (2009, June 20). China on the march, again. *Fortune.*

Kiplinger, K. (2010a, April). A stubborn U.S. budget. *Kiplinger's Personal Finance.*

Kiplinger, K. (2010b, May). We're leaving our children a shameful legacy. *Kiplinger's Personal Finance.*

Klein, P. (2009, July–August). The matter with myths. *The American Spectator.*

Kotkin, J. (2010a). *The next hundred million: America in 2050.* New York: Penguin.

Kotkin, J. (2010b, January 23–24). The kids will be alright. *The Wall Street Journal.*

Krauthammer, C. (2009, October 19). Decline is a choice. *The American Spectator.*

Krepenevich, A. F. (2009). *Seven deadly scenarios.* New York, NY: Bantam.

Krieger, L. M. (2010, April 18). California's university system: What went wrong? *San Jose Mercury-News.*

Kroeber, A. (2010, April 11). Four myths about China's economy. *The Washington Post.*

Krugman, P. (2008, May 31). Embedded vs. non-embedded inflation. *The New York Times.*

Krugman, P. (2010, May 30). Taking on China. *The New York Times.*

Lachman, D. (2010a, February 25). Greek apples California oranges. *Australian Financial Review.*

Lachman, D. (2010b, March 6). A Greek tragedy. *International Economy.*

Laffer, A. B. (2009a, June 11). Get ready for inflation and higher interest rates. *The Wall Street Journal.*

Laffer, A. B. (2009b, September 22). Taxes, depression, and our current troubles. *The Wall Street Journal.*

Laffer, A. B. (2010c, June 7). Tax hikes and the 2011 economic collapse. *The Wall Street Journal.*

Laffer, A. B., & Moore, S. (2009, May 18). Soak the rich, lose the rich. *The Wall Street Journal.*

Laffer, A. B., Moore, S., & Tanous, P. (2008). *The end of prosperity.* New York, NY: Threshold Editions/Simon & Schuster.

Laffer, A. B., Moore, S., & Williams, J. (2010). *Rich states, poor states.* ALEC-Laffer State Economic Competitiveness Index. Washington, DC: American Legislative Exchange Council.

Landler, M., & Sanger, D. E. (July 29, 2009). China seeks assurances that U.S. will cut its deficit. *The New York Times.*

Lauricella, T. (2009a, April 27). For inflation tips, look to "5yr5yr breakeven." *Wall Street Journal.*

Lauricella, T. (2009b, July 10). Failure of fail-safe strategy sends investors scrambling. *The Wall Street Journal.*

Lauricella, T. (2010, March 26). Debt fears send rates up. *The Wall Street Journal.*

Lazear, E. P. (2010, January 28). The spending "freeze" that isn't. *The Wall Street Journal.*

Lee, J. (2010, February 1 & 8). Don't underestimate India's consumers. *Bloomberg Businessweek.*

Legislative Analyst's Office (LAO) (California). (2006, December). *Cal Facts.*

Lehmann, R. (2009, April 13). Prepare for inflation. *Forbes.*

Lewis, J. T., & House, J. (2010, May 14). Portugal approves tax increases, salary cuts. *The Wall Street Journal.*

Lewitt, M. (2009, June 1). The full faith and credit economy. *HCM Market Letter.* Harch Capital Management.

Light, L. (2009a, July 9). Catching the gold bug. *The Wall Street Journal.*

Light, L. (2009b, December 12–13). Funds take a shine to gold. *The Wall Street Journal.*

Lim, P. J. (2010, March). Why diversification will work again. *Money.*

Lind, M. (2010, January 5). The Clintonites were wrong. *Salon.*

Linden, A. (2009, July 21). A fiscally conservative Generation X. TheStreet.com. Retrieved from http://secure2.www.thestreet.com.

Longman, P. (2004a). *The empty cradle.* New York, NY: Basic Books.

Longman, P. (2004b, May/June). The global baby bust. *Foreign Affairs.*

Lowry, R. (2010, April 13). Tax hikes forever. *New York Post.*

Luskin, D. L. (2010, April 15). George W. Bush's 2010 tax miracle. *The Wall Street Journal.*

Lustig, R. J., ed. (2010). *Remaking California.* Berkeley, CA: Heyday Books.

Magnus, G., & Cates, A. (2010, May 11). *Sovereign debt: A structural crisis and its implications for growth.* New York, NY: UBS Investment Research.

Malanga, S. (2009, June 12). Notable and quotable. *The Wall Street Journal.*

Malpass, D. (2009, October 8). The weak dollar threat to prosperity. *The Wall Street Journal.*

Mandelbaum, M. (2010, May/June). Overpowered? *Foreign Affairs.*

Maps of India. (n.d.). India: Per capita income of states, 2005–2006. Retrieved from http://www.mapsofindia.com/maps/india/percapitaincome.htm

Mariner Books. (n.d.). A memo by the CEO of Oaktree to clients.

Marks, H. (n.d.). *Tell me I'm wrong.* Oaktree Capital.

Mauldin, J. (2009a, March 24). Roadmap to inflation and sources of cheap insurance. *John Mauldin's Thoughts From the Frontline.* Dallas, TX: Millenium Wave Investments.

Mauldin, J. (2009b, July 9). The great reflation experiment. *John Mauldin's Thoughts From the Frontline.* Dallas, TX: Millenium Wave Investments.

Mauldin, J. (2010a, February 12). Between dire and disastrous. *John Mauldin's Thoughts from the Frontline.* Dallas, TX: Millenium Wave Investments.

Mauldin, J. (2010b, May 1). The future of public debt. *John Mauldin's Thoughts From the Frontline.* Dallas, TX: Millenium Wave Investments.

Mauldin, J. (2010c, May 28). Six impossible things. *John Mauldin's Thoughts From the Frontline.* Dallas, TX: Millenium Wave Investments.

Mayer, C. (2009a, October 29). What the "man who made too much" says about gold. *Daily Wealth.*

Mayer, C. (2009b, December). A billionaire investor shares his best idea. *Capital & Crisis.*

McClintock, T. (2009, June 4). Warnings from the left coast. *Orange County Register.*

McIntyre, D. A. (2010, February 25). As Moody's targets Japan, the sovereign debt crisis moves closer to the U.S. *24/7 Wall Street.*

McKee, M. (2010, February 1 & 8). As the economy recovers, what is "normal"? *Bloomberg Businessweek.*

McKinnon, J. D. (2010, January 28). Big budget deficits demand number crunching and more. *The Wall Street Journal.*

McKinnon, J. D. (2010a, April 12). To fix deficit, tax man must knock on many doors. *The Wall Street Journal.*

McKinnon, J. D. (2010b, July 12). U.S. ponders tax that has VAT of political trouble. *The Wall Street Journal.*

Meichty, S. (2010, May 14). Italy's stagnant growth makes debt burden heavier. *The Wall Street Journal.*

Melloan, G. (2009a, June 20). Why "stimulus" will mean inflation. *The Wall Street Journal.*

Melloan, G. (2009b, June 24). A weakened U.S. goes to the G-20. *The Wall Street Journal.*

Melloan, G. (2009c, August 4). Bernanke's exit strategy. *The Wall Street Journal.*

Melloan, G. (2009d, November 24). Government deficits and private growth. *The Wall Street Journal.*

Meltzer, A. H. (2009a). *A history of the federal reserve.* Vol. 2, book 2. Chicago, IL: University of Chicago Press.

Meltzer, A. H. (2009b, May 4). Inflation nation. *The New York Times.*

Meltzer, A. H. (2009c, August 17). Will the Fed play politics? *Fortune.*

Meltzer, A. H. (2009d, October 23). Preventing the next financial crisis. *The Wall Street Journal.*

Meltzer, A. H. (2010a, January 28). The Fed's anti-inflation exit strategy will fail. *The Wall Street Journal.*

Meltzer, A. H. (2010b, May 21). Privatization can help Greece. *The Wall Street Journal.*

Meltzer, A. H. (2010c, June 30). Why Obamanomics has failed. *The Wall Street Journal.*

Mian, A., & Sufi, A. (2009, November). *House prices, home equity-based borrowing, and the U.S. household leverage crisis* (NBER Working Paper No. 15283). Cambridge, MA: National Bureau of Economic Research.

Miller, M. (2009, January 12). Take it from McCain's advisers: The GOP would raise taxes. *The Wall Street Journal.*

Miller, R. (2010a, March 22 & 29). "The new normal" vs. "the new mix." *Bloomberg Businessweek.*

Miller, R. (2010b, May 24). Central bankers can't return to simpler times. *Bloomberg Businessweek.*

Millman, J. (2010, January 25). Oregon tax vote shows states' plight. *The Wall Street Journal.*

Minger, J. (2009, June 19–20). Cash crops: Buying farmland for income. *The Wall Street Journal.*

Mishkin, F. S. (2009, June 22). How to get the Fed out of its "box." *Wall Street Journal.*

Moeller, P. (2010a, January 18). 8 possible Social Security benefit changes. *U.S. News & World Report.*

Moeller, P. (2010b, March 7). Whatever we're doing, it's not working. *U.S. News & World Report.*

Moffett, M., & Cowley, M. (2010, April 16). Argentine pins hope on swap. *The Wall Street Journal*.

Mogambo Guru (pseud.). (n.d.). The truth on gold. *Daily Reckoning*. Retrieved from http://dailyreckoning.com/the-truth-on-gold/

Monthly Labor Review. Retrieved from http://www.bls.gov/opub/mlr/2008/04/art2full.pdf

Montier, J. (2009, March 24). Roadmap to inflation and sources of cheap insurance. *John Mauldin's Outside the Box*.

Moore, S. (2009, September 28). Our $2 trillion bridge to nowhere. *The Wall Street Journal*.

Mulligan, C. (2009a, June 10). Inflation and government spending. *The New York Times*.

Mulligan, C. (2009b, June 17). What monetary policy cannot do. *The New York Times*.

Mulligan, C. (2009c, June 24). The next inflation: When, why and so what? *New York Times*.

Mulligan, C. (2009d, July 1). Investors will help determine the next inflation. *The New York Times*.

National Intelligence Council. (2009). *Global trends 2025: A transformed world*. Central Intelligence Agency.

Newcombe, R. (2009, July 10). Why we'll leave L.A. *The Wall Street Journal*.

NIA. (2009, December 28). Inflation biggest threat to U.S. economy in 2010. National Inflation Association.

Nixon, S. (2009, December 11). The other exit strategy for central bankers to consider. *The Wall Street Journal*.

Noonan, P. (2009, October 31–November 1). We're governed by callous children. *The Wall Street Journal*.

Noonan, P. (2010, January 23–24). The new political rumbling. *The Wall Street Journal*.

Norman, J. (2010, April 16). Calif. businesses urge regulatory reform. *Sacramento Bee*.

Novy-Marx, R., & Rauh, J. D. (n.d.). *The liabilities and risks of state-sponsored pension plans*. Cambridge, MA: National Bureau of Economic Research (NBER).

O'Brien, K. (2010, April 8). Who's afraid of a little Tea Party? Everyone, fortunately. *Cleveland Plain Dealer*.

O'Grady, M. A. (2010a, May 15–16). The Fed's monetary dissident. *The Wall Street Journal*.

O'Grady, M. A. (2010b, May 17). Venezuela's monetary mayhem. *The Wall Street Journal*.

Ody, E. (2010, April). Why you need TIPS. *Kiplinger's Personal Finance*.

OECD (2007–2008). *Central government debt.* Retrieved from http://stats.oecd .org/index.aspx

Opdyke, J. (2009, July 25–26). How to build a portfolio wisely and safely. *The Wall Street Journal.*

Opdyke, J. (2010, March 6–7). Should you join the next gold rush? *Wall Street Journal.*

Overholt, W. H. (2008). *Asia, America, and the transformation of geopolitics.* Santa Monica, CA: RAND Corporation & Cambridge University Press.

Patterson, S. (2009, May 9–10). Berkshire swings to loss of $1.5 billion for quarter. *The Wall Street Journal.*

Peaple, A. (2010, February 18). Chinese whispers for treasurys. *The Wall Street Journal.*

Pesek, W. (2010, January 25). After the stimulus binge, a debt hangover. *Bloomberg Businessweek.*

Pessin, J. L. (2009, December 8). Playing the new "Roth" angle. *The Wall Street Journal.*

Peterson, J. (n.d.). The correlation of gold versus other markets (final part). Retrieved from http://www.gold-eagle.com/editorials_05/peterson061307 .html

Peterson, P. G. (1994). *Facing up.* New York, NY: Touchstone/Simon & Schuster.

Peterson, P. G. (2009, November 16). Business is missing in action. *Businessweek.*

Peterson-Pew Commission on Budget Reform. (2009, December 14). Red ink rising: A call to action to stem the mounting federal debt. Retrieved from http://budgetreform.org/document/red-ink-rising

Peuquet, J. (2009, December 16). In a debt hole, let's stop digging. *New York Daily News.*

Porter, M. 1985. *Competitive Advantage.* New York, NY: Free Press.

Powell, R. (2009, October 29). This retirement- plan building block is cracked. MarketWatch. Retrieved from http://www.marketwatch.com

Prestowitz, C. (2005). *Three billion new capitalists.* New York, NY: Basic Books.

Putnam Investments. (2010, January 26). Survey shows Americans unsure about retirement income needs.

Rachman, G. (2009, May 25). When austerity does not come easily. *Financial Times.*

Rachman, G. (2010a, January 11). Bankruptcy could be good for America. *Financial Times.*

Rachman, G. (2010b, January 25). When nations turn to hoarders. *Financial Times.*

Rampell, C. (2009, December 11). Many see VAT option as a cure for deficits. *The New York Times.*

Ranson, D. (2010, May 17). The revenue limits of tax and spend. *The Wall Street Journal.*

Reinhart, C. M., & Rogoff, K. S. (2009a, December 31). *Growth in a time of debt.* National Bureau of Economic Research (NBER).

Reinhart, C., & Rogoff, K. S. (2009b, December 31). Growth in a time of debt. *American Economic Review and Proceedings.*

Reinhart, C. M., & Rogoff, K. S. (2009c). *This time is different: Eight centuries of financial folly.* Princeton, NJ: Princeton University Press.

Reinhart, V., & Reinhart, C. (2010, May 9). Five myths about the European debt crisis. *The Washington Post.*

Research Affiliates. (2009, June 18). A complete toolkit for fighting inflation.

Reynolds, A. (2010, June 10). Don't believe the double-dippers.

Richardson, J. (1997). *Willie Brown.* Berkeley, CA: University of California Press.

Romero, P. J. (2005, July). Mugged by statists. *Brainstorm.*

Romero, P. J. (2007, Summer). Racing backwards: The fiscal impact of illegal immigration, revisited. *The Social Contract.*

Roubini. (2009, August 24). The exit strategy from the monetary and fiscal easing.

Rowley, J. (2010, March 15). Congressman calculator. *Bloomberg Businessweek.*

Rublin, L. (2009, June 15). Too far, too fast. *Barron's.*

Ruffenach, G. (2009, November 14–15). Have you learned your lessons yet? *Wall Street Journal.*

Russell, R. (2009, June 27). Competitive devaluations to spur on gold. *Dow Theory Letters.*

Russell, R. (2009, December 9). *Dow Theory Letters.* La Jolla, CA.

Salas, C., & Miller, R. (2010, June 7). In search of the ideal jobless rate. *Bloomberg Businessweek.*

Samuelson, R. (2008a). *The great inflation and its aftermath.* New York, NY: Random House.

Samuelson, R. (2008b, November 10). A darker future for us. *Newsweek.*

Samuelson, R. (2009a, May 18). Obama's risky debt. *The Washington Post.*

Samuelson, R. (2009b, July 13). The consequences of big government. *The Washington Post.*

Samuelson, R. (2010, February 12). Politics, at your expense. *Newsweek.*

Santoro, M. (2009, September). *Will the demand for assets fall when the baby boomers retire?* Congressional Budget Office background paper.

Sasseen, J. (2009, November 16). A tax hike by any other name. *Businessweek.*

Saunders, L. (2010a, February 27–28). The right way to squirrel money from the tax man. *The Wall Street Journal.*

Saunders, L. (2010b, June 19–20). Is a Roth IRA safe from taxes? *Wall Street Journal.*

Saxena, P. (2009, December 29). The debt bomb. *Daily Reckoning.*

Schiff, P. (2007). *Crash proof.* Hoboken, NJ: Wiley.

Schrag, P. (2006). *California: America's high-stakes experiment.* Berkeley, CA: University of California Press.

Scott, M. (2010, January 25). Europe's delicate dilemma. *Bloomberg Businessweek.*

Seib, G. (2010a, January 19). U.S. shifted party, not ideology. *The Wall Street Journal.*

Seib, G. (2010b, April 27). I'm America. I'm an addict. *The Wall Street Journal.*

Setser, B. (2008, February 16). The perils of a weak dollar. Boston Globe. Retrieved from the Council on Foreign Relations website, http://www.cfr.org

Setser, B. (2009). *Understanding China's External Portfolio, Council on Foreign Relations working paper.* Retrieved from http://www.cfr.org/publication/ 18149/

Setser, B. W., & Pandey, A. (2009a, May). *China's $1.5 trillion bet: Understanding China's external portfolio.* Council on Foreign Relations Press. Retrieved from http://www.cfr.org/publication/18149/

Setser, B., & Pandey, A. (2009b, May). *China's $1.7 trillion bet: Understanding China's external portfolio.*

Setser, B., & Pandey, A. (2009c, May 26). *Quarterly update: Foreign exchange reserves in Brazil, Russia, India and China (BRIC).* Council on Foreign Relations. Retrieved from http://www.cfr.org/cgs

Sforza, T. (2010, April 9). State pensions massively underfunded. Stanford study concludes. *Orange County Register.*

Shelton, J. (2009, October 14). The message of dollar disdain. *The Wall Street Journal.*

Shelton, J. (2010, May 27). Recovery starts with sound money. *The Wall Street Journal.*

Siegel, J. J. (2009, October 28). Efficient market theory and the crisis. *The Wall Street Journal.*

Signature Capital Partners. (2009, May 28). Macroview: Treasury turmoil, inflation, and deflation.

Sjuggerud, S. (2009a, June 12). A government boondoggle that can save you thousands on your taxes. *Daily Wealth.*

Sjuggerud, S. (2009b, September). The only 100% tax-free retirement plan in America. *True Wealth.*

Sloan, A. (2009a, August 17). The next great bailout. *Fortune.*

Sloan, A. (2009b, November 8). What's still wrong with Wall Street. *Time.*

Smith, G. (2010, January 25). Reasons to cry for Argentina. *Bloomberg Businessweek.*

Sonders, L. A. (2009, June 15). *Deficits, the dollar and exit strategies*. Charles Schwab & Co.

Stansberry, P. (2009, November 24). The bankruptcy of the United States is now certain. *S&A Digest*.

Stansberry, P. (2010a, May 21). Why gold is a sure long-term bet. *Daily Wealth Premium*.

Stansberry, P. (2010b, May 22). The single most important financial step you can take right now. *Daily Wealth Premium*.

Starr, K. (2010). *Coast of dreams: California on the edge, 1990–2003*. New York, NY: Vintage.

Steil, B. (2010, April 26). Don't blame the euro for Greece's woes. *Financial News*.

Steil, B., & Swartz, P. (2010, June 14). Dangers of U.S. debt in foreign hands. *Financial News*.

Stern, L. (2010, May 3). Retirement: The new math of personal finance. *Newsweek*.

Stewart, K. (2008, April). The experimental consumer price index for elderly Americans (CPI-E): 1982–2007. Retrieved from http://www.bls.gov/opub/mlr/2008/04/art2full.pdf

Steyn, M. (2010, February 26). Our own Greek tragedy. *Washington Times*.

Stimulus spending: How to get more bang for the buck. (2010, March 22 & 29). *Bloomberg Businessweek*.

Stoeferle, R. (2010, June 24). Gold—the optimal investment in deflation and inflation. *Mineweb*.

Sunshine, M. (2009, June 15). *What if the Fed isn't printing money like a drunken sailor?* Retrieved from http://www.riskcenter.com

Szymanski, E. (2009, August 2). Now is the best time to start your planning for Roth IRA conversion. *Trenton Times*.

Tergesen, A. (2009, December 6). Get ready for 2010—the year of the Roth IRA. *The Wall Street Journal*.

Things that make you go "hmmm." (2010, January 25). BTIG Singapore.

Thomas, E. (2010, February 5). Obama's other deficit. *Newsweek*.

Thomas, K. (2009). *Go Roth!* Elgin, IL: Fairmark Press.

Thomsett, M. (1986). *Webster's New World investment & securities dictionary*. Washington, DC: Webster's New World.

Tilson, W., & Heins, J. (2010, March). Buy and hold is risky. *Kiplinger's Personal Finance*.

Trabandt, M., & Uhlig, H.(2010, April). *How far are we from the slippery slope? The Laffer Curve Revisited* (European Central Bank Working Paper No. 1174).

Tully, S. (2009, June 22). We owe *WHAT*? The next crisis: America's debt. *Fortune*.

Turk, J., & Rubino, J. (2004). *The collapse of the dollar and how to profit from it.* New York: Currency Doubleday.

Twenty generational tips for building trust with clients. (2009). *Generational Adviser.* The Boomer Project.

U.S. Census Bureau. (2010). *Statistical abstract of the United States: 2011 (130th Edition). International investment position by type of investment.* Washington, DC. Retrieved from http://www.census.gov/compendia/statab/tables/09s1249.xls

Vaneman, R. (2010, March 11). In praise of moderation, E*TRADE Capital Management. Retrieved from https://us.etade.com

Walker, M., & Fidler, S. (2010, February 1). Experts see another global dip ahead. *The Wall Street Journal.*

The Wall Street Journal. (2009a, May 1–2). The recovery so far.

The Wall Street Journal. (2009b, May 15). Geithner's revelation of the obvious provokes response (letters to the editor).

The Wall Street Journal. (2009c, July 14). The small business surtax.

The Wall Street Journal. (2009d, July 17). A reckless Congress.

The Wall Street Journal. (2009e, August 17). Fannie Mae, Enron, the sequel.

The Wall Street Journal. (2009f, October 9). The dollar adrift.

The Wall Street Journal. (2009g, October 12). Q&A: Reinhart and Rogoff on the crisis, the "mother of all moral hazard."

The Wall Street Journal. (2009h, October 26). The spending rolls on.

The Wall Street Journal. (2009i, October 30). A recovery at last.

The Wall Street Journal. (2010a, February 5). Q&A: Carmen Reinhart on Greece, U.S. debt and other "scary" scenarios.

The Wall Street Journal. (2010b, April 15). Europe's VAT lessons.

The Wall Street Journal. (2010c, March 26). The government pay boom.

The Wall Street Journal. (2010d, May 10). The euro's tribulations.

The Wall Street Journal. (2010e, June 26–27). The Keynesian dead end.

Wall Street lays another egg. (2008, December). *Vanity Fair.*

Walsh, M. W. (2010, March 24). Social Security to see payout exceed pay-in this year. *The New York Times.*

Wang, P. (2009, October). Strategies for a slow-go market. *Money.*

Weil, D. (2009, May 4). Buffett sees massive inflation to handle staggering debt. *Newsmax.*

Wessel, D. (2010a, March 4). Perils of the California model. *The Wall Street Journal.*

Wessel, D. (2010b, April 8). A big, bad . . . "great" recession? *The Wall Street Journal.*

Where's the inflation? (2009, November). *Money.*

Whiskey and Gunpowder. (n.d.). *The 7 deadly ingredients for the coming U.S. hyperinfl ation . . . and how to protect your money.* Retrieved from http://whiskeyandgunpowder.com/archives/

Whitehouse, M. (2010, January 4). Deficit, budget woes need solutions as U.S. nears the precipice. *The Wall Street Journal.*

Wiggin, A., & Incontrera, K. (2008). *I.O.U.S.A.* (book and DVD). Hoboken, NJ: Wiley.

Williams, G. (2009, December 8). Things that make you go "hmmm." BTIG Singapore.

Williams, G. (2009, December 10). Things that make you go "hmmm." BTIG Singapore.

Williams, G. (2010, January 25). Things that make you go "hmmm." BTIG Singapore.

Williams, J. (2010, May 1). Gold, silver and currencies favored as hyperinflationary Great Depression nears. *Mineweb.*

Williams, W. (2010, May 18). Who has the right to live in the U.S.? *Orange County Register.*

Wines, M. (2010, May 2). How bad is inflation in Zimbabwe? *New York Times.*

Wood, C. (2009, November 30). Is the U.S. economy turning Japanese? *Wall Street Journal.*

Woolridge, A. (2010, April 15). The world upside down. *The Economist.*

World Bank. (2011, February 25). India at a glance. Retrieved from http://devdata.worldbank.org/AAG/ind_aag.pdf

Wright, S. H. (2009, April). Immigration and wage inequality. *NBER Digest.*

Zakaria, F. (2008). *The post-American world.* New York, NY: Norton.

Zeng, M. (2009, December 31). Treasury debt sales top $2.1 trillion. *The Wall Street Journal.*

Zhao, C. (2009, October 30). *Benign or malignant neglect?* Montreal, Canada: BCA Research.

Zhao, C. (2010, June 4). *Asset allocation in a high risk world.* Montreal, Canada: BCA Research.

Zigler, B. (2009, December 24). Gold stock volatility's double edge. Hard Assets Investor. Retrieved from http://www.hardasetsinvestor.com

Zing, M. (2009, December 31). Treasury debt sales top $2.1 trillion. *The Wall Street Journal.*

Zingales, L. (2009, October). Capitalism after the crisis. *National Affairs.*

Zuckerman, M. (2009a, July 14). The economy is even worse than you think. *The Wall Street Journal.*

Zuckerman, M. (2009b, October 23). Drowning in debt: Obama's spending and borrowing leaves the U.S. gasping for air. *New York Daily News.*

Zuckerman, M. (2010, May 21). The bankrupting of America. *The Wall Street Journal.*

Zweig, J. (2009, June 30). The time to tame inflation is well before it strikes. *The Wall Street Journal.*

Zweig, J. (2010a, January 30). Placing investing chips in the right countries. *The Wall Street Journal.*

Zweig, J. (2010b, May 20). When the global debt shuffle hits home. *The Wall Street Journal.*

Index

Announcing the Business Expert Press Digital Library

Concise E-books Business Students
Need for Classroom and Research

This book can also be purchased in an e-book collection by your library as
- a one-time purchase,
- that is owned forever,
- allows for simultaneous readers,
- has no restrictions on printing,
- can be downloaded as PDFs from within the library community.

Our digital library collections are a great solution to beat the rising cost of textbooks. E-books can be loaded into their course management systems or onto students' e-book readers.

The **Business Expert Press** digital libraries are very affordable, with no obligation to buy in future years.

For more information, please visit **www.businessexpertpress.com/librarians**. To set up a trial in the United States, please contact **Sheri Dean** at sheri.dean@globalpress.com; for all other regions, contact **Nicole Lee** at *nicole.lee@igroupnet.com*.

OTHER TITLES IN OUR ECONOMICS COLLECTION
Series Editors: **Philip J. Romero and Jeffrey A. Edwards**

Managerial Economics: Concepts and Principles by Donald N. Stengel

Working With Economic Indicators: Interpretation and Sources by Donald N. Stengel and Priscilla Chaffe-Stengel

With Forthcoming Titles Including...

Business and Energy: A Managerial Perspective on Cost, Availability and Impact on Profit by Herb Shields

International Economics: Understanding the Forces of Globalization for Managers by Paul A. Torelli

Game Theory: Managing Action and Reaction in the Strategic Management of the Firm by Mark L. Burkey

Applying the Logic of the Five Forces Model to Your Products and Services: How Strong is Your Firm's Competitive Advantage? by Daniel R. Marburger

Innovative Pricing Strategies to Increase Profits by Daniel R. Marburger

CPSIA information can be obtained at www.ICGtesting.com
Printed in the USA
BVOW03s1612050913

330222BV00003B/15/P